# COGNITION AND EROS

# COGNITION AND EROS

## A CRITIQUE OF THE KANTIAN PARADIGM

# ROBIN MAY SCHOTT

The Pennsylvania State University Press
University Park, Pennsylvania

First published in 1988 by Beacon Press

First paperback edition published in 1993 by The Pennsylvania State
University Press, Barbara Building, Suite C, University Park, PA 16802

Library of Congress Cataloging-in-Publication Data

Schott, Robin May
        Cognition and eros : a critique of the Kantian paradigm /
        Robin May Schott.
                p.        cm.
        Originally published: Boston : Beacon Press, 1988.
        ISBN 0-271-00936-5 (pbk.)
        1. Kant, Immanuel, 1724–1804. 2. Objectivity—History—18th
        century. 3. Knowledge, Theory of—History—18th Century.
        4. Asceticism—History. 5. Sensuality—History. 6. Women—
        Sexual behavior—History. I. Title.
        [B2798.S32 1993]
        128'.3—dc20
                                                        92-34926
                                                        CIP

# CONTENTS

# PREFACE

THIS PROJECT BEGAN AS AN INVESTIGATION INTO THE RELATION BE-
tween cognition and eros in Kant's theory of objectivity, which has
become paradigmatic for modern views about knowledge. Kant
posits a split between cognition, on the one hand, and feelings and
desires, on the other hand. The question arose whether this splitting off of feeling and sensuality from cognition captures the essence of knowledge, as Kant claims, or whether it requires the
knower to perform distorting operations on him- or herself in order
to conform to the conditions of objective knowledge. I hypothesized
that the split between cognition and eros in Kant's philosophy was
not a natural and necessary condition for knowledge, but entailed a
suppression of the erotic dimension of existence.

In focusing on the suppression of eros in Kant's thought, I am
invoking a specifically un-Kantian term. My use of eros here is
purposely broad, encompassing a range of meanings including

feelings, desires, sensual pleasures, and explicit sexual activity. These features are commonly linked in the ascetic religious and philosophical tradition, to which Kant is heir, in opposition to the quest for spiritual or rational purity. As a prolegomena to my discussion of Kant, therefore, I will consider interpretations of feeling, desire, and sexuality that have become central in the Western religious and philosophical tradition. It is beyond the scope of this project, however, to explore the tensions and shifts in the historical interpretations of these concepts in depth. Moreover, this study does not propose a theory of the erotic. In such a project one might examine whether sexuality is the source of all feelings and desires or is one of many sources, or one might examine whether emotions are an aspect of embodied experience or are separable from this domain. Instead, my project is to probe the model of objectivity on the basis of which both the history and theory of eros have appeared as philosophically insignificant. Despite the philosophical devaluation of eros, the interpretation of emotion, desire, and sexuality as polluting has in fact been central to the construction of rationality on the basis of purity. Because of the perceived threat to rational control posed by emotion, desire, and sexuality, a fundamental opposition has been established between eros and cognition. Although there is a form of eros in Greek and Christian thought that appears as de-materialized love, I am concerned with its insistently embodied incarnation. In this latter sense, the erotic is commonly linked with the mind's passionate abandonment to emotional and sensory stimulation. This study seeks in part to explore why feeling and desire are viewed as an overwhelming force and what implications this view holds for the conceptualization of knowledge.

The hostility toward sensuality manifest in Kant's view of objectivity appeared, moreover, to be correlated with a dismissal of women as sexual beings, who are incapable of rational thought. Since knowledge must be freed of erotic interferences, women, as sensual creatures, must be excluded from philosophy. The project of viewing Kant's theory of knowledge in the context of women's historical absence from philosophy was motivated by the conception of philosophy as an articulation of relations in the social world. Critical social theory, stemming from Marx, treats philosophy not as existing in a realm of pure abstraction, as philosophers frequently interpret their own thought, but as reflecting and justifying the distribution of power in the world outside of philosophical thought. Although critical theorists have analyzed the philosophical implications of economic forms of power, I sought to expand this scope by considering sexual forms of power as well. I embarked on this project to probe how the philosophical hostility to sensuality sustained the hierarchical valuation of the sexes out of which the commitment to purity was born.

In exploring these hypotheses, the inquiry took an unexpected turn. Originally, I had anticipated discussing Kant's thought as paradigmatic of the split between cognition and eros, and proceeding to treat thinkers since Kant who have been critical of his conception of knowledge. But in embarking on the study of Kant, it became apparent that I myself was so schooled in this philosophical tradition of objectivity that I lacked the tools necessary to critically view Kant's assumptions about knowledge. Although I intended to display the specific commitments involved in the operations that had been accepted as natural and essential components of the philosophical enterprise, I found that the Kantian method of achieving objectivity by establishing universal forms of knowledge itself appeared to me as inescapably necessary.

It became devastatingly apparent that, in order to gain perspective on this view of knowledge, it was imperative to delve into the history out of which Kant's thought developed. If philosophy is a reflection of the social world, as Marxist theoreticians claim, it cannot be divested of the history either of its own concepts or of the society in which its ideas developed. To understand these historical connections, it is insufficient to merely thematize the relation between history and philosophy in an abstract manner, empty of content. It becomes necessary to get down into the mud, as Plato would say, to dirty one's hands with history.

This recognition led to an investigation of the origins of the concept of purity, which frames Kant's discussion of the formal conditions of knowledge. I sought in Plato a clue for answering the following questions. From what must the intellect be purified? Why is the body viewed as polluting? How does the philosophical commitment to purity, which enters the philosophical tradition in the clas-

sical Greek period, reflect religious and social practices that prevailed outside of the domain of philosophy?

This historical turn provided the first substantive indication of
the meaning of purity in philosophy. The emphasis on distancing
thought from sensuality grew out of an ascetic practice by which
men sought to transcend the vicissitudes of the phenomenal world,
to escape the mortal fate implicit in the natural life cycle of human
beings. Moreover, the most threatening moments of birth and death
were connected, through myth and ritual, with an interpretation of
women's sexuality as polluting.

Consequently, the project took on a genealogical character.
Questions arose concerning the significance of these original ascetic impulses for the modern world. How was the ascetic commitment to purity, evident in early Greek and Christian thought, transmitted to modern philosophy? What role did the institutions of the
church and the university play in the transmission of asceticism?
How did views about purity and pollution themselves become transformed in their modern incarnation?

This historical study provided the foundation from which to read
Kant. His emphasis on purity in systematic philosophy displays the
inheritance of the ascetic hostility toward the body and toward
women. But in spelling out the consequences of this suppression of
sensuality in Kant's philosophy, the inquiry followed another unexpected avenue. Although Kant is indeed part of an ascetic tradition inherited from both Greek and Christian sources, as his biography indicates, the particular form of asceticism manifested in his
thought was shaped by modern conditions. Specifically, it became
apparent that Kant's discussion of objectivity reflected the reified
social relations that characterized the emerging capitalist order in
which persons and things became reduced to objects of exchange
in the marketplace. The desensualization of existence demanded in
the world ruled by commodity relations is itself a form of asceticism.

The coexistence of the themes of reification and asceticism in
Kant's thought suggests that there exists an intimate relation between the fetishistic consciousness of market society, which subor-
dinates relations between persons to relations between things, and
the ascetic hostility towards sexuality. Implicit in the ascetic impulse is a dialectic that results not in the liberation of the soul from

the material world, but in an objectification of both persons and things. Correspondingly, intrinsic to the fetishism of commodities is a suppression of sensuality that results in a distortion of the erotic interests of human beings. Therefore, the ascetic posture in philosophy has lent itself to the purposes of a world built on commodity relations, and it has been transformed by this world as well.

In reflecting on the themes of asceticism and fetishism, it became possible to view concretely what initially appeared only as abstractions: the historical content of philosophical concepts; the manner in which they reflect and sustain relations in the social world; and, in particular, the nature of the sexual relations between men and women that these concepts validate. The philosophical paradigm of objectivity not only entails an operation on the part of objective thinkers who must divest themselves of their sensual existence, but it has broader social implications as well. This philosophical ideal has historically justified the exclusion of women from institutions of higher education, which serve as avenues for social power, and from other domains of public activity for which women have been viewed as insufficiently rational. Furthermore, this paradigm has an impact on human beings generally by making normative the objectifying social relations between persons and things that are generated in a world ruled by commodity production.

# ACKNOWLEDGMENTS

ALTHOUGH ACKNOWLEDGMENTS APPEAR AT THE VERY BEGINNING of a work, in fact they stand at the end of a long process. Thus, they serve as an occasion to reflect on the persons with whom one has shared some or all of this effort. First, I would like to thank my friend and mentor George Schrader, who has been part of this project at every stage. Through his warmth and his wisdom he has taught me more of both philosophy and life than one can acknowledge either here or in person. He has given me where appropriate the encouragement and criticism that has seen me through the long process of completing this work.

My family has shared the frustrations and joys of this process, as have several friends: Monique Breindel, Jonathan Oberman, and Carol Heim have encouraged me throughout the years of working on this project; John Cumbler has shared generously his time and his professional experience; Judith Cumbler, Kathy Bean, Linda

Eiseman, Eric Hill, and Gisela Kolb have all provided much valued personal and professional support during my years in Louisville; Kathleen Keest and Irit Rogoff both tolerated me and urged me on during the final stages of this project.

For financial support I would like to thank the American Association of University Women for funding early stages of this research, the American Council of Learned Societies and the National Endowment for the Humanities for supporting the final stages of this work, and the University of Louisville for providing funds that enabled me to devote several summers to research. I would also like to thank the Center for European Studies at Harvard University, where I was in residence during the completion of this work, for providing a stimulating and congenial environment. I would like to thank John Flodstrom, Seyla Benhabib, and Allen Wood for supporting my efforts to gain research time to complete this work.

I would like to thank Virginia Keown for her patient and painstaking work in preparing the manuscript in the face of the seemingly endless revisions and the repeated frustrations engendered by computer technology.

I would also like to thank my editors at Beacon Press: Caroline Birdsall has taught me valuable lessons about editing, and Deborah Johnson has through her warmth and professional judgment made the process of publishing most pleasurable.

**I**

# HISTORICAL ANTECEDENTS
# OF ASCETIC PHILOSOPHY:
# GREEK AND CHRISTIAN ORIGINS

# 1

# PHILOSOPHICAL ORIGINS
# OF ASCETIC PHILOSOPHY:
# PLATONIC VIEWS OF
# WOMEN AND EROS

IN THE *CRITIQUE OF PURE REASON*, KANT ATTEMPTS TO GROUND
the system of all pure knowledge. Knowledge that is pure, in his
view, is free of all sensible or empirical content and provides the
necessary condition for the possibility of knowledge at all. Kant's
emphasis on the purity of knowledge and of reason occurs with
alarming frequency and raises the question of what is implied by
his insistence on purity. From what must reason be purified? What
pollution in the sensible, empirical world threatens the project of
establishing a foundation for philosophical truth?

The question concerning the meaning of purity in Kant's thought
leads us to consider the philosophical origin of his association of
purity and truth, which becomes paradigmatic for modern discussions of knowledge. Although Kant claims that philosophy has no
history, the association of purity and truth is in fact deeply embedded in the history of Western philosophy. A genealogical approach

reveals that the association of purity and truth is not a necessary a priori connection, but emerges from a specific historical context stamped by unequal relations between men and women. By studying the historical origin and evolution of the concept of purity, we can hope to make visible beliefs about sensuality and female nature that inform this commitment to purity. Through this inquiry it is possible to examine the assumptions about sensuality and sexual relations that underlie the modern philosophical commitment to purity and that previously may have remained unacknowledged.

By beginning a genealogy of the concept of purity with Plato's formulation of the link between purity and truth, it is possible to see how the value of purity enters into the philosophical tradition. From this study of origins it will then be possible to consider what traces of this classical conception remain in Kant's treatment of knowledge, and what shifts have occurred in the value of purity as it has been transmitted to the modern world. In Plato's view, pure thought is achieved by cutting oneself off from all of the sensations of the body, which serve only to impede the soul's quest for truth. In the *Phaedo*, for example, Socrates argues that man pursues the truth, "by applying his pure and unadulterated thought to the pure and unadulterated object" (*Phaedo* 66a). Plato writes: "The person who is likely to succeed in this attempt [at seeking knowledge] most perfectly is the one who approaches each object, as far as possible with the unaided intellect . . . cutting himself off as much as possible from his eyes and ears and virtually all the rest of his body, as an impediment which by its presence prevents the soul from attaining to truth" . . . (*Phaedo* 66a). He adds, "We are convinced that if we are ever to have pure knowledge of anything, we must get rid of the body and contemplate things by themselves with the soul by itself" (*Phaedo* 66d–e). Implicit in the Platonic ideal of truth, therefore, is a conception of the body as a contamination, which the soul must control and ultimately transcend in order to attain the purity of thought necessary for true knowledge.

The opposition between the purity of truth and the pollution of the body is linked in Plato's thought to an interpretation of women as exemplifying the harmful attributes of physical existence, which interfere with rational control. Plato repeatedly characterizes women as dangerously influenced by sensations, feelings, and appetites. Plato's ideal of knowledge, therefore, must be understood in the context of its denigration of the body and of women, with the consequence that phenomenal existence in general is viewed as a corruption of the purity of the world of ideas.

In the *Timaeus*, Plato offers a version of the story of creation that posits male superiority over female nature by virtue of men's ability to control sensations and feelings. In the first act of creation, in which all souls are born without disadvantage, human nature appeared in the form of the "superior race" that would be called "man" (*Timaeus* 42a). Since the souls of men were implanted in bodies, they possessed both the faculty of sensation and the feelings of love, fear, and anger. Those who conquered these sensations lived righteously; those who were conquered by these feelings lived unrighteously (*Timaeus* 42b). Plato describes the creation of women in the following way: "Of the men who came into the world, those who were cowards or led unrighteous lives may with reason be supposed to have changed into the nature of women in the second generation. . . . Thus were created women and the female sex in general" (*Timaeus* 90e–91e). According to this account, then, primordial human nature is male, and those souls who have conquered bodily passions retain the privileges of this superior race. Women are by definition the embodiment of those souls who have succumbed to temptation and live unrighteously. The creation myth in the *Timaeus* vividly portrays the projection onto woman's nature of man's failure to control his sensations and feelings.

In the *Republic*, Plato also portrays women as primarily ruled by desires. Plato introduces women in the class of individuals in whom the worse part rules the better. In book 4 he contrasts "the mob of motley appetites and pleasures and pains one would find chiefly in children and women and slaves and in the base rabble of those who are free men in name," with "the simple and moderate appetites which with the aid of reason and right opinion are guided by consideration . . ." (*Republic* 431c). Elsewhere in the dialogue Plato confines the lamentations of grief to women and to inferior men (*Republic* 387e–388a), and he exhorts young men seeking to become "brave, sober, pious, free" (*Republic* 395c) against imitating women. He writes, "We will not then allow our charges, whom we expect to prove good men, being men, to play the parts of women and imitate a woman young or old wrangling with her husband, defying heaven, loudly boasting, fortunate in her own conceit, or involved in misfortune and possessed by grief and lamentation—still less a woman that is sick, in love, or in labor" (*Republic* 395d–e). Women in general, therefore, display the emotional abandonment that men must avoid if they are to become suited to civic liberty. Although some men also assume such attributes ("inferior men" [388a], tyrants [579b]), all but the "most worthy" (388a) women are characterized in this manner. Thus, women as a group are identified with the qualities of the worst men. In the *Laws*, Plato argues for the inclusion of woman in the institution of the public table, not because she is equal to man, but because her weakness necessitates legislative control. He comments, "Woman—left without chastening restraint—is not, as you might fancy, merely half the problem; nay, she is a twofold and more than a twofold problem, in proportion as her native disposition is inferior to man's" (*Laws* 781b).

Woman's inferior nature, evident in her inability to moderate her desires, mandates a political order in which men and women have unequal political rights. In identifying women primarily with bodily sensations and passions that must be subjected to rational control, the Platonic ideal of knowledge has the consequence of justifying philosophically the politics of Greek society in which women were subordinated to male rule. Although the *Laws* ascribes a legal status to women that was an improvement over contemporary Athens, it is still not one of equality with men.[1] Plato views the equal rights that obtain between men and women in a democratic city as a characteristic of its "anarchic temper" (*Republic* 562e–563b), not as a goal of the ideal political order.

Despite this generally negative evaluation of female nature, in book 5 of the *Republic* Plato makes the suggestion that women, too, can enter the guardian class. The guardians would rule in the ideal republic because they would have developed the rational legislation in their own souls that would enable them to provide the rational rule for other classes in the state. In the history of political theory, Plato's suggestions about female guardians have appeared as a radical defense of the possibility of female equality.[2] However, in evaluating the significance of Plato's admission of women into the guardian class, one must examine the conditions under which this occurs. Plato ultimately allows for female guardians only on the condition that they separate out what is specific to female nature from their identity as guardians. Plato introduces the issue of female guardians only after the completion of the "male drama" (*Republic* 451c), in which the nature of justice, education, and the duties of the guardians have already been discussed. Women, therefore, are not included in his original description of the happy city. The ideals that rule the Republic are conceived in relation to an all-male society. Moreover, Socrates indicates his trepidation at embarking on this discussion of women. He speaks of his doubts (*Republic* 451a) and disavows any claim to be speaking "with knowledge" (*Republic* 450d). Socrates only turns to the "female drama" in order to consider men's "possession and use" of women and children (*Republic* 451c). The assumption that women are the property of men, which operated in Greek social practices, persists in this philosophical argument for "equality." Although in eliminating private cohabitation Plato challenges the traditional, private "possession and use" of women, he does not challenge the premise that women's function is defined by their usefulness to men. The definition of women's nature in terms of her function as wife is evident in the Greek word *gynē* itself, which means both wife and woman.[3] Women become guardians in the *Republic*, it appears, to serve as wives of the guardian men. Moreover, the guardian wives in the ideal republic, like the women in Greek society, serve primarily to breed legitimate offspring. Because one ought not to "breed from all indiscriminately" (*Republic* 459a), Plato seeks to establish the conditions by which "the best men must cohabit with the best women" (*Republic* 459d).

Plato's discussion of female guardians in book 5 of the *Republic* represents a marked shift from his characterization of women elsewhere in the dialogue. Since women's passionate nature is responsible for their inferior status, both in origin and in law, the only condition under which women can become "equal" to men is apparently through the renunciation of sexual desire. No mention of women as desiring or emotional beings occurs in this portion of the dialogue, in contrast to Plato's earlier description of women as appetitive and pleasure seeking. Women's sexual relations with men are totally controlled by the state. The state regulates intercourse and reproduction, much as it regulates the maneuvering of military troops. The state decides with whom one mates, on what occasions, and during what years of one's life. Although male sexuality is similarly constrained by the political order, Plato acknowledges the continued existence of male sexual desire. For example, he considers intercourse with women a suitable reward for bravery in action (*Republic* 460b). No comparable incentive, however, is mentioned for women who excel. Thus, female sexual desire appears to pose such a threat to the state that it must be thoroughly neutralized. The traditional functions of motherhood are also taken over by the state. After a child is born, officers either deposit it in separate quarters or dispose of it if the child is deformed (*Republic* 460c). When the mother is full of milk, she will be brought to the nursery; but precautions will be taken to prevent any mother from knowing her own child. Maternity becomes, according to Socrates' listeners, a "soft job" (460d). Thus, women are admitted into the guardian class only under the condition that they become "desexualized."[4] Their sexual nature becomes reduced to a mere biological act, devoid of love for either mate or offspring.[5]

It is under such a desexualized regime that Plato argues that women can share the same tasks as men. Although men and women have different natures insofar as their sex is concerned (*Republic* 453b), Plato rejects the view that these sexual differences influence their natural capacities to rule. He argues,

> If it appears that the male and the female sex have distinct qualifications for any arts or pursuits, we shall affirm that they ought to be assigned respectively to each. But if it appears that they differ only in just this respect that the female bears and the male begets, we shall say that no proof has yet been produced that the woman differs from the man for our purposes, but we shall continue to think that our guardians and their wives ought to follow the same pursuits. (*Republic* 454d–e)

In this passage, Plato claims that men's and women's reproductive capacities have no bearing on their pursuits as guardians. One's "qualifications," not one's role in sexual reproduction, determines one's social function. Thus a man and woman who have a physician's mind have the same nature, but a male physician and a male carpenter have different natures (*Republic* 454d). This argument is based on Plato's more general view that the body is a foreign contamination impinging on the soul's fulfillment of its highest nature, and that the soul must detach itself from the body: "It seems that so long as we are alive, we shall continue closest to knowledge if we avoid as much as we can all contact and association with the body, except when they are absolutely necessary, and instead of allowing ourselves to become infected with its nature, purify ourselves from it until God gives us deliverance" (*Phaedo* 67a). Consequently, bodily identity is ultimately irrelevant to an individual's soul. Factors such as whether one is male or female, black or white, rich or poor—all concrete features of one's identity—are set aside when considering the nature of the soul. Plato attempts to relegate sexuality to the same level of insignificance as being bald or hairy (*Republic* 454c).[6] Thus, women can participate in the same pursuits as men if they reject their identity as sexed creatures, as men have sought to do.

But Plato is never entirely successful in his attempt to desexualize the women guardians and thus to ground women's equality with men. He qualifies his claim that women should share in all tasks with men, with the disclaimer that they remain inferior. He writes, "There is no pursuit of the administrators of a state that belongs to a woman because she is a woman or to a man because he is a man. But the natural capacities are distributed alike among both creatures, and women naturally share in all pursuits and men in all—yet for all the woman is weaker than the man" (*Republic* 455d–e).[7] Plato stresses that he is concerned with likenesses and differences in nature only insofar as they are pertinent to the pursuits themselves (*Republic* 454c). If sexual identity were insignificant, it would not determine one's qualification to rule. Yet Plato continues to regard women as weaker in all respects than men. He implies that women's weakness is not merely physical but extends to the qualities necessary for intellectual activity or political leadership. Thus for Plato, femaleness is ultimately inseparable from women's rational and legislative capacities. His attempt to designate sexuality as a purely physical activity with no implications for women's nature founders. Although Plato leaves room for individual exceptions, women in the guardian class ultimately remain inferior to male guardians because of the physical and intellectual weakness inhering in their sex.[8]

Plato's attempt to desexualize the female guardians of the *Republic* coheres with his view in the *Phaedo*, that the soul must be "freed from the shackles of the body" (*Phaedo* 67d).[9] The fact that sexual identity nonetheless remains inescapable for female guardians arouses scepticism in the reader regarding Plato's commitment to equality between guardian women and men. Women, unlike men, remain associated with a body that hinders them from excelling in their pursuits.

Some commentators suggest that Plato's discussion of desire in the *Symposium* indicates that he moved away from the view evident in both the *Phaedo* and the *Republic* that the body is primarily an obstacle to the soul's quest for knowledge.[10] The *Symposium* is concerned with the nature of eros, which for Plato encompasses love for beautiful bodies as well as love for knowledge. Through the education of eros, the seeker after wisdom discovers that what is common to all these forms of love is love of beauty, and through this progression at least certain souls will attain the ultimate knowledge of beauty. Consequently, interpreters often view this account as demonstrating the interdependency of sensual desire and cognition. It is desire, which originates in the love of bodies, that guides the seeker after wisdom toward knowledge. According to this view, the education of desire in the *Symposium* does not entail its suppression.

Contrary to this interpretation, I would argue that the highest love in the *Symposium* is not merely an enrichment of eros, but is an abandonment of the sexual and human orientation evident in the earlier forms of desire.[11] Alcibiades admires the "manliness and self-control" (*Symposium* 219d) Socrates shows in resisting his sexual advances. In the *Phaedrus*, Plato also contrasts the truly philosophical lovers with those who, in a "careless hour," choose the part of their souls that the "multitude account blissful," and "achieve their full desire" (*Phaedrus* 256c). Thus, explicit sexual satisfaction is renounced by the truly philosophical soul. In fact, once eros has climbed even to the lowest rung on the ladder of knowledge, it cannot be equated with sexual desire.[12] The passion for an individual body gives rise to noble discourse (*Symposium*

210a), because this passion is not for the beauty of the body itself but for that common element of beauty that leads beyond love for the body. Even at this first step of erotic education, it is the form of beauty, not the sensual qualities of the body, that gives rise to discourse. Eros at this stage is already contrasted with the desires of the vulgar whose "procreancy is of the body" (*Symposium* 2083) rather than the spirit. Thus, the love that plays so central a role in the *Symposium* presumes a desensualization of desire.[13]

Love, in its highest form, becomes an intellectual love of universal, pure forms, which in Plato's view underlie the realm of phenomenal existence. Diotima, the priestess who became Socrates' teacher about love, distinguishes it from the ordinary meaning of eros as sexual love for another individual. Instead of this interpretation of eros, Plato deliberately broadens its scope.[14] As Diotima comments, "What we've been doing is to give the name of Love to what is only one single aspect of it . . ." (*Symposium* 205b). Instead, we should view eros as an encompassing form of desire, a longing for what one lacks, that is held in common by all mankind (*Symposium* 205b). Socrates recounts Diotima's speech about love as follows:

> For "Love, that renowned and all-beguiling power," includes every kind of longing for happiness and for the good. Yet those of us who are subject to this longing in the various fields of business, athletics, philosophy and so on, are never said to be in love and are never known as lovers, while the man who devotes himself to what is only one of Love's many activities is given the name that should apply to all the rest as well. (*Symposium* 205d)

In Diotima's account, philosophers are the most perfect lovers, since they seek above all knowledge of the good. In treating knowledge as the highest form of love, she distinguishes between those whose "procreancy is of the body, who turn to woman as the object of their love," and "those whose procreancy is of the spirit rather than of the flesh . . ." (*Symposium* 208e–209a). The contrast between sensual and philosophical love indicates that knowledge is devoid of sensuous components. It becomes love of the pure form of beauty, "unsullied, unalloyed, and freed from the mortal taint that haunts the frailer loveliness of flesh and blood. . . ." (*Symposium*

211e). Love of knowledge deprives the lover of his interest in sensuous beauty. The individual turns away, not only from the "charm of gold, of dress" (*Symposium* 211d), but also from love of another individual. Gregory Vlastos objects to Plato's denigration of human love in the following way: "It does not provide for love of whole persons, but only for love of that abstract version of persons which consists of the complex of their best qualities. . . . The high climactic moment of fulfilment—the peak achievement for which all lesser loves are to be "used as steps"—is the one farthest removed from affection for concrete human beings." [15] In the process of education, the lover ultimately transcends the original experience of love. Socrates quotes Diotima: "Starting from individual beauties, the quest for the universal beauty must find him ever mounting the heavenly ladder, stepping from rung to rung—that is, from one to two and from two to *every* lovely body, from bodily beauty to the beauty of institutions, from institutions to learning, and from learning in general to the special love that pertains to nothing but the beautiful itself—until at last he comes to know what beauty is" (*Symposium* 211c).

Although it has been suggested that this final appreciation of love allows us to love the beauty in individuals that is incarnate in the world, [16] Diotima explicitly argues that beauty can best be appreciated as a disincarnate form. Diotima is concerned with the ultimate appreciation of beauty "subsisting of itself and by itself in an eternal oneness" (*Symposium* 211b). Although lovely things partake of this form, they are loved only insofar as their beauty can be abstracted and contemplated on a general level. [17] Socrates' resistance to Alcibiades' charms epitomizes the consequences of this philosophical love. Whether out of genuine indifference or self-control, Socrates' behavior indicates that there is no place for sexual love in the higher reaches of the philosopher's journey. [18] Desire is diverted from its sensual origin into an intellectual contemplation of the loveliness of form. [19]

In the *Symposium*, Plato identifies the sensual form of love with female qualities. For example, in one of the early speeches in the *Symposium*, Pausanias distinguishes between the love of earthly and heavenly Aphrodite. Earthly Aphrodite, who possesses both male and female qualities, governs the passions of the vulgar. The vulgar are those who are attracted by women as well as men, whose desires are of the body rather than the soul, and who court only the shallowest people (*Symposium* 181b). Heavenly love, on the other hand, has nothing of the female, but has attributes that are altogether male. Heavenly love inspires those who turn to males, rather than females, "preferring the more vigorous and intellectual bent" (*Symposium* 181c). Thus, it is only the vulgar desires of the body that lead to love of women, but such love is considered inferior to the love of men, which is "innocent of any hint of lewdness" (*Symposium* 181c). Aristophanes' speech also contrasts the original females who are descendents of Earth to the males who are descended from the sun (*Symposium* 190a–b).[20] Men who are attracted to women indicate their descent from the hermaphrodite sex. They possess only vulgar passions and are exemplified by the adulterer (*Symposium* 191d). Men who are attracted to men, however, reveal their descent from the original male sex. They are "the only men who show any real manliness in public life" (*Symposium* 192a).

Although Socrates begins his speech with the admonition that none of the previous speakers has given the truth about love, his criticism does not appear to extend to their characterization of women. He too implies that female sexuality is an obstacle to the soul's higher pursuits. In his rendition of Diotima's teaching, he describes the mother of Love as Need, who endows her son with a "harsh and arid" character (*Symposium* 203c). It is only Love's father, Resource, who endows him with his desire for wisdom and truth (*Symposium* 203d). Moreover, Socrates' account of Diotima's speech echoes the view expressed earlier in the dialogue that vulgar love of the body is oriented toward women and human propagation, whereas the love of a man leads to a more lasting form of fatherhood (*Symposium* 208e, 209c). Diotima refers only to "man," "manhood," and "fatherhood" in describing the seeker of wisdom. It appears that the lover of wisdom can be neither a woman nor a lover of women.

Given this restriction, it is naturally puzzling that Socrates' teacher of love is herself a woman. If women do not appear among those eligible to become educated "lovers," how did Diotima attain her status? The condition under which Diotima can participate in philosophical wisdom parallels the desexualized condition under which women can enter the guardian class in the *Republic*. Diotima is not merely a woman; she is a priestess. According to Greek religious practices, those women eligible to serve the gods were either virgin or past child-bearing years.[21] In several instances in the dialogues, Plato adopts earlier religious myths or rituals in altered form. In this case, Plato admits into the dialogue the role of the priestess as a mouthpiece for the gods, along with the presupposition that she has become desexualized, in order to transform her into the mouthpiece for philosophy. Hence, it is the abdication of her sexuality that allows Diotima access to wisdom.

Thus, women's sexuality appears as an obstacle for both men and women to the spiritual progression of eros. Although Plato argues that the soul must seek to escape the body, ultimately the sex of the body determines the soul's fate.[22] Despite his claim to account for asexual souls, only the male is treated as asexual. Although it is the men at the drinking party who must learn to educate their desires in order to free themselves of their bodies, this demand for men's self-control has consequences for the way women's sexuality is interpreted. Men must seek conditions under which control can be exerted: thus they avoid any form of intercourse with women.[23] The absence of female participants from the symposium on love implies that women are incapable of educating their desires. This philosophical exclusion of women reinforces the commonly held views of Greek society that women were not fit to be educated or to gather and converse publicly with men. Although men must learn self-control, women are not even candidates for learning the philosophy of love.

The imperative to deny sensuality in all its forms is reflected in Plato's interpretation of knowledge. The goal of eros is the wisdom that resides only in the abstract vision of beauty itself. Diotima describes the very "soul" of beauty in the following way: "It is an everlasting loveliness which neither comes nor goes, which neither flowers nor fades, for such beauty is the same on every hand, the same then as now, here as there, this way as that way, the same to every worshipper as it is to every other" (*Symposium* 211a). Since the soul of beauty is eternal and identical to every worshipper, it must necessarily abstract from the sensual qualities of phenomenal existence, which are evanescent and idiosyncratic. The turning away from the pleasure of the flesh, which is necessary for knowledge of beauty, echoes the *Phaedo*'s rejection of the body as a contamination that interferes with the soul's quest for purity.[24] In this dialogue, Socrates argues on his deathbed that in order to attain "pure knowledge," we must "get rid of the body" instead of "allowing ourselves to become infected with its nature . . ." (*Phaedo* 66d–67a). The turning away from sensual pleasure, required in the pursuit of wisdom, leads to a turning away from the sensuous world in general. The phenomenal world, including bodies, laws, and institutions, is loved only insofar as it leads beyond itself to an appreciation of the single form of beauty. In its quest for purity, Platonic thought reveals the common origins of the philosophical interpretation of human sensual desire and of the sensuous world in general. In Plato's view, both must be ultimately transcended. Yet despite Plato's overt rejection of sensuous existence, sexuality determines who can and cannot pursue the path of knowledge; for it is the interpretation of women as inescapably erotic that forecloses to them this possibility.

Plato's ideal of truth is based on a commitment to pure, formal Ideas, which are eternal and unchanging. This purity of knowledge evolves within a framework in which all things bodily, including those qualities associated with women's bodies, are denigrated. The phenomenal world is systematically devalued in relation to the realm of pure thought. Aristotle's materialist orientation, however, appears to signify a departure from the commitment to purity in classical philosophy. Aristotle rejects the Platonic conception of Ideas. Instead of positing form as ideally separable from the phenomenal world, Aristotle considers the composite of form and matter to be that which creates substance (*Metaphysics* 1043a17–18). However, he does maintain a categorical distinction between the formal and the material elements, the rational and the passionate, the active and the passive. In all cases the rule of form over matter, reason over passion, and active over passive remains unquestioned. Although Aristotle recognizes the interdependency of these elements, he maintains a hierarchical relation between them that echoes Plato's denigration of the body and its passions. For example, in the *Politics* Aristotle writes, "It is clear that the rule of the soul over the body and of the mind and the rational element over the passionate is natural and expedient; whereas the equality of the two is always hurtful. The same holds good of animals in relation to men. . . . Again, the male is by nature superior, and the female inferior, and the one rules and the other is ruled" (*Politics* 1254b5–15). The body, or the passionate element, requires the surveillance and control of the soul, or the rational element. When the body appears to rule over the soul, this is a sign of a "corrupted" nature, of an "evil and unnatural condition" (*Politics* 1254a38, 1254b2).

Aristotle's claim that the rule of the rational over the passionate is natural is also used to justify the rule of the male over the female. He identifies the male with the rational elements that must, according to what is natural and expedient, dominate the passionate nature of females. In the *Generation of Animals* Aristotle characterizes the male and female principles by the contrasts between form and matter, active and passive (*Generation of Animals* 716b11). Although both the female, material principle and the male, formative principle are necessary for reproduction, the female remains inferior to the male. Aristotle writes, "the female, in fact, is female on account of inability of a sort . . ." (*Generation of Animals* 728a18). The female's inability resides, according to Aristotle, in her incapacity to create semen. Thus, in the biological writings he takes the male as the standard against which the female is measured and found deficient. The natural hierarchy that Aristotle establishes between reason and passion, form and matter, active and passive, male and female extends beyond the natural organism into the social domain. These principles influence not only physical existence, in Aristotle's view, but the "mental characteristics of the two sexes" (*History of Animals* 608a21–22). Since women are fundamentally passionate (e.g., compassionate, jealous, querulous [*History of Animals* 608b8–16]), they must be excluded from participation in the polis, the sphere of rational self-determination. Their domain is circumscribed by the household, which is the realm of natural necessity, and which must be subordinated to political rule. Men, on the other hand, as primarily rational creatures, find their proper and fullest sphere of activity in the political domain.

Despite their differences, Plato and Aristotle share certain philosophical commitments. Although Aristotle is critical of Plato's conception of pure Ideas, he retains the Platonic conception of the body as a source of unruly passions that must be subordinated to rational control. Moreover, he retains the identification of the physical, passionate, and irrational with women's nature, thus justifying the sexual politics of Greek society. Since for both thinkers, reason must rule the body, and not be ruled by it, philosophical thought itself appears to be devoid of sexual identity. Qua philosopher, the thinker is a rational, not a sexual, being. And yet, although these philosophers have claimed the universal, hence asexual character of their thought, at the same time this "asexual" mode has been a privilege limited exclusively to men. Both Plato and Aristotle have claimed, in effect, that men can transcend sexual existence in a way that is foreclosed to women. But what is the origin of this need, demonstrated by these male philosophers, to transcend sexuality? Why does their transcendence depend on women's remaining mired in sexual life? Do the philosophical categories that are developed, not only in the political sphere, but in the theories about knowledge, reveal a genuine transcendence of sexuality? Or do these categories under the guise of universal reflection instead reflect the particular experience of men in a specific historical context? Examining the social and religious practices of the period will illumine how sexuality in general, and female sexuality in particular, is handled by philosophical reflection.

**2**

# SOCIAL AND RELIGIOUS ANTECEDENTS OF ASCETIC GREEK PHILOSOPHY

THE PHILOSOPHICAL IDEAL OF PURE KNOWLEDGE, AS IT ORIGI-
nates in Plato's thought, is linked both to a conception of the body
as a source of pollution and to an association of women with this
polluting sphere. Although within the philosophical tradition, the
interpretations of both women and the body as polluting appear inseparable, in fact the linking of these concepts seems to reflect the
social and religious practices that prevailed at philosophy's inception. I will investigate the historical development of those practices
and their link with the philosophical ideal of purity by asking how
this association between women and embodiment entered the philosophical tradition. Do we see, on an empirical level, practices that
are reflected in the philosophical treatment of knowledge? Does the
demand for purity in philosophical thought build on religious antecedents? If so, what light do religious practices shed on the source
of the body's pollution?

These questions assume that concrete factors of existence, such as religious practices, sexual relations, and political institutions are not outside the sphere of culture in which philosophy operates. The inside/outside metaphor does not properly describe the relation of philosophy to the empirical world. Rather, like Gadamer, I assume that philosophy is a reflective appropriation of cultural and historical traditions.[1] It is by no means universally accepted, however, that philosophy reflects the historical concerns of a period. On the contrary, philosophers often believe that philosophical thought is protected from the external events of the world. Historical context is at best considered an interesting footnote to philosophy and is usually dismissed as belonging to the history of ideas. From this point of view, philosophy appears as a purely rational construct. Those committed to this vantage point will demand justification on the level of "pure" thought of the relevance of social practices to philosophy. Yet perhaps it is not the attempt to bring together the apparently separate spheres of life and thought that requires justification. Instead, one might fruitfully consider why these different dimensions of life are initially split apart. This handling of the empirical and intellectual as opposed spheres itself expresses the understanding of philosophy inherited from Plato. If philosophy deals only with pure truth, then philosophers must detach themselves from the empirical world and raise questions only on the level of abstraction. But the demand that knowledge be pure may itself reflect social practices and beliefs about purity and pollution. Consequently, one must critically question this philosophical tradition, which has not questioned its own commitment to pure thought.

The inquiry into the social and religious antecedents of the Greek philosophical ideal of purity leads to an investigation of the treatment of the body in the period prior to and contemporaneous with Plato. I will examine the beliefs and practices concerning sexual desire, reproduction, and death, which governed the relations between men and women. These attitudes toward the body are evidenced both in the popular religious practices of the fifth and fourth century B.C. and in the ascetic practices of the elite Orphic cult, which emerged by the sixth century B.C. and systematically combined different elements of popular Greek religion. In the more widespread religious practices, only specific activities, such as intercourse or birth, were considered polluting. The performance of purification rituals was sufficient to eliminate or contain this contamination. But in the Orphic cult, the demand for purity became generalized as a way of life. For the Orphics, the performance of purification rituals was no longer sufficient to achieve purity. Instead, spiritual purity could derive only from the absolute rejection of all things polluting—sexuality, death, and women.

The threatening character of sexual desire is clearly indicated by commonly held beliefs concerning eros, which the Greeks believed to be an extremely dangerous force. The desire for sexual gratification was seen as a disturbance that upset the healthy balance between body and soul. Sexual desire was considered to be a force external to the soul, which entered the body through the eyes.[2] By surrendering to desire, the soul lost its mastery over the body. Thus, sexual desire could lead men to commit adultery. If the woman involved in an act of adultery was related to a citizen, the man who committed the crime could be punished by immediate death.[3] Moreover, since overt displays of enthusiasm for women led a man to be suspected as a potential adulterer, they were strictly condemned. Not only did eros pose a threat to the controlling, law-abiding aspect of the soul, but it also offered no guarantee of satisfaction. Because unrequited desire was viewed as a great misery, eros also could be hated as a sickness.[4] It was believed that the disorder caused by the disease of love led to insanity. According to the Sophist Prodikos, eros "doubled" was madness.[5]

Although eros was dangerous to both men and women, its effects were not uniform. Women were believed to be especially vulnerable to erotic influence. Women's erotic nature, according to Hesiod, was the source of her deceptive character. He warns, "Let not a woman with buttocks attractively covered deceive you, charmingly pleading and coaxing while poking into your barn. He who trusts in women is putting his trust in deceivers."[6] Presumably, women were more carnal than men because they derived greater pleasure from sexual activities. Hesiod relates the story of Teiresias, the blind prophet, who had lived both as a man and as a woman. When Zeus and Hera asked which sex got the more pleasure from intercourse, he answered that women got nine-tenths of the pleasure and men one-tenth.[7] In a rage, Hera then blinded him for having revealed women's secret. However, since this story is based on the betrayal of women's secret, it also suggests that women's greater lustful nature was contrary to appearances. The theme of women's enslavement to sexual desire recurs throughout Greek literature. For example, the comic dramatist Anaxandrides wrote, "To be a slave of pleasure is the behavior of a licentious woman, not of a man." And Jason, in Euripides' *Medea*, both reproaches and excuses Medea by saying that the bed is the focus of a woman's life.

Although eros was considered to be a threatening and alien force to both sexes, restrictions on sexual activity applied primarily to women, not men. Greek men did not practice abstinence or limit sex to procreation. In fact, men had a multiplicity of sexual relations available to them while women's opportunities for sexual gratification were limited to intercourse in marriage. According to the orator Demosthenes, "We [men] have hetairai for pleasure, concubines for our day-to-day physical well-being, and wives in order to beget legitimate children and have trustworthy guardians of our households."[8] Whether men found sexual satisfaction with their wives or not they could with impunity have sexual relations with their servant girls or boys, with male or female prostitutes, and with other citizen men. The only prohibitions concerned relations with the wife, widowed mother, unmarried daughter, sister, or niece of a citizen.[9] If an adulterer were caught, he could be dealt with however the wronged male saw fit.

In contrast to male sexual freedom, women's options were severely limited. Women in the family of a citizen were strictly protected by their fathers if they were unmarried, and by their husbands after marriage. The belief prevailed that a son inherited his qualities solely from his father.[10] Since there was no effective contraception, it was necessary for men to ensure that women did not have intercourse outside the bounds of producing legitimate offspring. Consequently, girls and boys were kept apart after an early age. This segregation was so extreme that the orator Lysias spoke of his "sisters and nieces . . . ladies who have lived so respectably that they are embarrassed at being seen even by members of the family."[11] For these reasons, it was unusual for women to obtain sexual satisfaction outside the boundaries of marriage. Moreover, since marriages were predominantly arranged, especially among the upper classes, relations between husband and wife were often extremely frustrating for both partners. There was frequently a grave disparity in age between husband and wife. It was not uncommon for a girl of fifteen to marry a man in his middle thirties, offering her dolls as a sacrifice before the wedding ceremony. Although marital relations may have been unsatisfying for men, the prevalence of homosexual relations and commercial sex among men indicate that they sought sexual gratification outside the limitations of marriage. Despite the myths of women's unrestrained sexual desire, however, these avenues were closed to women.

Ultimately, for the Greeks, it is not sexuality in general, but women's sexuality in particular that is feared and must be controlled. The beliefs about women's enslavement to sexual pleasure and their ensuant moral failings appear, then, not to describe but rather to justify the social subordination of women to men.[12] Popular practices and beliefs concerning sexuality expressed an androcentrism, a bias that still often occurs in modern discussions of Greek life. For example, some scholars describe the sexual life of Greek men as extremely healthy, completely ignoring the ramifications of these practices for women.[13]

The social practices that construed female sexuality as threatening were complemented by the mythological representation of women as the source of all evil. This attribution of evil and illness to women's acts is most tellingly displayed in the story of Pandora, which is one of Hesiod's favorite tales.[14] Pandora, the first woman, was created by Zeus to take revenge on Prometheus for his crime of stealing fire. According to the gods' designs, Pandora was created to be beautiful in appearance and to be filled with evil in her heart. The gods gave Pandora a jar containing the world's evils and illnesses. When she opened the jar, death and disease were unleashed on the race of men who had previously lived without misfortune. Among other evils, Pandora brings the cruel lesson of deception to men, who discover too late that what is beautiful on the outside harbors evil on the inside.[15] The story of Pandora symbolizes the Greek perception that the evil of death is hidden beneath the beautiful appearance of life. Since the race of women sprang from Pandora, women carry the taint of evil attributed to Pandora's act.

This interpretation of women as dangerously sexual creatures who are responsible for the world's misery suggests an underlying hatred and fear of women in Greek society. Yet the prevalence of female divinities on Mount Olympus might indicate, on the contrary, a generally positive attitude toward women. Despite the presence of goddesses in Greek mythology, the hostility toward female sexuality is reflected even in the images of the deities. Athena is, for example, a revival of the ancient figure of the earth mother Kore, but she appears in a wholly desexualized form. Athena abdicates her female sexuality in her complete identification with her father. The story of Athena's birth reveals her loyalties:

> For mother have I none that gave me birth,
> and in all things, save wedlock, I am for the male with all my
>   soul,
> and am entirely on the father's side.[16]

All ties with the mother are sundered, as Athena emerges not from a woman's womb, but flashes like lightning from Zeus's brow.[17] Moreover, wise and strong as Athena is, her power is never considered comparable to that of the male deities. It is said that Zeus heard the prophecy that his first child would be "the equal of her father in wise counsel / and strength," and his second child would be a son who would be "king over gods and mortals."[18] Zeus swallowed his first wife, Metis, to prevent her from giving birth to a son who would fulfill this dire prophecy. A daughter, no matter how strong, posed no threat to the father's power in Greek mythology.

Although it was necessary for mortal children to be born of women, many of the major deities were able to avoid this fate. The story of Dionysos's birth also reflects the desire to dispense with the mother. Zeus struck Semele with thunder and lightning when she was six months pregnant. Hermes rescued Dionysos and sewed him up in Zeus's thigh for three months longer. Dionysos could claim that he, too, was not of woman born.

Apollo, worshipped by the Greeks as the god of purification, also shunned women and urged their subjugation. He was known both as a woman-hater[19] and a homosexual.[20] On his temple at Delphi was inscribed the maxim, "Keep woman under the rule."[21] In light of this characterization of Apollo, it is ironic that he uttered his oracle through the mouth of a priestess. But, although the Delphic oracle was a woman, she in no way represented a position of power for women in Apollonian religion. The oracle uttered incomprehensible sounds, which were then translated by the "holy ones." She became merely a tool of the male priests, who were thereby able to wield their influence on the state.[22]

The rituals concerning women's sexuality indicate that the devaluation of women expressed in myth affected the everyday life of Greek society.[23] As the noted anthropologist Frank Turner writes, rituals teach the members of a culture "what the values, rules, behavioral styles, and cognitive postulates of their culture are."[24] The early Greeks believed that contact with women during childbirth was the strongest, most contaminating pollution. Purification rituals were performed to wash away this material contamination. Women who had just given birth were excluded from the temple for forty days, and those who had contact with them were excluded for two days.[25] Sexual intercourse was believed to render both men and women unclean for a shorter period. Furthermore, menstrual blood was thought to contain a dangerous power.[26] In one agricultural ritual, a menstruating woman would walk about in the garden, in order to destroy weeds and injurious insects. Thus, the rituals regulating sexual behavior taught that women's sexuality was a powerful and dangerous force.[27]

Implicit in the constellation of beliefs and practices regarding female sexuality in Greek culture is the view that women posed a threat to the social order. Men feared that women's intractable sexual desires would undermine their social function of reproducing legitimate offspring, unless they were confined to the household under the watchful eyes of fathers and husbands. The suppression of women's sexuality served as one of the primary vehicles for maintaining the social oppression of women in Greek society. Because of the apparent necessity for male control over female sexuality, women were excluded from citizenship and from participation in economic life.

This regulation of women's sexuality also had implications for men. Men sought to control sexual pollution both through their authority over women, the source of contamination, and through control over their own desires. The construction of male sexual identity on the basis of control or mastery is correlated with the demand to control women. Men, by virtue of being male, determined the fate of their wives and daughters. A father decided who his daughter would marry, and a husband determined the sexual satisfaction of his wife. Furthermore, Greek citizens held sexual power not only over their families, but also over the foreign and slave population. Although citizens could be prosecuted or killed for adultery with a citizen's wife, no danger accompanied sexually using women of a foreign or servile status.[28] The male citizen exerted his authority sexually over both family and slaves as a means of buttressing his dominant social position.

Greek men could contain sexual pollution by overt domination of women or by avoidance of women altogether through homosexual relations or abstinence. Although men had a variety of sexual options outside of marriage, they also received warnings about the debilitating effects of overindulging in commercial sex.[29] They were encouraged to emulate the military ideal and practice self-control and discipline. This ascetic response to sexuality is echoed in Plato as the prerequisite for philosophical thought.

Greek beliefs regarding sexual pollution are grounded in the view that sexuality, and in particular women's sexuality, is a dangerous force. But what is the origin of this fear that is inscribed in sexual practices? What light do other purification rituals shed on this interpretation of sexuality as a pollution? Purification rituals in classical Greece occur not only around sexuality; they appear prominently around the area of death as well. An exploration of the relation between sexuality and death in popular Greek culture suggests that sexuality became imbued with the fears that surrounded contact with the dead. Consequently, women's role in the care and worship of the dead provides a clue for understanding the belief in the threatening nature of female sexuality.[30]

Death was believed to be one of the primary sources of contamination in ancient Greece. The pollution that hovered around death expressed a fear of dead men in particular and of the threat of death in general. The dread that surrounded contact with the death appears to have imbued Greek attitudes towards sexuality. Since sexuality is that life-giving activity that sends human beings to their mortal fate, it carries implicitly the threat of death. Women are implicated in this fear of sexuality in part because of their visible role in reproduction.

Purification rituals concerning death in early Greek religion sought to ward off the injurious influences generated by the dead. When a death occurred, the family of the deceased was surrounded by a taboo that excluded them from the temple for twenty to forty days. Those who had visited a house of mourning were excluded from the temple for three days. Those who had seen a corpse or taken part in ceremonies connected with a funeral were forbidden to visit the gods for an indeterminate time.[31] To be in the neighborhood of death was felt to be materially contaminating, and purification rituals served as protection by washing away this contamination.

The power of the dead is also acknowledged in the widespread worship of the dead. The early Greeks believed that after leaving this life, a pale image or ghost of the person remained in the physical shape it had during life.[32] The ghosts of individuals could return and help their kin and friends and bring harm to their enemies. These spirits made regular pilgrimages from their home below ground during certain annual festivals. For example, the wine festival of the Anthesteria devoted to Dionysos and the joy of opening and drinking the new wine was also informed by solemnity and dread.[33] For three days, the spirits of the dead were believed to rise up and fill the city with pollution. To protect themselves from danger, men chewed buckthorn and annointed their doors with pitch, and on the third day of the festival they called upon the spirits to depart. The significance of the dead for this festival is also evident in the prominent presence of the wine jars, which every Greek knew represented the grave jars in which the souls of the dead were sheltered.

Why in the midst of the rites of spring did the spirits of the dead play such a significant role? Did the spirits return to the city to contaminate men during the planting of the seeds, when the earth was most vulnerable to contamination? Did the dead play a positive role in the celebrating of spring? Jane Harrison suggests that the Anthesteria focused not on the threatening aspect of death, but on the continuation of life made possible through death. During the festival, a "panspermia" was prepared, which consisted of a pot in which every kind of seed was cooked, and of which none could partake. The panspermia was the offering of the seeds to the souls of the dead, meant in part to appease and be rid of them. But it was also prepared so that the dead could take the seeds down below the earth, tend them, give them body, and send them back to the living in the autumn. The spring then, is the dead man's time, for the seeds belong with him under the ground.

Thus, the festival of the Anthesteria reveals an understanding of death as part of the cycle of life. The dead nourish the seeds; the earth takes the seeds and gives them body. This view of death as necessary for the continuation of life implies a belief in a form of reincarnation: the dead return incarnate in the new life that they nourish. This cyclical view of nature explains how Hermes can be both the god of ghosts and the underworld, and the god of fertility of flocks and herds. One prayer says of him, "When he shines forth the earth blossoms, and when he laughs the plants bear fruit, and at his bidding the herds bring forth young." The role of the dead in nurturing the seeds underground is more familiar to us as the function of the earth mother. Aeschylus writes of "Earth herself, that bringeth all things to birth, and, having nurtured them, receiveth their increase in turn."[34] This perception of the earth as bringing all things to life is an abstraction from these earlier beliefs concerning the role of the dead in generation.

Although death is intricately related to life and fertility, the solemnity of the Anthesteria suggests another, more threatening dimension of death. This negative aspect of death is evident also in the Thargelia, the festival of the first fruits. During the Thargelia, great care was taken to keep away, as unlucky, the spirits of the dead.[35] Jane Harrison explains the coexistence of both life-giving and life-threatening aspects of death through the double nature of the Greeks' belief in an afterlife. The mana or strength of a man was believed to join his ancestors; through the reunification of his spirit with the ancestral group he would begin the cycle of life again as a tribesman or animal.[36] But for individual identity, there remained only the unhappy fates of the Keres. These ghost-like remnants of the individual soul, pale and weak, became carriers of evil and disease.[37] This unhappy view of life after death is expressed in the pessimistic notion of moira, or fate. The Greeks believed that the moira of death was assigned to each person on the day of birth.[38] Thus, alongside the belief that the dead participated in the renewal of life is the fear of the end of one's individual life, which is never fully assuaged by the belief in reincarnation. From this dread arises the belief in the pollution of death. Since the only form of immortality possible in early Greek thought occurred through group identity, the increased individuation in Orphic religion and Platonic philosophy strengthened the imperative for the individual to seek immortality in a new form. The purity of the individual's soul became the means for achieving immortal existence.

Women played a particularly prominent role in Greek practices associated with death. The task of caring for the corpses and mourning for the dead fell to women. Women were responsible for purifying the household contaminated by the risen spirit of the dead during the festival of the Anthesteria, and in general for pouring "libations to the dead."[39] The story of Pandora also emphasizes this connection between women and death. Pandora's jar represents both the wine jar of the Anthesteria and the grave jar in which the spirits of the dead were stored. According to the myth of Pandora, woman is the agent of death; without woman there would be no mortality.

This association of women and death occurs in other cultures, like that of the Highland New Guineas.[40] Anthropologists have speculated about the psychological motivation for the association between women and death. In the cycle of fertility and decay, that which emerges from the earth eventually returns to it. The Highland tribes, like the early Greeks, perceive the earth both as womb and as tomb. Just as the earth embodies both the beginning and end of life, so too do women's reproductive organs. If women possess graves in their vaginas,[41] it is because sexual intercourse for men involves reentry into that from which they emerged. Furthermore death, like birth, is a moment of transition and change. Its pollution can be read as a fear of ambiguity and change, which either directly or symbolically affects the whole community. Purification rituals provide a means for controlling this threat.

Thus, cross-cultural comparisons suggest that the link between women, death, and fertility occurs cosmologically, psychologically, and mythically. But the belief in the cyclical relation between death and fertility, evident in the Greeks and the Highland tribes, is insufficient to explain the attribution of pollution exclusively to women in popular Greek culture. Men were also thought to play a dominant role in reproduction; as stated earlier, the Greeks thought that a son inherited his qualities strictly from his father.[42] Aristotle systematizes this prevailing view of reproduction in the *Generation of Animals*, where he argues that men provide the soul, the active principle for generation that gives form to the material of the body, while the passive principle is supplied by women. But if men's participation in reproduction is at least as vital as women's, how do men escape the polluting implications of fertility?

In order to understand how men escape the pollution entailed by sexual reproduction, it is necessary to turn to one of the most deeply entrenched ritual practices in Greek culture: that of the pharmakos, or scapegoat. The ritual of the pharmakos delineates a practice that is reflected not only in the popular understanding of women, death, and fertility, but in the philosophical representation of these categories as well. Purification by means of the scapegoat ritual appears most prominently in the festival of the Thargelia. An individual was singled out, ladened with all of the pollution of the city, and sent forth (usually to his or her death) in order to cleanse the city for the protection of the new crop.[43] Although this festival did not choose women in particular as scapegoats, there were occasions when women exclusively were used as scapegoats.[44] For example, the Locrian tribute consisted in sending two maidens each year either to their death or to servitude and celibacy. Their sacrifice served to atone for the original crime of rape committed by one of their country's heroes. Harrison calls the pharmakos *the* typical purification of the whole year, familiar to every Greek.[45] It is a ritual in which a pollution is artificially created in order to purify the city of all defilement. This pattern of artificially concentrating pollution on a single figure reappears in the Greek treatment of sexuality and death. Since men had political, economic, and religious authority in Greek society, they could seek to detach themselves from and to control unwanted features of human existence by assigning pollution to a subordinate group. If women become the symbolic embodiment of the pollution arising from birth and death, and men distance themselves from this polluting sphere, then the male community will be rid of this threat.[46]

The use of the scapegoat pattern in assigning pollution to women signifies a shift from previous views regarding fertility and death. In early Greek culture, death and fertility had an ambiguous status. On the one hand, they were considered to be dangerous elements that must be rooted out, and on the other they were recognized as necessary for the sustenance of life. This ambiguity concerning death and fertility reflects the double meaning of early conceptions of taboo. In Greek, the verb *arasthai* means both "to pray" and "to curse." Similarly, in Latin, the word *sacer* means both "sacred" and "accursed."[47] Among primitive peoples the "power" that is recognized as taboo can be either good or evil, depending on how it comes into contact with people. It is therefore set aside from ordinary usage and must be treated with extreme caution. Like a sacred power, fertility brings both good and evil.[48] When ideas of taboo became associated with belief in the gods, they became transmuted into ideas of purity and impurity.[49] Purification rituals, such as that of the scapegoat, resolve this original ambiguity in the meaning of taboo by segregating out the "evil" from the "good."

Another central ritual in early Greek culture, directed toward the pollution associated with birth, is that of the "new birth." This practice is echoed in the story of Dionysos, who was reborn from his father's thigh. This myth describes a practice common in male initiation ceremonies, in which a boy is reborn (e.g., by reenacting a birth so that a boy appears to emerge from a goat) in order to rid himself of the pollution and danger that accompany his original biological birth. The ritual of new birth is a means of sundering the boy's ties of dependency on women by socializing him into the dominant male community. Through this rite of passage, childbirth is "masculinized" and decontaminated.

Rituals in general are rites of passage.[50] They accompany important changes, such as birth and death, and serve as ceremonies of transition.[51] The ritual is a mimetic art: it imitates and repeats an act that has already been done or an act that is desired.[52] By imitating an aspect of birth or death, rituals provide a means of subjugating natural conditions to the rule of human culture. By reappropriating these ritual events, the uncontrollable becomes, in some sense, controlled by human acts. The rituals of the scapegoat and the new birth signify the desire to rid the population of the evil and disease that threaten it with death.

Thus, the early Greek fear of women's pollution and the dangerous nature of female sexuality corresponds to the rituals surrounding fertility and death. This fear of sexuality appears to arise primarily from the fear of death. Death nurtures new life, yet rebirth itself inevitably ends in death. Women come to embody this pollution through a pattern of thinking that is grounded in the rituals of the scapegoat and the new birth. These beliefs about women's sexuality appear not only in popular but also in philosophical thought. Therefore, the function that the ritual fulfills in distancing and controlling the threatening moments of life is repeated in the reflective distancing from birth and death enacted in Platonic philosophy.

In the ascetic religious cult of Orphism, which emerged in the sixth and fifth century B.C., as well as in the philosophical thought that was informed by this ascetic religion, one finds an emphasis on rebirth and conversion to the way of truth, which assured these religious and philosophical devotees of immortality. The Platonic forms, which represent the qualities of universal and unchanging being, signify a rejection of temporality and mortality, of birth and death, which are the essential features of life itself. The central role of new birth in both Orphic religion and Platonic philosophy suggests that the exclusion of women from these ascetic forms was by no means incidental. On the contrary, the repudiation of women was the foundation on which their view of spiritual purity was established. Women's sexuality in Platonic thought, as in early Greek religion, represents these threatening moments of life from which philosophy seeks to purify itself. It was only by denying the fact of being born of a woman that purification and immortality was possible for the male initiates.

The religious cult of Orphism not only transmitted early Greek beliefs about the pollution of fertility, death, and women to philosophical thought but it is also considered a precursor to Western forms of religious spirituality. The Orphic religion was well established by the fifth century B.C., and if not widely practiced, it was widely known. Plato passes down to us the Orphic verse, "Many bear the wand, but few become Bakchoi" (*Phaedo* 69c). Many joined in the worship of Dionysos, the god served by Orphic religion, but few carried out all of the practices necessary for attaining the ultimate goal of union with the god.[53]

Orphism is commonly referred to as the first spiritual religion in Greece. The early Christian church saw Orpheus as the prototype of Christ.[54] Moreover, the Orphic view of religion as a way of life, the belief in conversion, original sin, and communion with God,[55] all suggest strong parallels with Christianity. The unprecedented character of Orphism lay in its transformation of purification from an external ritual act to an internal spiritual principle. For the Orphics, purification became both a way of life and a way of death. Although the full practice of Orphism, involving initiation and an exacting code of conduct, was not widespread, it played an important role in the history of both religion and philosophy. In particular, Orphism had a powerful influence on Plato's thought. The Platonic emphasis on the progression of the soul toward purity echoes the new Orphic stress on spiritual as opposed to ritual purity.

The ritual of new birth, which played a prominent role in earlier Greek religious practices, also recurred in the religion of Orphism. One of the primary tenets of Orphism was the necessity of initiating its followers into the cult's mysteries, from which women were absolutely prohibited. The male initiate underwent a conversion to a new life, in which he followed an ascetic code of conduct prohibiting marriage and contact with corpses. If the Orphic followed all of the cult's precepts, he would ultimately escape from the cycle of life and attain immortality. Distanced from the cycle of life by his commitment to purity, the Orphic priest seeks to divest himself of his mortal shell in order to uncover the divine in man. Women, however, are viewed as inescapably linked to the life cycle. It is through woman that birth occurs, and from birth results death. For the male initiate who seeks immortality, to escape life means to escape woman.

Nowhere is this aversion toward women more explicitly revealed than in the myth of Orpheus. Orpheus's wife Eurydice was killed by the bite of a snake (the snake is known to have been a symbol of fertility and is also thought to have been a vehicle for the dead).[56] After Orpheus failed in his attempt to lead Eurydice back from the underworld, he completely shunned the company of women; he is designated by some as the originator of homosexual love. There are several versions of how his death took place, but all concur that Orpheus died at the hands of women. According to one version, Orpheus was killed by the Maenads, women who worshipped Dionysos. Enraged by Orpheus's attentions to Apollo, Dionysos sent the Maenads to vent his fury. By another account, the women of Thrace murdered Orpheus because he refused to initiate them into his mysteries, and he enticed their husbands away from them.[57] Since Orpheus showed his hostility toward women by refusing to let them participate in his rites, the sacred precinct around the shrine of Orpheus is still forbidden to women. The practice of tattooing Thracian women was also said to be the punishment inflicted on them by their husbands for the murder of Orpheus.[58]

The intense misogyny of Orphism is linked to a change in early Greek religious beliefs in ideas about immortality. Earlier forms of Greek religion sought immortality through the reincarnation of life, made possible by the dead. In the Anthesteria, the dead nurture the seeds, which bring forth life, and the living, who are nurtured on these seeds, eventually join the ancestral dead. The Orphics preserved a sense of life as cyclical, in which death led to reincarnation. But the belief in reincarnation provided no comfort to the Orphic, who saw this renewal of life merely as a form of punishment for men's original sin. According to the Orphic story of creation, the race of Titans was guilty of the horrible crime of killing the infant Dionysos and tasting his flesh. By way of retribution, Zeus slew them with a thunderbolt, and out of their smoking remains arose the race of mortal men.[59] Because of this origin, mankind has a composite nature, partly reflecting his wicked ancestors and partly reflecting the godly being whom the Titans swallowed. Man's aim in life, therefore, is to purge the titanic element from his nature in order to exalt the divine. The Orphic ascription of evil to the body is justified mythologically by this story of creation. Since the Titans who killed the god contribute the fleshly attribute of human existence, the body represents that inheritance of evil. Guthrie describes the Orphic denigration of the body as follows: "The belief behind it is that this present life is for the soul a punishment for previous sin, and the punishment consists precisely in that, that it is fettered to a body."[60]

Until man sufficiently purifies himself by following the Orphic code of conduct, he remains on the wheel of life, merely to be reborn after death in another incarnation. The follower of Orphism believes his conversion to this new religion is itself a sign that he is on his last life and will imminently escape from this cycle. Ultimately the Orphic will become one of the gods and live eternally in their midst. Thus, the fundamental doctrines of the Orphic religion suggest that man achieves immortality not through reincarnation on the wheel of life; he can attain ultimate divinity only by means of living righteously. Although the belief in reincarnation is preserved in Orphic religion, no longer does it assuage the dread of death. Instead, rebirth itself is seen as a punishment. In the Orphic vision immortality cannot be achieved through the participation in the ancestral community, but only through the individual's transcendence of the life cycle. Thus, this new emphasis on individual immortality introduced by Orphism is linked at its inception with an intensified hostility both toward women and toward life itself.

The Orphic focus on redemption of the individual ascetic reflects the transformation of societal bonds in this period. The strong ties of kinship groups had begun to break down by the sixth century B.C. to be replaced by the stronger bonds of the city-state.[61] The individualism of the Orphic religion can be understood as a response to the decay of family ties and as a refusal to transfer the bonds of loyalty to the state.[62] Just as Orphism emerged from the disintegration of traditional family ties, so it rejected the conceptions of life and death linked to these communal ties. The life of the natural, material world, instead of being both worshipped and feared, became the object of contempt. Orphic asceticism inverted the understanding of man's relation to nature evident in the more popular forms of Greek religion. Instead of standing in awe at the situatedness of human beings in nature's cycle of growth and decay, the ascetic sought to deny this origin.

Since the Orphics believed that the pollution of life is omnipresent, the Orphic followers sought to purify the soul of the body through constant vigilance in order to attain immortality. Our knowledge of their ascetic practices derives from two important sources. The Orphic rules of asceticism are those familiar to us as "pythagorean." Diogenes Laërtius describes these as follows: "Purification, they say, is by means of cleansings and baths and aspersions, and because of this a man must keep himself from funerals and marriages and every kind of physical pollution, and abstain from all food that is dead or has been killed."[63] Moreover, the fragment of Euripides' *Cretans* makes the following reference to Orphic prohibitions: "Clothed in raiment all white, I shun the birth of men nor touch the coffins of the dead, and keep myself from the eating of food which has had life."[64] The Orphic creed mandates the avoidance of funerals, coffins, and marriages, which signify the fundamentally polluting qualities of death and sexuality. In order to escape this pollution, the Orphic undergoes a process of conversion, like the ritual of rebirth found in certain religions, through which the initiate is inducted into an all-male society and sunders his preexisting ties with women. The Orphic becomes initiated into the Way, a path of truth, righteousness, and salvation by which the Orphic could determine his fate after death and eventually escape from the wheel of life. The elite who are converted to this way of life will attain divinity, while the masses of ignorant people will be left to rot in the mud of Hades.[65] Although Orphism is still based on ritual observance,[66] the purpose of these observances is not to please the gods. Instead, the Orphic is propelled from within by the goal of achieving his own divinity through a spiritual commitment to an ascetic way of life. Commentators such as Guthrie and Harrison recognize in Orphism a "spiritual" form of religion akin to Christianity, and its practices may well elucidate the underpinnings of the Christian concept of spirituality. Moreover, since misogyny is explicit in Orphism through its exclusion of women, a pattern to be repeated both in the philosophical tradition and in the Christian priesthood, and since it is embedded in the basic doctrines concerning purity and immortality, which negate the cycle of life heralded by women, this hostility to women evident in the origin of asceticism may be the hidden practice of our modern religious and philosophical commitment to purity.

All of these features of the Orphic conception of spiritual purity—conversion to a way of truth, the striving for individual immortality, the denial of the body—express the fundamental features of asceticism, which in the *Genealogy of Morals* Nietzsche calls "this hatred of humanity, of animality, of inert matter; this loathing of the senses, of reason even; this fear of beauty and happiness; this longing to escape from illusion, change, becoming, death, and from longing itself. It signifies, let us have the courage to face it, a will to nothingness, a revulsion from life, a rebellion against the principal conditions of living."[67] The Orphic attempt to achieve immortality by escaping the wheel of life appears as a response to the dread of death. More generally, it may be a means of detaching oneself from the threat posed by change, by the existence of a world outside of one's control. Ascetic practices, like earlier purification rituals, provide an instrument for asserting control over the ominous changes in life, for mediating the terror of life and death. By following rigidly defined rules of conduct, the individual is assured of progressing along the path of salvation. As Nietzsche writes, asceticism serves as a "safety valve for pent-up emotion."[68] All feelings of doubt, fear, anxiety, and desire can be purged from the ascetic soul as energy becomes directed solely toward the pursuit of purity.

Orphic asceticism retains the association of women with the life process evident in earlier Greek religious practices. When life itself is felt to be a threat, and one seeks to escape life, then women, who are taken to represent the life process, appear as dangerous and polluting. Misogyny, therefore, becomes a vehicle for the ascetic rejection of the body in its urge to transcend the changes of life brought on by temporal existence.

Thus, the Orphic emphasis on the Way, the path of salvation, leads to a detachment from the ordinary course of life. By establishing a rigid distinction between the world of "purity" and the pollution of sensuous existence, Orphism seeks a purpose in reality beneath the flux of appearance. The remarkable parallel between Orphic and Platonic beliefs about purity and pollution indicates

that these ascetic religious practices informed the Greek philosophical tradition. The goal of the philosopher, like that of the Orphic follower, is to achieve purity of the individual soul. Purity can
be achieved, according to Plato, only when the soul rids itself of
the contamination of the body, which is ultimately possible only
through death. However, Plato substitutes philosophy for religion
as the practice of purification. As Socrates says in the *Phaedo*:

> Perhaps these people who direct the religious initiations are not so
> far from the mark, and all the time there has been an allegorical
> meaning beneath their doctrine that he who enters the next world
> uninitiated and unenlightened shall lie in the mire, but he who
> arrives there purified and enlightened shall dwell among the gods.
> You know how the initiation practitioners say, "Many bear the em-
> blems, but the devotees are few"? Well, in my opinion these de-
> votees are simply those who have lived the philosophical life in
> the right way. (*Phaedo* 69c)

In order to dwell among the gods, the philosophical soul must not
only hold the body in contempt but must also relegate the world of
the senses in general, the world of change and becoming, to the
realm of mere illusion.

Orphic influence is also evident in Plato's treatment of reincarnation. In the *Meno*, Socrates says, "I have heard from men and
women who understand the truths of religion. . . . Those who tell it
are priests and priestesses of the sort who make it their business to
be able to account for the functions which they perform. . . . They
say that the soul of man is immortal. At one time it comes to an
end—that which is called death—and at another is born again,
but is never finally exterminated. On these grounds a man must
live all his days as righteously as possible" (*Meno* 81a–b). Socrates' speech echoes the Orphic belief that a man's soul will be
reborn, and that the fate of a good man is different from the fate of
an evil one after death. Socrates continues his account with a reference to the "ancient doom" for which we must give satisfaction to
the Queen of the Underworld. This phrase refers not to anything
done by the individual, but can only refer to the original sin im-
parted to man by his Titan heritage. These mystical references in-

dicate that Plato shares the Orphic view that mortal men must undergo punishment and purification.[69]

The doctrine of reincarnation appears not only in the dialogue's mythical allusions but is also necessary for the philosophical doctrine of recollection that Socrates presents. The soul can gain knowledge through recollection because it "has been born many times, and has seen all things both here and in the other world, has learned everything that is" (*Meno* 81c). Plato thus gives philosophical significance to the religious belief in the reincarnation of the soul.

The most detailed account of reincarnation occurs in the *Phaedrus*. Plato writes: "For a soul does not return to the place whence she came for ten thousand years, since in no lesser time can she regain her wings, save only his soul who has sought after wisdom unfeignedly, or has conjoined his passion for a loved one with that seeking. Such a soul, if with three revolutions of a thousand years she has thrice chosen this philosophical life, regains thereby her wings, and speeds away after three thousand years" (*Phaedrus* 248e–249a). Plato's suggestion that the philosophical life marks the end of one's existence on the wheel of life echoes the Orphic belief that its adherents are in their final incarnation. Consequently, death is to be embraced rather than feared. In the *Phaedo*, Socrates consoles his friends who are mourning his imminent death by saying, "As it is, you can be assured that I expect to find myself among good men. I would not insist particularly on this point, but on the other I assure you that I shall insist most strongly—that I shall find there divine masters who are supremely good" (*Phaedo* 63c). The escape from life for the philosophical soul, like for the Orphic soul, holds the promise of residing with the divine masters.

Plato also sees the body as the source of evil from which the soul must be liberated. In the *Phaedo*, he writes, "And purification as we saw some time ago in our discussion, consists in separating the soul as much as possible from the body, and accustoming it to withdraw from all contact with the body and concentrate itself by itself, and to have its dwelling, so far as it can, both now and in the future, alone by itself, freed from the shackles of the body" (*Phaedo* 67c–d). Separating the soul from the body requires abstaining from the "so-called pleasures connected with food and drink" (*Phaedo* 64d), from sexual pleasures, and from the pleasures of ornament. This abstention reflects the asceticism introduced by the Orphics. Plato carries this mistrust of the body from the realm of everyday practices to that of perception. Not only physical pleasures, but physical sensations are to be mistrusted. The soul attains truth "when it is free of all distractions such as hearing or sight or pain or pleasure of any kind—that is, when it ignores the body and becomes as far as possible independent, avoiding all physical contacts and associations as much as it can, in its searching for reality" (*Phaedo* 69b–c).

Orphic asceticism consisted in a denial of the value of the body, of sexuality, and of mortality. Purity was considered the way of righteousness and salvation. In Platonic philosophy, ascetic detachment from the body is also necessary for the soul to achieve salvation through the attainment of knowledge. The philosophical demand for purity is reflected in the exclusion of emotion and sense experience from the quest for truth. Truth, according to Plato, is achieved by applying "pure and unadulterated thought to the pure and unadulterated object" (*Phaedo* 66a). If the soul is to reattain its affinity with the realm of pure Ideas, with reality, it must avoid these bodily interferences. Philosophy is the means of "liberation and purification" (*Phaedo* 67e).

Thus, Orphic influence is evident in Plato's insistence on purity, in both the mind that thinks and the object that is thought. The dualism of the *Phaedo* expressed the necessity for the soul, which is potentially divine, to be liberated from the pollution of the body. This denigration of the body pervades Plato's ontological and epistemological commitments. The contrast between the purity of thought and the pollution of embodiment informs "the most characteristic part of Platonism, the sharp separation of the lower world of *sensa* from the heavenly world of the Ideas."[70] Both the soul and the Ideas possess eternal being; both the soul and the Ideas exist purely when they are no longer embedded in the phenomenal world.[71] Only because of this affinity between the soul and the Ideas is knowledge of reality possible.[72]

Thus, the emphasis on purity in Platonic thought reflects the as-

ceticism inherited from Orphic religion. This philosophical commitment to purity leads to a de-eroticization of eros. Love is detached
from its sensual origins and becomes the pure contemplation of
beauty. Furthermore, this asceticism leads to a conception of truth
as existing apart from the phenomenal world of change, sensation,
and emotion. The Platonic practice and concept of purity is also
deeply rooted in the misogynist heritage of Orphism; Orphic misogyny is apparent in the exclusion of women from their cult, in
their mythical account of Orpheus's death, and in their avoidance
of sexuality and contact with the dead, which common rituals and
beliefs had linked with women. Women were excluded from philosophy as they had been from the ascetic religious cult. No women
participate in the conversations around which the dialogues are
built. Although Diotima is the great exception, as a priestess she is
desexualized, and she herself does not undergo the process of education within the dialogue. Moreover, only two women were ever
admitted to Plato's Academy.[73] Concomitant with this exclusion of
women from the activity of philosophy is a philosophical system
built on the purification of the soul from the body and of truth from
phenomenal existence. The Platonic demand for pure knowledge,
which is ultimately attainable only through death, echoes the Orphic goal of achieving a purity that will provide an escape from life.
Like the Orphics, in detaching the soul from the body, Plato seeks
to deny that man is a sexual and hence a mortal being. By conversion to the way of truth, the philosophical soul can escape the mortal fate linked to being born of woman.

Nietzsche describes the consequences for the truth-seeker when
truth itself is constructed on such an ascetic foundation: "The
truthful man . . . is led to assume a world which is totally other
than that of life, nature, and history."[74] The ascetic view of truth
expresses, in Nietzsche's view, a will to dominate life in order to
denature it. Nietzsche notes as well that philosophy's opposition between pure truth and sensuous, fickle existence has linked women
with the latter domain. Hence the startling opening line of *Beyond
Good and Evil:* "Supposing that truth is a woman. . . ."[75] Philosophers have been bumbling and inept in their courtship of truth. If
they seek to court truth in a more convincing manner, the opposi-

tion they draw between pure truth and sensuous existence, between reason and desire, and between masculinity and femininity must be transformed.[76]

In Nietzsche's view, therefore, asceticism is a form of nihilism. Life is determined negatively by the prohibitions one must obey. The Platonic dialogues themselves contain a nihilistic element, since Plato constructs his ideal realm of truth on the negation of the ordinary realm of appearance. However, there is a tension in Plato's own view about the possibility of entirely cutting ties to the world of phenomenal existence. The ascetic goal of purifying the soul through detachment from the body cannot be fully realized within the context of human, temporal existence. Plato insists that those who have studied philosophy must return to the cave, return to the realm of managing human affairs. He comments, "When they have thus beheld the good itself they shall use it as a pattern for the right ordering of the state and the citizens and themselves throughout the remainder of their lives . . ." (*Republic* 540a–b). Only when the proper ordering of the state and education of the populace has been achieved can the philosopher depart to the Islands of the Blessed (*Republic* 540b). Thus, the philosopher cannot escape mortal existence entirely through the purification of his own soul, but ultimately he must seek to embody the ideal order in the phenomenal world. However, Plato's deprecation of phenomenal existence, with its implication that the world inherently resists the philosopher's ideal, suggests that purity ultimately may be an unrealizable goal.

**3**

# AUGUSTINE'S VIEWS OF WOMEN
# AND SEXUALITY

IN GREEK RELIGION AND PHILOSOPHY, WOMEN REPRESENTED THE
pollution associated with the body and sexuality because of their
role in giving birth to life, which brings with it the threat of death.
Both Plato and Aristotle denigrate women as the embodiment of the
dangers posed to reason by sexuality. Since women are considered
to be ruled primarily by passions, they are deemed unsuited for
rational pursuits. A similar alignment appears in Christian views
about women and sexuality, stemming from both Greek and He-
brew religions.[1] By turning to key thinkers in the Christian tradition, we may illuminate the assumptions in which modern Western
religious conceptions of purity are rooted. Moreover, because of the
intimate connection between the church and educational institutions in the medieval and early modern period, an inquiry into
Christian views provides a foundation for interpreting the significance of purity in modern philosophy. This discussion will raise

43

the question whether the transmission of the concept of purity from classical sources to modern thought brings with it the misogynist underpinnings of philosophy's ascetic forebears.

Asceticism has remained one of the prominent themes in Christianity. Although not all of its followers are required to renounce sexual activity, until the Reformation all those who dedicated their lives to religion adhered to a life of celibacy. Like the ancient Greeks, the church fathers primarily associated the dangers of sexuality with women's nature. Although both men and women were subject to the torments of sexual desire, women were seen as more likely than men to remain under its sway. In order to be pure, therefore, men had to avoid contact with women. Women could also achieve a kind of purity by preserving their virginity. But because of their biblical role as temptress, women were viewed as naturally closer to sexual danger than men, and hence as justly subordinated to men in this world. Although the church fathers indicted Eve in particular, and women in general, for the sexual scourge that beset mankind, they also demanded that men control their sexual feelings. One avenue for discouraging male desire was to deprecate women as objects of desire. Ultimately, ascetic Christian views of sexuality contributed to the philosophical construction of reason as a form of transcendence and mastery over sexuality in particular, and sensuousness in general.

Augustine, born in 354, was one of the most influential figures of the early church. His views about sexuality, lust, women, and embodiment constituted an important dimension of Christian teachings. Not only did he figure prominently among his contemporaries, but his stature and influence increased through the Middle Ages. In the fifteenth century, he was described by the Bishop of Florence as a luminary in church history: "What the sun is to the sky, St. Augustine is to the Doctors and Fathers of the Church."[2]

Augustine's treatment of sexuality is intimately linked to his understanding of man's fall from grace. Sexual desire is one form of the more general state of desiring that Augustine calls concupiscence, or lust. In *The City of God*, Augustine comments that concupiscence is "the generic word for all desires."[3] The pleasures of all the senses—taste, hearing, smell, and sight—readily pose the dangers of temptation and desire to the soul.[4] The danger that lies in gratifying our senses is that we are led to seek such pleasures for their own sake rather than appreciating them as God's creation.

This general state of desire—whether it is lust for sensual gratification, for money, or for power—is itself the punishment man bears for his disobedience to God. In *The City of God*, Augustine notes that man's failure in paradise to abstain from one kind of food is all the greater since he was not yet compelled by lust to violate this command. He writes that man "found no resistance to its observance in lust, which only afterwards sprung up as the penal consequence of sin" (*CG* 14.12.460).

Consequently, all forms of lust are viewed as the punishment for the evil will, which initiated the human fall from grace. With the onset of desire, the senses pose the constant temptation of pleasure. Although hunger is no sin when we need to satisfy our appetite for our health, generally we are tempted to eat, not just to preserve health, but for the sake of pleasure itself (*Confessions* 10.31.235). Thus, in the process of satisfying our needs we are caught in the "snare of concupiscence" in which we experience the "ominous" enjoyment of gratifying our greed. Likewise, although Augustine accords a valuable role to music, he warns against the dangers of indulging in the pleasures of sound. In speaking of musical enjoyment, he writes, "But I ought not to allow my mind to be paralyzed by the gratification of senses, which often leads it astray. For the senses are not content to take second place. Simply because I allow them their due, as adjuncts to reason, they attempt to take precedence and forge ahead of it . . ." (*Confessions* 10.33.238). Thus, sensuous gratification can threaten the proper mastery of reason over the senses. Men become enamored with worldly things, become their slaves, and consequently are led away from God. In fact, sense experience in general, by which we seek empirical knowledge of the world, is in Augustine's view merely another form of the "lust of the eyes" (*Confessions* 10.35.242).

Although concupiscence is a general term referring to all desires, sexual desire remains the preeminent form of lust.[5] In *The City of God* Augustine comments, "Although, therefore, lust may have many objects, yet when no object is specified, the word lust usually suggests to the mind the lustful excitement of the organs of generation" (*CG* 14.16.464). The bodily movements that signify sexual desire were the first consequences of human's loss of grace (*CG* 14.17.465). Not only is sexual desire the most immediate sign of corruption, but it also incarnates, as no other desire does, the act of disobedience for which mankind is punished. Because of man's disobedience to God, he now suffers disobedience within himself, for neither his mind nor his flesh obey his will (*CG* 14.15.463). In sexual desire the soul can neither master itself, so as to eliminate the temptation, nor master the body, "so as to keep the members under the control of the will . . ." (*CG* 14.23.471). Whereas in other forms of desire, resistance occurs within the soul (e.g., the feeling of gluttony), in sexual desire the body itself resists the mastery of the soul. Sexual lust is most shameful because the soul's "will and order are resisted by the body, which is distinct from and inferior to it, and dependent on it for life" (*CG* 14.23.471). Thus sexual desire embodies the disobedience that precipitated and forever marks man's fall from grace.[6]

Augustine's treatment of concupiscence in general, and sexual desire in particular, reflects an ascetic imperative inherited in part from the Greeks.[7] He believed that leading a life of continence would bring him closest to God's will. In the *Confessions*, Augustine writes of the need to control sexual desire in the following way: "You [God] command us to control our bodily desires. . . . Truly it is by continence that we are made as one and regain that unity of self which we lost by falling apart in the search for a variety of pleasures. For a man loves you so much the less if, besides you, he also loves something else which he does not love for your sake" (*Confessions* 10.29.233). In Augustine's view, the temptations of the flesh pose a danger not only to our whole-hearted devotion to God, but they also interfere with the proper functioning of our mind. In *The City of God*, where Augustine describes lust as leading to the "greatest of all bodily pleasures," he comments, "So possessing indeed is this pleasure, that at the moment of time in which it is consummated, all mental activity is suspended" (*CG* 14.16.464). Thus, ideally, one must eradicate lust altogether. Augustine pleads to God to eliminate the "fire of sensuality," which provokes him even in his sleep (*Confessions* 10.30.234). And in *The City of God* he notes that any friend of wisdom would see that the purpose of sexuality, the procreation of children, would be better served if it were motivated by will and not lust (*CG* 14.16.465). Thus, the "natural" sexuality that he envisions in paradise would have been completely devoid of desire. Although Augustine admits that before the Fall, Adam and Eve did not practice coitus, he argues that had they continued to live together without sin, they still could have fulfilled God's injunction to increase and multiply (*CG* 14.23.470). In prelapsarian sex, since the body was still thoroughly subjugated to the rule of the will, the body would have remained purified of desire.

In *The City of God*, Augustine discusses how it is possible for Adam to have sown the seed, and Eve to have received it, without being excited by the shameful feeling of lust (*CG* 14.24). Augustine admits such a state is difficult to imagine since desire has become inseparable from the sexual act. However, he argues that if man had not sinned, he could have controlled sexuality by will alone, rather than by the passions. Augustine illustrates how the will can move various parts of the body. For example, one can will movement in one's hands and feet and even in those parts that are "composed of slack and soft nerves" (*CG* 14.24.472), including the face, mouth, and lungs. He notes, as further evidence, that some men have remarkable abilities to vomit, fart, and sweat at will (*CG* 14.24.473). Ideally, had man not forfeited his state of grace, sexual intercourse would have been just such an activity. Instead, his loss of control over his body, manifest in sexual desire and death, is man's punishment for his disobedience to God.[8] But in the state of paradise, Adam could have sown his seed like the artisan employed in mechanical operations (*CG* 14.24.470) or the farmer sowing the earth (*CG* 14.24.471). Augustine writes:

In such happy circumstances and general human well-being we should be far from suspecting that offspring could not have been begotten without the disease of lust, but those parts, like all the rest, would be set in motion at the command of the will; and without the seductive stimulus of passion, with calmness of mind and with no corrupting of the integrity of the body, the husband would lie upon the bosom of the wife . . . the male semen could have been introduced into the womb of the wife with the integrity of the female genital organ being preserved, just as now, with that same integrity being safe, the menstrual flow of blood can be emitted from the womb of a virgin. (*CG* 14.26.475)

In Augustine's discussion of prelapsarian sex, the problem that must be resolved is how a man can have an erection without being motivated by desire. Augustine mentions the willful control of organs composed of slack and soft nerves, in order to suggest that man could have had willful control of his penis. It is noteworthy that Augustine does not concern himself with the question of whether a woman could engage in sexual activity without being motivated by desire. Unfortunately, too often women have had difficulty in avoiding unwanted sexual contact. Women's experience in sexual relations is not visible from Augustine's point of view. His concern is with the husband lying on the wife's bosom, and not with the woman.

Thus, Augustine speaks as a man, addressing other men, regarding the need to eliminate sexual desire. Women appear primarily as the objects that incite men's desire. For example, Augustine's discussion of resurrection contrasts the "natural" female body, which will not excite lust but instead will call forth praise, with the body that occurs in our unresurrected state (*CG* 22.17.839). Augustine argues against the view that women would be resurrected as men (*CG* 22.17.839). This latter view implies that woman's body is intrinsically a corruption that would be eradicated in the state of blessedness. Instead, Augustine argues that the vice in women's bodies lies in carnal intercourse and child-bearing. Thus, Augustine condemns woman's provocative and procreative body because it is a source of transgression for man. Since women arouse desire in men, their earthly bodies are deemed unnatural.

Augustine's treatment of sexuality in the states of blessedness, corruption, and resurrection indicates that ideal human relations are devoid of desire. Moreover, it implies that sexuality cannot be a vehicle for human love but serves only as an interference with it. Consequently, Augustine maintains a place for sexuality in human life only as a narrow and corrupted form of human expression. For Augustine, ideal sexuality is devoid of all feeling and desire, and it finds its sole justification in the procreation of children. As Rosemary Radford Ruether comments, "In Augustine's view, then, rightly ordered sex is properly such as to be depersonalized, unfeeling and totally instrumental. It relates to the female solely as a body to be used for procreation."[9]

Augustine's conception that sexuality should be only a vehicle for procreation is part of his more general desensualization of the body. The ideal body, as Augustine's condemnation of concupiscence makes clear, is devoid of desire for sensual pleasures. Although gratification of the senses is necessary to maintain a level of health or satisfy modest needs, seeking pleasurability as an end in itself is a sickness. Despite Augustine's rejection of lust, it has been argued that he maintains an appreciation for the sensuous nature of the human body.[10] For example, in *The City of God* he argues in detail that not just the soul, but the body, too, will be resurrected (*CG* 22.25.855). And he comments that although the body is "made for the service of a reasonable soul" (*CG* 22.24.853), the beauty of the body indicates that in its creation "comeliness was more regarded than necessity" (*CG* 22.24.854). Moreover, he stresses that the flesh is not alien to our nature (*CG* 15.7.487); hence it must be healed, not rejected. It is not the body itself, but the corruptibility of the body that is a burden to the soul (*CG* 13.16.424). Consequently, before the body was tainted by man's disobedience, man could enjoy his senses without sin. Augustine describes paradise in the following way: "Man then lived with God for his rule in a paradise at once physical and spiritual. For neither was it a paradise only physical for the advantage of the body, and not also spiritual for the advantage of the mind; nor was it only spiritual to afford enjoyment to man by his internal sensations, and not also physical to afford him enjoyment through his external senses. But obviously it was both for both ends" (*CG* 14.11.458).

However, Augustine's appreciation is for the ideal body that is purified of all desire, and "in every respect subject to the spirit" (*CG* 22.24.855). The mortal body that human beings have in this worldly existence is condemned in Augustine's philosophy. Only when we transcend our present mortal existence will our flesh be transformed to a wholly spiritual being. Thus, the body is valued insofar as it serves as an instrument of the soul, and it can be infused throughout with a spiritual nature. The body does not contain its good in itself, but "the soul is the good of the body."[11] Augustine's treatment of the body is analogous to Plato's treatment of eros in the *Symposium*. Although Plato viewed eros as central in gaining knowledge, ultimately eros became a wholly intellectual, desensualized form of desire.[12] Similarly, the resurrected body embraced by Augustine is not the desiring body that animates human existence but a spiritualized being wholly devoid of lust.

Consequently, Augustine's ascetic treatment of the body does not lead to an enhancement of our existence as sensuous beings but to a transcendence of fundamental characteristics of our physical life. In the *Confessions*, when Augustine describes the qualities embraced by his love of God, they are not material beauty, earthly light, the sweetness of harmony, or the fragrance of flowers. Instead, this love of God brings with it a "light that is not bound by space," a "sound that never dies away," a fragrance "that is not borne away on the wind," a food "that is never consumed by the eating," and an embrace that is "not severed by the fulfillment of desire" (*Confessions* 10.6.212). Although this physical imagery indicates Augustine's sensitivity to the sensual aspect of his being, these metaphors also suggest his struggle to conquer these feelings. A fragrance that never fades is not the ultimate fragrance for us; rather it could not be perceived as a fragrance at all. An embrace that is not severed by the completion of desire is not an embrace, but signifies a retreat into an inner life in which the temporal quality that constitutes sensuous life is denied. Augustine's vision of love of God brings with it not the fulfillment of our senses, but a condition in which the qualities of sensuous existence have disappeared.[13] Just as Augustine decries the temporality of the senses, which must be transcended, so he also distances himself from the fleeting qualities of emotions. Augustine describes paradise as a state that is devoid of the "vicissitudes of fear and desire," of sadness and joy (*CG* 14.26.474). Instead, the only kind of emotion suitable to the pristine state of paradise consists in gladness that flows ceaselessly from God. No passion, no extremes, no change of emotion is conceivable for the ideal human state. In short, the very qualities that characterize emotional life must be overcome.

Although Augustine suggests that the body in general must be subject to the rule of the soul, he also implies that women are less suited to fulfilling this task than men. As Ruether observes, Augustine assimilates the male-female relationship into the soul-body relationship.[14] Ruether writes that the female is "somehow made peculiarly the symbol of 'body' in relation to the male (i.e., in a male visual perspective) and is associated with all the sensual and depraved characteristics of mind through this peculiar 'corporality.'"[15] Women, as the object of male desire, are associated with the unruly passions that the male soul must seek to conquer. Augustine describes the need to avoid sexual contact with women as follows: "There is nothing I am more determined to avoid than relations with a woman. I feel that there is nothing which so degrades the high intelligence of a man than the embraces of a woman and the contact with her body, without which it is impossible to possess a wife."[16] In a manner reminiscent of early scapegoat rituals, Augustine resolves his own ambivalence about sexual desire by banishing women from his presence. As in Greek religion and philosophy, by heaping the pollution of sexuality onto woman as the source of temptation, man thereby purifies himself of this contamination. Consequently, Augustine's interpretation of female sexuality as a danger signifies above all a conflict about male sexuality.

Augustine's view that women are more closely linked to the corrupt body than men makes their subordination to men both natural and commendable. In his eulogy of the present order, Augustine treats woman as existing exclusively for man. He describes man as made in the "image and likeness" of God because he has the power of reason and understanding. Augustine continues,

> And just as in man's soul there are two forces, one which is dominant because it deliberates and one which obeys because it is subject to such guidance, in the same way, in the physical sense, woman has been made for man. In her mind and her rational intelligence she has a nature the equal of man's, but in sex she is physically subject to him in the same way as our natural impulses need to be subjected to the reasoning power of the mind, in order that the actions to which they lead may be inspired by the principles of good conduct. (*Confessions* 13.32.344)

If woman is made for man in the physical sense, one must consider what function her subordination to man fulfills. Her creation appears to embody in an external being the natural impulses that man seeks to control in himself. The physical subjection of women to men represents, in the physical world, the proper subordination of the appetitive to the rational element in the soul. Since Augustine views the physical world as a representation of God's spirit, the proper ordering of this realm must conform to the divinely ordained rule of reason over natural impulses. The subjugation of woman to man incarnates, in Augustine's view, the spiritual hierarchy that man must strive to achieve within his own soul. Since women's physical existence is designed for men, this external embodiment of the rule of the higher over the lower elements of the soul must enhance men's ability to achieve rational self-control. By means of their domination over women, men can learn to achieve that domination of reason within their own soul required for spiritual purity. Thus, as with the early Greeks, the purity of the male soul requires control over women, who represent the threatening elements of existence. However, Augustine does not identify women exclusively with the body, as does Orphic thought. He notes that in her mind and her rational intelligence, woman has a nature equal to man's. Despite this admission of women's rationality, women became, in Augustine's view, symbolically identified with the lower, instrumental uses of reason. Thus, women remain associated with those functions of the soul that signify the dimension of human existence that is not made in God's image.[17] Ultimately, although Augustine acknowledges women's rational intelligence, the domination of male over female remains a natural dimension of human existence, which is overcome only with resurrection.

Thus, as Simone de Beauvoir has argued, woman is represented as "other" in the Christian tradition. She is created for man, and she embodies the aspects of human nature more closely identified with the sensibility of the body. Although Augustine acknowledges woman's rational equality with man, he immediately adds that she is "physically subject to him." Woman's rational nature does not detract from her primary purpose, which is to be physically subjected to man in the way that man's natural impulses need to be controlled. Augustine's insistence on rational equality and physical subordination suggests that women's physical being stands in a different relation to their spiritual being than does men's. Only in the order of salvation, when female flesh is purified of corruption, can women attain the physical equivalence with men that they are promised spiritually. Whereas men's bodies reflect the superior element of the soul, women's bodies do not. Consequently, women alone experience a split between their rational soul and their embodied existence.[18] Although Augustine does not explicitly identify the weakness in women's bodies that necessitates male control, one might surmise that it lies in their inability to rationally control their reproductive capacities, evinced in menstruation and pregnancy. Because of women's experience of the natural life cycles of the body, they symbolize for Augustine that lack of willful control over the body that men must overcome.

Augustine's dual conception of women's spiritual and physical being leads him to attribute conflicting qualities to women's nature. He writes, "A good Christian is found in one and the same woman to love the creature of God whom he desires to be transformed and renewed, but to hate in her the corruptible and moral conjugal connection, sexual intercourse and all that pertains to her as wife."[19] A Christian man must love in woman the creature of God who must be transformed, but he must hate her wifely, sexual nature. Augustine also compares the relation of husband to wife to the mandate to love one's enemies.[20] Although Augustine maintains that marriage is honorable, nonetheless it leads to lesser goods than those achieved by a life of continence. He describes marriage in the following terms: "If it is a duty of the wise man (I have not examined this point) to seek to have children, he who takes a wife for this purpose seems more to be admired than imitated, for there is greater danger in trying than there is happiness in succeeding. I think, therefore, that in imposing on myself the decision not to desire, nor to seek nor to take a wife, I have done so for the good and just liberty of my soul."[21] Although women were created for the purpose of aiding in generation, Augustine also argues that after resurrection, this function will be transcended. Women's bodies will retain their "nature," not their "vice"; they shall be "superior to carnal intercourse and child-bearing" (*CG* 22.17.839). Thus the resurrection of women's true nature negates the function for which they were created. Women's essence, in Augustine's view, is contrary to the reality of their embodied existence. Not only are women subordinated to men in earthly existence, but they are uniquely divided within themselves between their earthly function and their "nature." These contradictory aspects are resolved only when earthly existence itself is overcome.

Augustine's contemporaries harbored few doubts about the naturalness of women's subordination because of woman's role in the fall from grace. Indeed, Augustine's views of woman's burden of sin are rather more tempered than those of other church fathers. For example, Tertullian, one of the early church fathers, offers a virulent account of Eve's behavior: "*You* are the Devil's gateway. *You* are the first deserter of the divine Law. *You* are she who persuaded him whom the Devil was not valiant enough to attack. *You* destroyed so easily God's image man. On account of *your* desert, that is death, even the Son of God had to die."[22] Tertullian attributes to Eve pernicious power. *She* persuaded Adam when the Devil would not; *she* destroyed man. In Augustine's account of the Fall, Eve does not retain such power. However, his modification of Eve's role itself reflects his assumption that women represent the inferior element of the soul. According to Augustine, Eve was deceived by the Devil, who chose the weaker partner in the human union. The Devil knew full well that Adam would never suppose the "devil's word to be truth" (*CG* 14.11.459). Adam chose to join with Eve with "his eyes open" out of the noble bonds of kinship (*CG* 14.11.459). He was not deceived about the truth of the devil's word but only about the consequence of his action. Hence, Eve's weakness relieves her of ultimate responsibility for sin, which falls on Adam's nobler shoulders. Only one with the full capacity for rational self-control can bear the burden of a disobedient will.

Although Eve is not responsible for the Fall, she remains the temptation or vehicle for sin in Augustine's account. Her behavior suggests that if woman had properly remained subordinate to man, human beings would not have been excluded from paradise. But since woman is created for man in Augustine's account, Eve's behavior nonetheless appears to satisfy a certain function for man. Just as women's subordination contributed to men's achievement of self-control, so women's insubordination gives expression to men's desire to transgress and to the consequent demand for punishment. What emerges from the story of the Fall is not Eve's transgression but man's own, arising from the failure of the rational component in the male soul to dominate.

Because of this act of disobedience in our first parents, sexual activity can never escape its sinful origin. Although the purpose of the marriage contract is the procreation of children, even when sex is performed for the sake of producing legitimate offspring, it is permeated by original sin. In the *Confessions*, Augustine observes the difference between his own love alliance and marriage in the following terms: "I found out by my own experience the difference between the restraint of the marriage alliance, contracted for the purpose of having children, and a bargain struck for lust, in which the birth of children is begrudged . . ." (*Confessions* 4.2.72). Only by transforming the satisfaction of lust into a necessary duty is the act forgiven its inherent sinfulness.[23] Even under these conditions, however, one cannot completely annihilate pleasure and satisfaction. Consequently, children are always born under the taint of original sin. Although Augustine argues in qualified terms that procreation is a "goal" of marriage, he suggests that God's commandment to increase and multiply may no longer apply to the Christian people. He declares that there are already enough souls to fill heaven. If men would remain celibate, the end of the world and the time of blessedness would be hastened.[24]

Augustine's identification of women's function with procreation, which inevitably is imbued with sin, reveals an androcentric bias in his analysis. Since woman symbolizes the element of existence that precipitates us into lust, man can identify himself with the superior aspect of rationality. Augustine's ascription of different natures to male and female provides a theoretical rationale for men's dominance over women. Although woman also is rational, woman's body appears as the symbolic representation of irrationality, whereas man's body appears as the symbol of rationality. Thus, the rational control that ascetic thinkers have sought as a religious and philosophical goal becomes incarnate in a physical existence that demands the social exercise of power. Augustine prefigures the identification of reason with mastery that became pronounced in the modern philosophical tradition since Bacon and Descartes. As in Augustine's writing, reason in modern philosophy is linked not only with rational control within the soul, but also with men's control over women in the social world.[25]

Augustine's demand that sexual desire be controlled reflects, in part, his personal conflicts about sexuality, which are revealed in the *Confessions*. Having struggled against his own desire for years before his "conversion," he recalls: "As a youth I had been woefully at fault, particularly in early adolescence. I had prayed to you for chastity and said 'Give me chastity and continence, but not yet.' For I was afraid that you would answer my prayer at once and cure me too soon of the disease of lust, which I wanted satisfied, not quelled" (*Confessions* 8.7.169). Augustine reports that he lived for years with a mistress, who remains unnamed, but whom he dearly loved and with whom he had a child (*Confessions* 6.15.131). During this period, Augustine was tormented by the impurity of his desires and the illegitimate nature of this union. In order to resolve his conflicts, he finally decided to marry a respectable partner and chose a girl still two years too young for marriage (*Confessions* 6.13.130). While waiting for her to become marriageable, still tormented by sexual passion, he took another lover. This act precipitated his "conversion," and he began a life of celibacy.

Some authors have suggested that the extremely personal origin of Augustine's theory of sexuality discounts it as representative of Christian attitudes.[26] Although Augustine's views on sexuality reflect his own struggle to control sexual passion, they also underlie his general views on original sin, redemption, and the relations between men and women, which remained highly influential until the twelfth century. Moreover, Augustine's own conflict between the desire for sexual love and the legitimacy promised by the marriage union was not idiosyncratic. In an age in which it was common for men of thirty, forty, or even sixty to marry girls of fifteen,[27] Augustine's view of marriage as primarily a union for the procreation of children would accord with contemporary practices. The enormous historical impact of Augustine's thoughts on sexuality indicates that his personal experience found resonance in the culture that embraced his ideas. As Lucien Goldmann suggests in *The Hidden God*, the very prominence of certain thinkers indicates that their ideas originate in a common social experience. Goldmann writes, "The men who express the vision [of their social class] on an imaginative or conceptual plane are writers and philosophers, and the more closely their work expresses this vision in its complete and integral form, the more important does it become."[28] Viewed in this light, the preeminence of Augustine's thought about sexuality and women indicates how profoundly he articulates commonly held beliefs and practices.

Although in Augustine's writings women appear as the primary agents of sexual desire, it is man's own problematic relation to sexuality that motivates Augustine's treatment of woman. Augustine taught that women are to be avoided, as he did in his personal life after his conversion,[29] since their bodies provoke lustfulness in men. Despite his attempt to eradicate lust, the astonishing number of references to sexual passion in the *Confessions* indicates that sexuality remains a central issue for him. Augustine seeks to resolve his own sexual conflicts by eliminating the threat to rational control posed by desire. Therefore, he idealizes a natural sex that is completely unfeeling. Prelapsarian sexuality is merely the necessary instrument for procreation, by which the man uses the woman the way a farmer sows his seeds. This desensualization of sexuality provides a means whereby man can control his own forbidden desires. This ascetic imperative leads men to distance themselves from women. Augustine's view of sexuality precludes the possibility that sexual relations can be a vehicle for personal intimacy.[30] Furthermore, for men to defend themselves against the threat of excitation, they must ultimately control all intercourse between men and women. Thus, Augustine construes the sexual identity of men in the form of domination and the identity of women in the form of submission. Although for Augustine both men and women possess rational souls, the social relationships between the sexes are determined not by rational equality but by sexual inequality. Augustine's drive to conquer sexuality motivates him to institutionalize a sexual hierarchy as determinative of human relations.

Augustine's commitment to the "natural" hierarchy between the sexes, which is only overcome with resurrection, derives from his view of sexual desire as a disease, his identification of women with both physical and spiritual sources of temptation, and his imperative to establish a chaste and pure heart. Men's willful control of their bodily passions is necessary for spiritual purity, and the exercise of their authority over women is requisite for such self-control. This commitment to the values of purity and control ultimately becomes transferred in the modern period from the religious to the philosophical domain. The opposition between purity and sensual desire expressed by Augustine is reiterated in prevailing philosophical conceptions of rationality, which have devalued the role of feeling and desire. This detachment from the body is historically grounded, as Augustine demonstrates, in a distinctly androcentric perspective. From this standpoint, men provide the standard of purity against which women are constantly found lacking. Women face the impossible task of becoming pure in the midst of their intrinsically defiling nature. Although this association of embodiment, pollution, and women reflects a distinctly male perspective, it has been presented in both religious and philosophical traditions as an unbiased, all-encompassing truth. Consequently, the origin of this ascetic commitment to purity in a particularly male-centered world has been lost from view.

# 4

# AQUINAS'S VIEWS OF WOMEN
# AND SEXUALITY

AUGUSTINE'S CONCEPTION OF PURITY IS BUILT ON A REJECTION OF the sexual pleasures of the body, which in his view interfere with spiritual well-being. Since Augustine regards women as more likely than men to be ruled by desire, spiritual purity requires that women be subordinate to men in earthly existence. Thus, historically, the ascetic commitments within Christianity are profoundly linked to the denigration of women. In the thirteenth century, Thomas Aquinas reestablished these earlier ascetic values on a thoroughly rationalistic basis. Whereas Augustine was concerned with the control of the will over the body, Aquinas sought the control exerted by reason. Aquinas's thought augurs the emergence of rationalism and the interest in natural science in the Christian world. His adoption of Aristotelian philosophy provided, in the words of one critic, "a 'scientific' basis to the earlier patristic attitudes . . . [which] guaranteed the survival of this antifemale anthropology."[1]

The Christian ascetic ideal that developed within the church was also widely appropriated in popular beliefs and practices. Asceticism became a guiding force not only in the cloisters, but in the everyday life of the Middle Ages. The practice of a harsh asceticism was commonly thought to certify one's holiness.[2] Ascetic practices apparently endowed the adherent with a spiritual power made possible by withdrawing from the body. The power of asceticism was thought to be so great that it was popularly believed that relics of "holy" ascetics could cause miracles. The widespread admiration for asceticism led to the rapid growth of monasteries and nunneries. In the period between the early years of the tenth and twelfth centuries, there was an enormous proliferation of religious orders. In England and Wales there were over 800; in London alone there were nineteen. In Paris there were twenty-two, and in the diocese of Cambrai in northern France there were more than eighty.[3] Aquinas himself entered a monastery at the age of five to receive his education and later became a Dominican monk. Those who did not enter a monastery themselves could still get credit in heaven by contributing financial support to monasteries. Economic reasons contributed in part to the flourishing of monastic life. The youngest sons of aristocrats were often destined for monastic orders because there was insufficient land to be divided among the sons. Likewise, daughters were often encouraged to enter nunneries in order to relieve their parents of the burden of paying an enormous dowry. There were also theological reasons for the growth of religious orders. The Catholic church possessed a dual ethics.[4] Although there was one code of conduct for those who lived in this world, there was a stricter code of purity for those who left the world to enter the monastery. Individuals with a passionate commitment to spiritual purity chose the path that lay outside of everyday life.

The pervasiveness of asceticism in this period suggests that Christian attitudes toward the body and sexuality—in particular, women's sexuality—became popularized. The growth of the cult of Mary with its glorification of virginity attests to the prevalence of the view that women must be purified of a corrupting sexuality. The worship of Mary emphasized the doctrine of virgin birth, which claims that Mary incurred no loss of virginity during the conception and birth of Jesus. Although Mary figured prominently in religious beliefs of the period, her stature in no way corresponded to an enhanced social position for women more generally in the Christian world.[5] Ordinary women who became mothers, and thereby lost their virginity, could not in their own minds or the minds of others be identified with this idealized image of the Mother. Mary was supernatural; she had undergone no struggle against the temptation of the flesh. Since the sanctification of virgin birth contrasted with the experience of real women, the worship of Mary did not raise women's status but provided further grounds for their subordination.[6]

As an alternative to fulfilling their function in Christianity through motherhood, women could enter the nunnery. According to the church fathers, marriage brings a thirtyfold of virtue, widowhood a sixtyfold, but virginity brings the one-hundredfold of virtue.[7] But even in the cloister, celibacy did not bring about equality for women. During the period of great monastic growth, women's position in monastic life actually suffered a sharp decline.[8] St. Bernard argued against the intrusion of women into the monastery. He declaimed, "To be always with a woman and not to have intercourse with her is more difficult than to raise the dead. You cannot do the less difficult: do you think I will believe that you can do what is more difficult?"[9] Although the nuns devoted themselves to virginity, they could never escape women's biblical role as temptress. In double monasteries, the sisters were not even allowed to sing offices, for fear that their voices might arouse male passion. Elaborate curtains were erected around a dying nun lest she see the priest who administered the last rites. In general, nuns were to speak as little as possible, since Eve's words had caused the Fall. Moreover, the nuns did not escape women's traditional work in the household, which they performed in order to free the brothers for prayer and study.[10]

Thus, ascetic religion circumscribed women's lives both inside and outside the cloister. It insured the subordination of wives to their husbands and of nuns to monks. The commitment to sexual purity inherited from Augustine, and the concomitant view that women are naturally subordinate to men, found further confirmation in Aquinas's treatment of sexual relations.

In the *Summa Theologica*, where Aquinas discusses the creation of woman, he poses the question of "whether woman should have been made in the first production of things."[11] Aquinas suggests that woman's existence is problematic because, as Aristotle says, she is a "misbegotten male"; because she is naturally subjugated to man; and because she is the occasion for sin. If God's creation is in all respects good, it is puzzling to Aquinas how such an imperfect being as woman could have been made in this original act of production. There must be a positive value in woman's existence that justifies her place in creation. Aquinas explains woman's role in the following terms: "It was necessary for a woman to be made, as the Scripture says, as *a helper* to man; not, indeed, as a helpmate in other works, as some say, since man can be more efficiently helped by another man in other works; but as a helper in the work of generation" (*ST* 1.92.1). Woman's role in biological generation alone justifies her creation. However, Aquinas pursues the question why human biology necessitates the existence of the inferior female sex. After all, he notes, there are animals with no sexual differentiation. Aquinas responds to this objection by suggesting that the biological differences between males and females allow for the separation across the sexes between the active and passive powers in generation. This distribution of powers makes possible man's pursuance of the noble, "vital operation" of intellection. Without sexual differentiation, presumably, generative capacities would not be restricted to merely one aspect of species life but would be omnipresent, allowing no room for this nobler activity. Although both males and females are necessary for procreation, with sexual dualism only one sex need be responsible for reproductive tasks. Since woman is created for her reproductive function, in Aquinas's account, she becomes virtually identified with this generative activity.[12]

Because of woman's primary identification with reproduction, man is freed to identify primarily with the nobler works of reason. The active power found in the male sex contributes not just to generation but can be directed toward the "vital operation" of reason. In assimilating the active principle in man to reason, Aquinas echoes Aristotle's treatment of sexual relations. Aristotle also associated the male with the active power and the female with the passive in the work of generation. Similarly, for Aristotle these biological principles have mental correlates: activity, or form, is expressed through rational self-determination; passivity, or matter, becomes manifested through the emotions. Aquinas reinforces this identification of male with the operations of reason when he claims that man serves as the "principle" of human existence. Aquinas writes, "As God is the principle of the whole universe, so the first man, in likeness to God, was the principle of the whole human race" (*ST* 1.92.2). If man is the principle of the human race, then he must contain, like God, all the perfections of human existence.[13] Since reason is the noblest function of human existence, intellectual operations must be contained in this first principle of the human race. Therefore, in the story of Genesis, man becomes identified with the intellect in a manner that is not necessary to woman, who is derivative from this first man.

Although woman's sexuality is necessary to carry out the work of generation and to provide the precondition for man's pursuit of intellectual activity, her sex is also considered a flaw. Not only is woman viewed as less suited than man to the nobler functions of reason, but she is also inferior to man on strictly biological grounds. Aquinas notes that the production of woman stems from a defect in the active force that produces man. This defect may be caused by internal deficiencies, or by external interferences such as a moist south wind (*ST* 1.92.1). Therefore, woman's necessary role in reproduction is also a mark of her deficient nature. She is indispensable for serving the end of nature in general but misbegotten as an individual. Although both male and female contributions are necessary to the perpetuation of the species, women are judged to be defective when measured by the principle of activity that characterizes men.

Woman's deficiency is manifested in her greater affinity with the passions than men have and in her weaker affinity with reason. In the *Supplement* to the *Summa Theologica*, Aquinas writes, "In women the humors are more abundant, wherefore they are more inclined to be led by their concupiscences. . . ."[14] In comparison, "A man has more of the good of reason, which prevails over all movements of bodily passions" (*Suppl* 62.4). Ultimately, because women tend to be ruled more by their passions than men, they carry greater responsibility for the sin of adultery. Aquinas writes, "The adulterous wife sins more grievously than the adulterous hus-

band . . ." (*Suppl* 62.4). The adulterous woman sins more seriously against the marriage because her sin makes the parentage of
the offspring uncertain. Aquinas imputes this "lesion to marriage"
solely to the wife, and he fails to consider that a man's act of adultery also makes parentage uncertain. The grievousness of adultery,
apparently, lies in its obscuring of paternity in particular, since the
identity of the mother remains certain. Therefore, woman's function within marriage serves not merely to reproduce the species in
general, but to reproduce offspring for a particular man. Ultimately
the heinousness of a woman's act of adultery lies in its violation of
the husband's rule within the marriage.

Because of women's inclination to be led by passion, marriage
cannot be a relationship between equals. Instead, Aquinas considers the proper marital relationship to be one of "proportional"
equality (*Suppl* 64.5). Aquinas writes, "Speaking of the first equality [of quantity], husband and wife are not equal in marriage; neither as regards the marriage act, wherein the more noble part is
due to the husband; nor as regards the household management,
wherein the wife is ruled and the husband rules" (*Suppl* 64.5). But
a proportional equality exists between husband and wife because
they are equally bound by the marriage tie. Aquinas compares this
proportional equality between husband and wife to the complemen-
tary relation between active and passive elements: "Although it
is more noble to be active than passive, there is the same proportion between patient and passivity as between agent and activity"
(*Suppl* 64.5). The noble, active quality of the man corresponds to
his role as the "head," which is the "principal member," yet is
bound to the other members (*Suppl* 64.5). By associating the male
with the active, dominant, intellectual qualities, and the female
with the passive, subordinate, lustful qualities, Aquinas justifies
his view that woman is naturally subordinate to man. Aquinas argues that woman's subjection to man existed even before the Fall.
He writes, "For good order would have been wanting in the human
family if some were not governed by others wiser than themselves.
So by such a kind of subjection, woman is naturally subject to man,
because in man the discretion of reason predominates" (*ST* 1.92.1).
Although Aquinas argues that men have a greater ability to exercise reason than women, he does not deny women's rational ability.

He claims, "The image of God, in its principal signification, namely the intellectual nature, is found both in man and in woman" (*ST* 1.93.4). Therefore, woman also has a rational soul. Moreover, Aquinas comments that intellectual nature itself is sexless. He writes, "The image of God belongs to both sexes, since it is in the mind, wherein there is no distinction of sexes" (*ST* 1.93.6). Yet Aquinas persists in claiming that in a secondary sense the image of God is found only in man and not in woman: "For man is the beginning and end of woman; as God is the beginning and end of every creature" (*ST* 1.93.4). In Aquinas's view, man fulfills a godlike role in relation to woman, since man is the "principle of the whole human race" (*ST* 1.92.2).

Thus, Aquinas presents an ambiguous picture of women's relation to reason. On the one hand, he argues that woman's subordination to man is natural because of her lesser "discretion of reason." On the other hand, he attributes to woman an intellectual soul, which is the image of God, and is itself without sexual differentiation. One commentator has sought to resolve Aquinas's paradoxical depiction of women by segregating different levels of existence. Børresen suggests that Aquinas, like Augustine, counterbalances his claims for women's physical subordination with claims for spiritual equivalence between the sexes.[15] However, this interpretation fails to consider the Aristotelian inheritance on which Aquinas builds, which makes a separation between physical and spiritual relations problematic. Rather, Aquinas's account of women's rational capacities never fully establishes their equivalence with men; sexual differentiation and inequality are reflected even in the manifestations of reason. Although Aquinas argues that the intellectual principle is in men and women alike, the practical exercise of reason is not the same for both sexes.[16] Women's sexual nature militates against the functioning of the rational principle, which operates more successfully in men. Aquinas observes that "the intellectual principle which we call the mind or the intellect has an operation *per se* apart from the body" (*ST* 1.75.2). If reason were wholly independent of the body, as this statement seems to imply, Aquinas would have no justification for claiming that women's sexual nature diminishes her rational discretion.[17] But in Aquinas's view, the intellectual soul is also the form of the body (*ST* 1.76.1).

Therefore, the inequality between men and women displayed on the physical level is in his view reflected in the operation of reason as well.[18]

Although Aquinas believed that women are more inclined to be led by their lust than men, he concurred with Augustine that sexuality readily poses the danger of sin to both sexes. In the *Supplement* he writes, "The intercourse of fornication is wrong in itself. Therefore, in order that the marriage intercourse be not wrong, something must be added to it to make it right, and draw it to another moral species" (*Suppl* 49.1). Aquinas gives the following explanation for holding "fornication" in disrepute: "Now there is a loss of reason incidental to the union of man and woman, both because the reason is carried away entirely on account of the vehemence of the pleasure, so that it is unable to understand anything at the same time, as the Philosopher says (*Ethic*, vii, 11); and again because of the tribulation of the flesh which such persons have to suffer from solicitude for temporal things (1 Cor. vii 28)" (*Suppl* 49.1). The evil lurking in the act of intercourse resides in the threat that sexual pleasure poses to the operation of reason. Aquinas postulates that such a threat did not exist in paradise before the body was corrupted. Consequently, like Augustine, he exempts from his warning against the dangers of sexuality that ideal sex that could have existed—but did not exist—in paradise. Aquinas writes that in the present state of life, coition involves a "certain deformity of excessive concupiscence, which in the state of innocence would not have existed, when the lower parts were entirely subject to reason" (*ST* 1.98.2). Our foreparents would have lacked this immoderate lust, which we experience in sexual relations. But lest we think that paradise was lacking in any respect, Aquinas stresses that moderation would not have curbed delight. He writes, "In the state of innocence nothing of this kind would have happened that was not regulated by reason, not because delight of sense would be less, as some say (rather indeed would sensible delight have been the greater in proportion to the greater purity of nature and the greater sensibility of the body) but because the force of concupiscence would not have so inordinately thrown itself into such pleasure, being curbed by reason, whose place it is not to lessen sensual pleasure, but to prevent the force of concupiscence from cleaving to it immoderately" (*ST* 1.98.2). Thus, prelapsarian sex would have allowed human beings to enjoy the sensible delights of the body without threatening the control of reason over sensibility; this loss of rational control is itself the concupiscence of original sin (*ST* 2.82.3).

Because of Aquinas's stress on the natural place of generation in the state of innocence (*ST* 1.98.1) and his claim that the sensibility of the body would have been enhanced under these circumstances, some commentators argue that his asceticism does not entail a hostility toward the body.[19] Yet in evaluating his treatment of the body, one must bear in mind his distinction between innocent life and life as we know it. In principle, as his discussion of prelapsarian sex indicates, sexuality can be governed by the dictates of reason. But the actual manifestation of sexuality in our lives poses a threat to rational governance. Only marriage can provide the rational directive that mediates this threat. Although even in marriage passion may appear to corrupt the order of reason, Aquinas notes that "the intensity of pleasure in the marriage act does not do this, since, although for the moment man is not being directed, he was previously directed by his reason" (*Suppl* 41.3). However, ultimately we can never regain in earthly existence the innocence of our animal body. Purity will be attained only in resurrection, when our body as well as our soul will be spiritualized and will no longer require the generative function of sexuality (*ST* 1.93.3).

Implicit in Aquinas's condemnation of sexuality is the assumption that an inverse relation exists between reason and passion. The presence of passion indicates a loss of reason. His emphasis on rational control marks a shift away from Augustine's concern with the rule of the will over the body. For example, in *The City of God*, Augustine describes prelapsarian sex in the following terms: "We must be far from supposing that offspring could not be begotten without concupiscence. All the bodily members would have been equally moved by the will, without ardent or wanton incentive, with calmness of the soul and body."[20] But in explicating this passage, Aquinas substitutes the legislation of reason for that of the will. He comments, "The force of concupiscence would not have so inordinately thrown itself into such pleasure, being curbed by reason" (*ST* 1.98.2). Aquinas supports his argument that pleasure interferes with reason by reference to Aristotle's discussion of pleasure in the *Nicomachean Ethics* (Bk. 7, chap. 11). Aristotle observes that "some people think that no pleasure is a good" (1151b8). One reason for holding this view is that "the pleasures are a hindrance to thought, and the more so the more one delights in them, e.g. in sexual pleasure; for no one could think of anything while absorbed in this" (1152b16–18). Although Aristotle argues that the interference of sexual pleasure with reason is not a grounds for rejecting it, this pleasure is harmful with respect to the particular end of reflection. And since in Aristotle's view the highest end of man is contemplation (1177a18), sexual pleasure contravenes this highest virtue. In turning to Aristotle, therefore, Aquinas buttresses his view about the inherent conflict between passion and reason.

Sexual pleasure also appears as a threat to thought because the object of knowledge, in Aquinas's account, is treated in terms of pure intellection. Aquinas characterizes the goal of human reason as the "knowledge of intelligible truth, which angels know" (*ST* 1.79.8).[21] The appetite for pleasure, if unregulated by reason, interferes with the quest for the knowledge of God's work that is accessible to angels. In order to attain intelligible truths, therefore, one must be free of the bonds and temporal concerns entailed in family life. Bound to wife and child, a man cannot fix his gaze on things eternal or on the conclusions drawn from them in scientific knowledge (*ST* 1.79.9).

Aquinas does not reject the passions as bad in themselves, but they are good only when they are directed toward the end posed by reason.[22] This proviso is linked in Aquinas's thought to the higher valuation of eternal truth over the finite and transient cares of material existence. Because human knowledge in its highest form is like the knowledge that "angels" possess, which transcends solicitude for temporal things, passion can only be viewed as posing a potential interference with reason. If, on the other hand, reason's primary goal were understood as knowledge of human experience, passion could be construed as itself a means of apprehending the world.[23] Aquinas's contrast between knowledge of intelligible truth and care for temporal things is grounded in an ascetic inheritance that views our present sensuous existence as marked by corruption. Not only "fornication" but solicitude toward one's spouse or child is deemed an interference with this higher form of knowledge. Aquinas notes that since children belong to the temporal sufferings of this world, they are more properly the concern of women than of men (*Suppl* 44.2). Women, therefore, remain mired in temporal cares while men are freed to pursue intellectual cognition, both of the material world and of immaterial things.

Although Aquinas consistently claims that women are more lustful than men, his analysis of the rules governing sexual intercourse reveals more about man's sexual behavior than woman's. For example, he argues that a husband must "pay the marriage debt" to his wife so she can be cured of her lust. He writes,

> By the payment of the debt a remedy is afforded against the wife's concupiscence. Now a physician who has the care of a sick person is bound to remedy the disease without being asked. Therefore the husband is bound to pay the debt to his wife although she ask not for it. Further, a superior is bound to apply a remedy for the sins of his subjects even though they rebel against it. But the payment of the debt on the husband's part is directed against the sins of his wife. Therefore sometimes the husband is bound to pay the debt to his wife even though she ask it not of him (*Suppl* 64.2)

Whether the wife expresses sexual desire or not, the husband is bound to perform his sexual duties in order to cure her as a doctor would treat a recalcitrant patient. In Aquinas's account, because the woman is guilty of the sin of concupiscence, the husband is effectively justified in behaving coercively toward her. In suggesting that even when men initiate sexual relations, they are acting for their wife's benefit, Aquinas discounts men's sexual desire as a motivation for intercourse. Men fornicate because of women's needs. However, if a woman's desire is explicitly expressed during menstruation, man should not pay the marriage debt because the woman is unclean and the offspring may be unnatural (*Suppl* 64.3). Nonetheless, the woman is required to pay this debt during menstruation if the husband asks for it. Aquinas quotes St. Paul: "The wife hath not power of her own body, but the husband" (*Suppl* 64.4). The woman is bound to have intercourse in this case, lest she be guilty of provoking her husband to commit adultery. As a rejoinder to the earlier argument for abstention during menstruation, he adds, it is "by no means so certain" that the offspring may be injured, "which perhaps would not be forthcoming" (*Suppl* 64.4). Thus, Aquinas argues that menstrual "pollution" should prevent intercourse when women desire it but not when men desire it. Implicit in his comments, as Aquinas's reference to St. Paul makes clear, is the view that men properly control sexual relations.

In Aquinas's discussion of the marriage debt, he treats the right to initiate sexual contact as residing entirely with the man. Aquinas does not consider whether the woman is bound to pay the marriage debt if the husband does not request it, in order to remedy his concupiscence. He assumes that woman's sexual desire is operative even if it is not expressed, but he does not presume that man's sexual desire is continuously present. Moreover, in suggesting that a man has the mandate to infer lust from woman's silence, Aquinas also indicates that men have interpretive powers lacking to women. Although Aquinas treats man's sexual activity solely in terms of a dispassionate duty, these marriage rules allow the man to initiate sexual relations at will. While renouncing male desire as a motive for sexual activity, Aquinas elaborates a code of conduct that justifies aggressive sexual behavior in men. Male sexual domination is deemed necessary because of women's incurable desire. Aquinas's treatment of sexual desire echoes the scapegoat motif of early Greek thought by attributing the unwanted corruption of sexual desire to a group that can be marginalized.

Just as men must retain rational control over their pleasures, lest they experience the sickness of concupiscence, so rationality in general in Aquinas's account is built on the transcendence of human desire. Since reason ultimately seeks intelligible truths, solicitude for temporal things would only contravene this search for truth. Although rationality seeks to grasp universal concepts of the material and immaterial world, only man can have such knowledge. The mind's heights can be achieved by men alone, on the condition of sexual abstinence. Aquinas quotes the following remark from Augustine: "I consider that nothing so casts down the manly mind from its heights as the fondling of women, and those bodily contacts which belong to the married state."[24] The womanly mind, by implication, is foreclosed from gaining knowledge of intelligible truths. Thus, Aquinas's conception of transcendent knowledge serves particular interests in the material world which it seeks to go beyond. Rather than being sexually indifferent, it reinforces the "natural" subordination of woman to man in the domain of worldly existence.

Aquinas's treatment of reason played a central role in transmitting Christian views of purity to science and philosophy. His discussion of rationality as the imperfect means of grasping truth, which is eternal in the divine intellect (*ST* 1.16.8), augurs the conception of scientific rationality that emerges in the modern period: the attempt to grasp the unchanging laws of nature. But in order to attain this highest goal, according to Aquinas, reason must exert its control over the passions; pleasure must be contained in order for knowledge to be acquired. This insistence on reason's control over passion reflects an ascetic commitment, which brings in its wake the antithesis between the purely intelligible object of knowledge and the nonrational concerns of human existence. Moreover, by positing the mastery of reason over the passions as a necessary condition for knowledge, and by sustaining the ascetic view that women are less capable of rationality than men, Aquinas implicitly endorses the hierarchical relations between the sexes as a precondition for the flourishing of reason. If rational knowledge involves a detachment from lesser, temporal concerns, and women are designed to serve these earthly affairs, then men's rule over women appears as the necessary social condition in which science can develop. Although it may seem a vast leap from the dominant views of the church in the fourth century or the twelfth century to modern philosophy or science, an eighteenth-century thinker such as Kant was deeply influenced by ascetic Christianity through the Protestant Reformation in Germany. Modern philosophical theories such as Kant's maintain the principles of the dominance of reason over passion and of pure truth over temporal existence. The continued power of these ascetic commitments within philosophy reinforces the inherited presupposition of these principles: that in the interest of reason, men must exercise their "superiority" over women.

# 5

# REFORMATION VIEWS OF WOMEN
# AND SEXUALITY

Despite reforms of the institution of monasticism, and despite a revaluation of marriage, the Reformation preserved the denigration of the lustful body so pronounced in both Augustine and Aquinas. The writings of Luther and Calvin indicate a continuity between Reformation views and the earlier Catholic concern for purifying the body of sexual desire. In fact, the Reformation intensified the ascetic tendencies evident in the Catholic church. Max Weber, in *The Protestant Ethic and the Spirit of Capitalism*, argues that the Reformation stopped the drain of asceticism from worldly life. According to the Protestant ethic, he writes, "every Christian had to be a monk all his life."[1]

Both Luther and Calvin, in fact, rejected the practice of monastic vows. Luther in particular encouraged nuns and priests to leave their religious communities and to marry. Their criticism of monasticism has led some scholars to argue that the Reformation had a healthier attitude toward sex and married life than the medieval church.[2] But the Reformers' rejection of chastity did not challenge the inherited value of sexual purity; it merely dismissed celibacy as a viable means for achieving this ideal.

In discussing questions of marriage and sex, Luther distinguishes between the "impure chastity" of those who are unsuitably bound to a religious order and the "pure chastity" of those who enter the holy estate of matrimony.[3] In writing to his father concerning his own experiences as a monk, Luther comments, "I lived . . . not without sin, it is true, but without reproach" (*LSC* 260). Vows of chastity taken, when we are by nature unsuited to them, lead only to greater unchastity. This danger of unchastity constantly torments us. In his "Treatise on Good Works," he writes: "The vice of unchastity rages in all our members: in the thoughts of our heart, in the seeing of our eyes, in the hearing of our ears, in the words of our mouth, in the works of our hands and feet and all our body. To control all these requires labor and effort."[4] In order to counteract this tumult, Luther advises us to avoid drunkenness, loafing, soft beds and clothes, excessive adornment, and intimate association with members of the opposite sex. He also recommends early marriage as a constructive measure to overcome the temptations of the flesh. Since God created us to marry and procreate, just as much as to eat, drink, and sleep, it is impossible for us to impede the fulfillment of these needs. Consequently, Luther supported the decisions of monks and nuns to break their vows of celibacy and to marry, as he himself did.

In his letter to Reissenbusch, Luther encourages the preceptor of the monastery in Lichtenberg to marry in the following terms: "Now, chastity is not in our power, as little as are God's other wonders and graces. But we are all made for marriage, as our bodies show . . ." (*LSC* 273). Since men are conceived, born, and nourished by women, he argues, it is impossible for them to keep away from women: "Therefore, whoever will live alone undertakes an impossible task and takes it upon himself to run counter to God's Word and the nature that God has given and preserves in him. The outcome is in keeping with the attempt; such persons revel in whoredom and all sorts of uncleanness of the flesh until they are drowned in their own vices and driven to despair" (*LSC* 273). Although Luther recommends marriage instead of celibacy, the purpose of his counsel is to enhance our ability to be continent. If one sought a life of chastity without the "special grace and miracle" (*LSC* 268) of God which makes it possible, this choice would lead to the raging, not the quietude, of desire. Marriage, in his view, provides the "remedy" for lust (*LSC* 292). Like Augustine and Aquinas, Luther also seeks to cure us of the defiling feeling of lust. But such a cure cannot be found in abstinence, as earlier thinkers suggested, since we desire most what we cannot have. Thus Luther does not disavow the goal of purity but argues that we must not judge purity by the external acts or works demanded by monastic vows. Instead, we must seek the continence of our hearts and consciences. Since most of us do not have the gift for chastity, a lifelong vow is foolish and is against God's commandment. Luther does not, however, denigrate the ideal of chastity itself. In counseling three nuns on whether to leave their convent, he remarks, "There is only one in several thousands to whom God gives the gift to live chastely in a state of virginity" (*LSC* 271). He advises the sisters to leave if they felt they did not possess "that high and rare gift."

Luther's rejection of the vow of celibacy corresponds to his general belief that salvation is attained not through external works, but through faith.[5] Monastic institutions exemplify Catholicism's emphasis on the external act. The monastic imposition of unnatural vows on human beings, in Luther's view, did not lead to chastity of conduct. Instead it brought about the corrupt behavior rampant in the church. It was not uncommon in the pre-Reformation world for clergy who had taken vows of celibacy to visit prostitutes and have concubines. Luther argued that even when monks lived without external misconduct, as he himself had, they did not live without sin (*LSC* 260). Chastity resides not only in the outward act but also in the inner state of mind. For example, he praises the chastity of the virtuous and modest wife who is obedient to her husband's bed and has a "continent mind" (*LSC* 261). It is the continence of mind that is commanded by God, not virginity and chastity. These latter qualities, Luther comments, are "to be praised, but in such wise that by their very greatness men are frightened off from them rather than attracted to them" (*LSC* 261).

Calvin agreed that virginity is "a virtue not to be despised," a "special gift of God."[6] He writes, "For first of all, the Lord distinguishes a class of men who have castrated themselves for the sake of the Kingdom of Heaven (Matt. 19:12)—that is, to permit them to devote themselves more unreservedly and freely to the affairs of the Kingdom of Heaven. Yet lest anyone think that such castration lies in a man's power, he pointed out just before that not all men can receive this precept, but only those to whom it is especially 'given' from heaven (Matt. 19:11)" (*Insts* 2.8.42). Like Luther, Calvin disapproved of monastic vows because they are too often made by those to whom God had not given the power of continence (*Insts* 4.13.18). To take a vow of celibacy when one is not suited to it, as few of us are, is to violate the nature given to us by God (*Insts* 4.13.3). Such a vow leads not to the purity of virginity, but merely to the practice of celibacy, which is corrupted by desire.

The Reformers consider marriage, rather than celibacy, as the antidote to our incontinence. As a result of the Fall, evil and concupiscence reside in all the members of our body. In Calvin's view, even those who seek to be most chaste, including the saints, are not freed from this corruption. He writes, "There remains in a regenerate man, a smoldering cinder of evil, from which desires continually leap forth and spur him to commit sin" (*Insts* 3.3.10). Man is freed from lust only when he is likewise "freed by death from the body of death . . ." (*Insts* 4.15.11). However, both Luther and Calvin argue that marriage provides a partial remedy for our lustful nature. Luther describes marriage as a "medicine," a "hospital for the sick."[7] Calvin claims that God ordained marriage as a "necessary remedy to keep us from plunging into unbridled lust" (*Insts* 2.8.41). Marriage "covers the baseness of incontinence"; but for that reason it should not provoke "uncontrolled and dissolute lust" (*Insts* 2.8.44) within matrimony. Thus, sexual desire is seen by the Reformers as an illness and a corruption, which must be cured or covered over. Although Calvin acknowledges that it is possible to treat the pleasures of the senses with mistaken strictness, since God created beauty, he immediately adds that we must monitor this enjoyment. He comments, "The lust of the flesh . . . unless it is kept in order, overflows without measure" (*Insts* 3.10.3). It is the acknowledgment of the inevitability of temptation, and hence the pessimistic evaluation of human sinfulness, that underlies Calvin's defense of marriage. As a result of original sin, human nature is characterized by depravity and corruption. Calvin comments, "For our nature is not only destitute and empty of good, but so fertile and fruitful of every evil that it cannot be idle . . . whatever is in man, from the understanding to the will, from the soul even to the flesh, has been defiled and crammed with this concupiscence" (*Insts* 2.1.8). Since desire resides in our flesh, even the saints are not freed from sin until they are divested of their mortal bodies (*Insts* 3.3.10).

In Calvin's eyes, it is not sufficient to resist temptation in order to free oneself of sin. He writes:

> But between Augustine and us we can see that there is this differ-ence of opinion: while he concedes that believers, as long as they dwell in mortal bodies, are so bound by inordinate desires that they are unable not to desire inordinately, yet he dare not call this disease "sin." Content to designate it with the term "weakness," he teaches that it becomes sin only when either act of consent follows the conceiving or apprehension of it, that is, when the will yields to the first strong inclination. We, on the other hand, deem it sin when man is tickled by any desire at all against the law of God. Indeed, we label "sin" that very depravity which begets in us desires of this sort. (*Insts* 3.3.10)

For Augustine, sin requires the consent of the will; the struggle against temptation does not itself constitute a sin. Calvin, on the other hand, regards the very "tickle" of desire as a transgression. His stringent condemnation of desire derives from the Reforma-tion's concern with man's "inner state." Since salvation is a matter of faith, not of works, external acts of will cannot assure us of sal-vation. Righteousness requires a judgment of the heart, of one's inner intent. Only when these innermost feelings are righteous is one pure. Although this goal is unattainable so long as man is bound to his mortal body, it remains the guiding light for the reli-gious man. A continent or chaste mind consists in the absence of any "inordinate desire."

The believer must learn to fight "manfully" every day against the pricks of desire, which are inherent in our flesh (*Insts* 4.15.11). Calvin chastises the "natural man," who "refuses to be led to recognize the diseases of his lusts" (*Insts* 2.2.24). One must strive for purity through the constant struggle against the desires that the natural man enjoys. Thus, Calvinism embodied a systematic code of conduct that regulated every moment of existence. Through unrelenting discipline, Calvinism sought to reshape both the "natural" man and the world and to eliminate all emotion and sentiment not inspired by religious faith, in order to serve the glory of God.[8]

Concurrent with their valuation of purity, the Reformers believed that women achieved chastity through obedience to their husbands. In Luther's view, just as all children are subject to the authority of God, so all wives are subject to their husband's authority, which signifies God's glory. Luther chastises Stephen Roth for being too lenient with his wife and suffering the consequences by her recalcitrance. He writes, "Certainly when you saw that the fodder was making the ass insolent (that is, that your wife was becoming unmanageable as a result of your indulgence and submissiveness), you should have remembered that you ought to obey God rather than your wife, and so you should not have allowed her to despise and trample underfoot that authority of the husband which is the glory of God, as Saint Paul teaches" (*LSC* 277). In Calvin's view, the husband's right over his wife extends even to physical abuse. He advises a woman, persecuted by her husband for her religious beliefs, not to leave her husband. A woman ought not to leave her husband, he notes, "except by force of necessity; and we do not understand this force to be operative when a husband behaves roughly and uses threats to his wife, nor even when he beats her, but when there is imminent peril to her life."[9]

Protestant thinkers viewed the husband's authority over his wife as sacred because, like the early Greeks and the church fathers, they defined woman's nature by her role in reproduction. In his letter to three nuns, Luther describes woman's function in the following words: "A woman does not have complete mastery over herself. God so created her body that she should be with a man and bear and raise children" (*LSC* 271). Luther argues that childbearing is the sole redeeming feature of women's sinfulness. He characterizes the female sex as "weaker, carrying about in mind and body several vices. But that one good, however, covers and conceals all of them: the womb and birth."[10] However, when a woman misuses her sexual function, he has nothing but contempt for her. For example, he describes prostitutes as "dreadful, shabby, stinking, loathesome, and syphilitic" (*LSC* 293). Luther shows no mercy for a woman of this kind, who is to be accounted a "murderer" and should be broken on the wheel and flayed for contaminating young men (*LSC* 293).

Woman's religious vocation is to care for her children and to be obedient to her husband. Luther chastises women who seek piety instead by "running to churches, fasting, counting prayers." He advises "dear Greta" to do her best in bearing children, and if she dies in childbirth, she dies in holy work.[11] Although both Luther and Calvin argue for a universal priesthood of believers, women are specifically excluded from proclaiming the word.[12] Calvin refers to Tertullian in justifying the exclusion of women from the priesthood. Calvin writes that Tertullian "held that a woman was not allowed to speak in the church, and also not to teach, to baptize, or to offer. This was that she might not claim for herself the function of any man, much less that of a priest" (*Insts* 4.15.21). Women's subordination to men is sustained even when Reformation thinkers treated marriage as a spiritual union, and not just for procreation or as a remedy for lust. Bucer, echoing Aquinas, describes woman as the "aid and the flesh of the man," while the man is the "head and saviour of the woman."[13]

Women are denigrated because they are identified exclusively with their function in sustaining the existence of the flesh, which is a subordinate aspect of human life. The Reformers maintained a contempt toward fleshly existence. Calvin calls the body the "prison house" of the soul, which ties men to earth and makes them grow dull (*Insts* 1.15.2). He considers the flesh to be "full of evil and perversity" (*Insts* 3.3.8), and he argues that it must be whipped like an "idle and balky ass" (*Insts* 2.7.12). Trapped within the body, the soul is blinded by the darkness and cannot see the light of its own immortality. The soul, the nobler part of man, can grasp the right, just, and honorable, which is hidden to the bodily senses. Calvin's imagery of the body as a prison of the soul, which is an obstacle to the purity necessary for the soul to seek truth, is drawn directly from Plato's *Phaedo*, as the translator and editor of the *Institutes* notes (*Insts* 3.6. n. 9).

The corruption of the flesh, in Calvin's view, derives not only from physical transgressions but also from the raging of lustful desire that is inherent in the mortal body. Therefore, to strive against sin requires that one constantly discipline desires that are a natural and inevitable component of physical existence. In the ideal state of grace, the resurrected body is completely cleansed of this contaminating desire. Calvin's praise of self-control derives largely from Stoic philosophy, which exerted a powerful influence on him in his early years.[14] His criticism of Stoicism was directed only against the absence of feeling evinced by the Stoics in religious faith. Ultimately, Calvinism strove for such a transformation of inner feelings that they would no longer require the discipline of the will.

The Calvinist emphasis on systematic self-control signifies what Weber terms a relocation of monasticism within everyday life. In eliminating the dual ethics of the Catholic church, the Reformation required all believers to exercise the stringent dictates of duty. This universal rule of behavior led to a methodical control of every moment of one's life. For the Calvinist, salvation consisted not in an accumulation of good works, but in the judgment every moment of one's life of being saved or damned.[15] The totality of one's life became the constant object of judgment. The Reformation's abolition of the monasteries and its doctrine of the priesthood of all believers meant that the ascetic rule applied to everyday life within the world. All worldly activities became ordered by the imperative to live purely and add to God's glory.

Thus, the Protestant worldview led to an antisensual attitude toward life. Whatever pertained to the flesh was suspect because it could lend nothing to the work of salvation. Religion's task was the "destruction of spontaneous, impulsive enjoyment." Furthermore, this worldview demanded an absolute adherence of individual conscience to its moral dictates. The early church had recognized that the individual was not a clearly defined unity, but that one's moral life was subject to conflicting motives. Although in principle the church demanded an ideal change of life, absolution tempered the demand to lead a life of perfection. The Reformation's rejection of this sacrament reflected its decreased tolerance for human error. All aspects of consciousness not in accord with its moral commands were to be suppressed. The asceticism of Protestant religion, with its general antisensualism and its imperative to control all feelings and desires according to a principle laid down by reason, is the most immediate religious antecedent for the modern philosophical ideal of rational consciousness articulated by Kant.

Although Protestantism sought to deny the sensual pleasures of life, its ascetic practices led unintentionally to consequences that violated its original purposes. The devaluation of material goods, combined with the rational control of conduct and the sense of work as a duty, led to an accumulation of wealth and a rationalization of economic life conducive to the development of capitalism.[16] As Weber describes the unintended consequences of this ascetic remodeling of the world: "Material goods have gained an increasing and finally an inexorable power over the lives of men as at no previous period in history."[17]

Similarly, the Reformation's intentional repression of sexuality may have led not to a disinterest in the body, but instead to a distorted form of interest. Both Luther and Calvin consider the body as harboring a disease that must be cured. This religious insistence on the body's need of cure from its infection parallels the renaissance of scientific and medical interest in the body during the seventeenth and eighteenth centuries. Foucault argues in *The History of Sexuality* that the bourgeoisie of this period were concerned to an unprecedented degree with their health and longevity, with how to avoid and treat illnesses. A new "technology" of the body developed in the midst of the flourishing of ascetic Protestantism.[18]

Thus, the emergent scientific interest in the body presents a secularized version of the religious concerns for purity and salvation. In the religious sphere the natural body is viewed as a corruption, requiring stringent regulations to remedy its concupiscence. Similarly, in the scientific view the body appears as an object that naturally tends to corruption, requiring the intervention of scientific treatment to rid it of its maladies. The value of purity is transmitted from religious belief to secular knowledge largely through the institutional connections between the church and the university. Purity becomes inscribed as a scientific value in the fundamental conception of the object of knowledge.[19] In examining the institutional pathway by which the value of purity is transmitted to secular knowledge, the prevailing posture of objective knowledge is itself revealed as a form of asceticism. This ascetic form of knowledge may generate a dialectic comparable to that observed by Weber in ascetic Protestantism. Although the intention of ascetic thought was to purify the forms of knowledge from the contamination of sensuous existence, ultimately this attempt created an alienated form of materiality, which held increasing sway over the activity of reflection.

# 6

# ASCETIC ORIGINS OF
# THE UNIVERSITY

THE HISTORICAL EMERGENCE OF UNIVERSITIES FROM CHURCH IN-
stitutions provided a vehicle for transmitting the ascetic value of
purity, with its implicit assumptions about sexual relations, from
religion to science and philosophy.[1] In Germany, for example,
scholarship and research took place entirely within the university
system,[2] which was deeply rooted in ecclesiastical life. Since the
universities literally grew out of the church, women were also excluded from these new institutions, just as they had been excluded
from preaching God's word. The secular conception of pure reason
and disinterested knowledge that emerged in this context reflects
the ascetic Christian commitment to purify the soul of the body's
pollution and to exclude women from the path of pure reason.

The medieval universities developed originally from monastic
institutions. Although monasteries served as the centers of education in the Benedictine Age,[3] in the eleventh century the task of

education was gradually shifted to the cathedral schools. The transference of educational activity from the monks to the secular clergy
has been called the great educational revolution of the period,
which presaged the later university movement.[4] In the period between 1150 and 1170, the first university developed in Paris out of
the cathedral schools and served as the model for all subsequent
universities in Europe.

The new universities maintained close connections with the
church.[5] The great educators of the Middle Ages, including Thomas
Aquinas, Albertus Magnus, and Bonaventura, were all monks. As
the new mendicant orders became less concerned with retreating
from the world and more concerned with Christianizing it, education became an increasingly important part of the monastic ideal.
Only by getting a hold on centers of education could they influence
the more educated and powerful classes. Dominic turned explicitly
to the universities as the most suitable recruiting ground for his
order so that he could secure for his preachers the highest theological training.[6]

Ecclesiastical influence was evident in both the foundation and
practices of the medieval university. The universities themselves
were established by papal bull. Moreover, the language of these
educational institutions was Latin, which was the language of the
Roman church. Far from being independent of the church's authority and rules, teachers were required to have ecclesiastical
sanction in order to teach.[7] Furthermore, the rules and discipline
regulating the everyday life of the medieval students and teachers
display the monastic character of the institution.[8] In Paris, every
student at the university was supposed to be a cleric and wear the
clerical habit. The adopting of clerical dress assured the wearer, as
long as he continued celibate, of exemption from secular courts.
The teacher, like the learner, was also required to be an ecclesiast.
The only serious obligation this imposed on him was celibacy. If he
had already been married, he could still attain a celibate status
by divorcing his wife. If a master married, he lost his regency. The
monastic discipline of the universities prohibited any kinds of
amusement. Silence, Bible reading, and fasting were required in
the students' halls. The monastic penalty of bread and water was
prescribed for any infringement of the rules such as arriving late at

meals or speaking in the vulgar (non-Latin) tongue. Rashdall comments that the "contempt of the body was too deeply rooted a sentiment of the religious mind for a pious college founder to recognize the necessity of bodily exercise and free vent for animal spirits."[9]

The institutional connections between church and university had an important impact on the content of education.[10] In the medieval university, academic study was dominated by theology, considered the queen of the sciences. No longer narrowly construed as scriptural interpretation, theology during the eleventh and twelfth centuries became the arena in which all scientific investigations were brought to bear on the conception of God, the universe, and the nature of human beings. Nonetheless, the preeminence of religious concerns remained unquestioned. The motivation for medieval science and philosophy was to provide a rational justification for faith in God. Under the dominance of theological concerns, all knowledge could be seen as unified into a single whole. This monolithic conception of knowledge made possible the gathering together of individual scholars and teachers to constitute a university.[11]

Thus the medieval university was fundamentally ecclesiastical in its origin, its discipline, and its views about the purpose of knowledge. One even finds explicit references to the university as modeled on the Kingdom of God. For example, Robert de Sorbon, founder of the Sorbonne, described the final examination on analogy with the Last Judgment, where God, as the Great Chancellor, refutes the sinner "in full university" before the world.[12]

One consequence of this medieval inheritance for modern universities has been the restriction of education for women until fairly recently. Given the ecclesiastical nature of the medieval universities, women were naturally excluded from their midst.[13] In fact, women's opportunities for receiving education generally declined with the rise of the new universities. When the monasteries served as centers of education, nuns had some limited access to learning. But with the shift of learning first to the cathedral schools and then to the universities, these possibilities were closed.[14]

The first universities in Germany, which were established in the fourteenth century, generally adopted the customs and institutions of the University of Paris. Although the German universities were founded by secular authorities, they too were fundamentally ecclesiastical in character. Papal bulls were necessary to permit the establishment of a new university, and the church possessed statutory control over instruction. Moreover, the large majority of members of the university were actual or potential clerics. Aside from a few governmental positions, the only available jobs for students were ecclesiastical. The salaries of the university professors were also paid by ecclesiastical stipends. And life within the university was modeled on the cloister. The church asserted its control over university education, and regarded the new institutions as secular endowments for spiritual ends.[15]

The creation of German universities was also directly linked to the growth of the Reformation movement in that country.[16] The German universities provided greater access to education for students than had been possible when university education required foreign study, and consequently they provided a platform for the spread of the ideas of Luther and other Reformers. In turn, the Reformation stamped its character on German university education. New Protestant universities such as Marburg (1527) and Königsberg (1544), where Kant studied and taught, were founded in the sixteenth and seventeenth centuries.[17] Moreover, the Reformation's demand that each individual have access to the Bible led to an expansion of religious education within the universities. The Protestant universities not only provided professional religious education for future priests but also provided religious instruction for laymen. Because of the Reformation's demand that all clergy be educated, the theological faculties in the Protestant universities were the largest of the faculties and controlled all of the instruction.[18] During the sixteenth and seventeenth centuries, the philosophical faculty was kept alive because philosophical and philological training was required as preparation for theological education.[19] Melanchthon, the famous Protestant humanist, was largely responsible for the ascendancy of the Protestant over the Catholic half in German education and culture. Friedrich Paulsen, a scholar of German university education, claims, "There can be no doubt whatever about the final outcome: German philosophy and science, German literature and culture grew up in the soil of Protestantism."[20]

In one sense, the Reformation has been credited with bringing about an increased secularization of study. The scholastic enterprise had aimed at the rational justification of faith. The goal of philosophy and science, therefore, was to support the "truth" as handed down by the religious authorities. The Reformation, by contrast, brought a separation of reason and faith. Luther viewed religion not as a matter for reason, but strictly for faith. Consequently, philosophy and science were no longer bound to serve as the rational supports for religious belief, and knowledge in the universities became increasingly secularized. Literary and scientific instruction achieved an independent status, since they were no longer primarily aimed at saving souls.[21]

Thus, the Reformation's emphasis on individual faith is generally understood to have liberated reason from the constraints of religious authority. But despite the fact that philosophy and science in Protestant universities no longer sought to justify truth as handed down by the church authorities, these disciplines did not divest themselves of the values inherent in this religious tradition. Instead, the religious goals of purity and universal truth were translated into the secular sphere. The emphasis on purifying the soul from desire in the Christian tradition is echoed in the philosophical and scientific focus on the purity of thought. The "universality" of knowledge was no longer founded in the comprehension of divine wisdom, but found new justification in the growth of scientific method. Paulsen notes that scholarship in modern German universities was based on the "unity of human civilization and scientific work."[22] Scientific practice, therefore, took over the function of unifying knowledge that had been previously fulfilled by the church. This transference of values from the religious to the secular sphere raises intriguing questions to the philosophical and scientific projects that emerged in this period. Although Christian thinkers have claimed to speak of the universal truths that are revealed in the light of God's wisdom, women have been precluded from attaining the knowledge accessible to male reason. Thus, Christian conceptions of spiritual purity can be linked to a distinctly androcentric bias. The institutional connection between the church and the university suggests that modern philosophy inherited from ascetic Christianity this commitment to exclude women from the pursuit of truth. Thus, the "universal" truths revealed in the light of reason may also be shown to reflect male-centered commitments.[23]

The influence of religious commitments on secular thought may have been especially pronounced in Germany where the university system, closely linked to the church, was the locus for philosophical and scientific work. In England, scholars such as Darwin, Spencer, Mill, Bentham, Ricardo, Hume, Locke, Hobbes, and Bacon were not connected with university life. But Wolff, Kant, Fichte, Schelling, Hegel, and Schleiermacher were all university professors.[24] The ecclesiastical character of the German university—the monastic life-style, the exclusion of women, the training for church-related jobs, and the dominance of the theological faculty—is reflected in the intellectual work produced under these conditions. The influence of ascetic religion is evident even in the increased stature of science. In the eighteenth century, philosophy sought to break away from its subservient role as the handmaiden of theology[25] by turning to the scientific method of discovery. The philosophy faculty fought even harder than the "hard" sciences for the secular, verifiable method of scientific discovery, in order to establish for itself a bulwark against the traditional faculties.[26] Science provided legitimacy within this largely ecclesiastical institution by its method for attaining pure and unchanging truth, which theology had sought in divine wisdom.

Thus, although science and philosophy claimed to establish universal, eternal truths, these claims must be viewed in the particular historical context in which they developed. The scientific thought that developed in the universities is not simply true or false but serves the particular needs of the society that generates it. In the modern period, educational institutions increasingly served as the organs that inculcated social values previously acquired through the church.

The university in eighteenth-century Germany also filled the practical function of providing the road of entry to positions of power for the middle class. Aspiring men of the middle class received training there for medicine, law, and government positions. The increased orientation of the universities toward professional training precipitated a crisis over its role. Those who saw university education as a humanistic enterprise opposed the government's view of it as primarily technical training. But even the humanists acknowledged the political significance of the university. Fichte, for example, envisioned the rule of academics, of philosopher-bureaucrats, over Prussia. He was not interested in reshaping the university to fit society, as the utilitarian reformers were; rather, he sought to reshape society to fit the university.[27]

In assessing the social function of German universities, it is also important to bear in mind their unisexual character. Women's exclusion from university life was considered so natural that neither the reformers of the time nor all but the most recent scholars of German education make note of it.[28] Women first received permission to attend university, under severely restrictive conditions,[29] on the eve of the First World War. By 1914, women constituted 7 percent of the student body in Prussia—marking a dramatic increase in their enrollment since 1900.[30] Thus, until the twentieth century, women were forbidden the study of philosophy and science and were prevented from receiving professional training, just as they had been excluded from the early cathedral schools. Although the Reformation had encouraged the expansion of education, this effort extended to women only insofar as they were taught the reading and arithmetic necessary to be religious mothers, whose duties included the frugal maintenance of the household.[31] Women's absence from the academy mirrored their exclusion from the priesthood and ministry. Viewed as sexual, irrational, sentimental creatures, women were deemed thoroughly unsuited to intellectual life.

Thus, university education determined whether individuals and groups had access to social authority and privilege. In particular, the asceticism of the university, evident in its early insistence on celibacy and its exclusion of women, reinforced the sexual relations made normative by the church, in which women were considered inferior to men in their reason and their labor. In both the structure and content of its education, the university became a medium of communicating ascetic values. In view of this social function, the university can be viewed as an ideological institution.[32]

The concept of ideology introduces a new level of analysis in this discussion. It provides an avenue for considering how the values and concepts that this institution has fostered are linked with the distribution of power in society more generally. The term "ideology" was originally coined in the late eighteenth century by the French theorists Cabanis and Destutt de Tracy to signify a theory of the generation of ideas from sensation.[33] But since Marx, it has referred specifically to the system of ideas that dominate the mind of an individual or a social group. These ideas legitimate the perspective of the ruling group by presenting it as universally valid; thus, they preserve the relations of domination and subordination that exist within the social group. Marx's theory of ideology suggests that philosophical, religious, or political ideas are shaped by material conditions, and they in turn sustain these conditions. Recent Marxists such as Althusser stress the role of institutions like the church and the educational system in serving as a vehicle for ideology. These institutions teach not only technical skills and familiarity with scientific and literary culture, but above all, rules of behavior. Through them individuals acquire the attitudes necessary for the day-to-day life of the established order. In other words, in the process of being socialized through these institutions, one learns submission to the ruling ideology.[34] Althusser argues that even though ideology shapes distorted perceptions of individuals' relation to their daily existence, these perceptions constitute the reality of daily experience for them.[35]

The concept of ideology is useful in interpreting how institutions like the university have taught values that have shaped both individuals' experience of the world and philosophical reflection on this experience. In particular, ascetic values have informed individuals' perception of their sexuality, of their bodies, and of relations between the sexes. This ascetic hostility to sexuality pervades the philosophical thought that emerged in the German universities and is typified, as we shall see, by Kant's treatment of sexual desire as objectifying and degrading. Moreover, modern philosophical thought has inherited the ascetic identification of women with the sensuous component of human existence in opposition to the qualities of rational self-determination.[36] This philosophical view of women's limited rational capacity justifies their practical exclusion from the university, and consequently from other forms of social activity. Thus, ascetic values have ultimately insured acceptance of existing sexual hierarchies.

Although modern philosophy and science have claimed to achieve universal, disinterested knowledge, in fact these very claims can be viewed as ideological. Philosophical systems do not transcend their conditions of existence, but as Terry Eagleton comments, each system "encodes within itself its own ideology of how, by whom, and for whom it was produced."[37] Marxists in general have demonstrated the class basis for theoretical claims to objectivity. They have pointed out that a set of ideas may be true for those whose position corresponds to the ruling interests; but from other positions, these same ideas are revealed as false. Class interests can be discerned in the practices of educational institutions as well. Although the educational system is thought to be neutral and disinterested, leading all individuals on the path to freedom and responsibility, those who are trained for management will have more freedom and responsibility than those who are trained for trades.[38] Thus, the knowledge-seeking enterprise appears as neutral and disinterested only to those who share the goals of the dominant group, not to those whose interests are opposed to the existing order.

A thinker such as Kant, who claims to formulate a purely disinterested theory of objectivity, has instead, as will be shown, been influenced by an interpenetration of ascetic values and economic interests. Although the conception of knowledge as purely objective, detached inquiry has refused to acknowledge itself as interested, it is constructed on the denial and displacement of erotic motivation. Such an approach not only conceives of knowledge as split off from sensual existence but also results in a deformation of one's sensual being. Ascetic ideology, therefore, has consequences not only for women who are excluded from the practice of knowledge but also for the male thinkers who become identified with this tradition. The thinker who identifies himself with the interests of pure reason and seeks to transcend his sensuous existence precipitates himself instead into a distorted relation to his own sensible being.

The discussion of Greek and Christian asceticism was motivated by the question concerning the origin of the association between purity and truth, which is so pronounced in Kant's thought. The concepts of purity and pollution originally emerged in a context that characterized sexuality, and in particular women's sexuality, as polluting; the desire for purity led male ascetics to detach themselves from this polluting sphere. In reading Kant, we can now consider whether his commitment to purity reflects this original ascetic impulse to escape the pollution of sensuous existence.

Pursuing a genealogical approach also opens another line of inquiry. How has the concept of purity been transformed historically? What is its function in the context of the modern world? These questions arise since genealogy does not study first origins in order to discover unchanging essences that are transmitted historically, but to examine how values shift with fundamental changes in social institutions and practices. Although Kant's attempt to purify reason from the contamination of emotion and desire echoes earlier ascetic views, the meaning of purity becomes bound up with other changes in the social world as well. The desensualization of cognition in Kant's thought contributes to an objectified interpretation of persons and things that serves the purposes of a world based on commodity relations. The shift from the religious to the economic dimension of purity in discussing Kant is motivated by the historical emergence of commodity relations, which served as a primary vehicle of asceticism.

In light of the historical transmission and transformation of asceticism, it will be important to bear in mind the following questions. To what extent has the denial and control of sexuality, which lay at the heart of the original ascetic impulse, been a precondition for the flourishing of capitalist relations? To what extent are ascetic demands for hierarchical relations between the sexes implicit in commodity relations? Is it possible to liberate ourselves from the sexual implications of this heritage while remaining within an economic structure that is ascetic in its roots?

**II**

# THE KANTIAN PARADIGM
# OF OBJECTIVITY

# 7

# BIOGRAPHICAL INTRODUCTION

IMMANUEL KANT, WRITING AT THE END OF THE EIGHTEENTH CEN-tury, is still widely considered the thinker who, more than any other, addresses the philosophical concerns of modernity. His attempt to build philosophy on a scientific basis in order to secure for it objective knowledge remains one of the dominant projects of modern philosophy.

Kant was born in Königsberg in 1724 and died there in 1804. The paucity of the accounts of Kant's life tells much about the manner in which he lived. Kant avoided all external change in his life. In a letter to his friend Herz, he wrote, "All changes make me anxious."[1] This attitude led him to turn down a professorship at Halle, one of the foremost Protestant universities in Germany. In his book, *Kant's Life and Thought*, Ernst Cassirer remarks that once Kant was established at the University of Königsberg, very little changed in his life until he died. Cassirer writes, "It is as if every occurrence and all progress were devoted purely and exclusively to his labors and withdrawn from him as a person."[2] Kant never married, and it is said that although he contemplated marriage once or twice, he lost the opportunity while reflecting on the matter. Kant's life was ordered according to a rigid schedule that precluded any spontaneity or disruptions. He would rise at five o'clock and work for two or three hours. He held lectures from seven or eight until nine or ten and would continue work until one o'clock. Then he would dine with one or two friends and occasionally with as many as five. Kant would then walk for an hour, spend the rest of the day in reading and meditation, and retire at ten o'clock.[3] This rational control of his life was exemplified in his abhorrence of emotional expressiveness. All emotions of a "soft-hearted kind," as he himself called them, were alien to his nature. Charlotte von Schiller once said of Kant that had he been able to feel love, he would have been one of the greatest phenomena of mankind; but since he could not, there was something defective in his nature. The only emotion that Kant recognized as valid was the ethical emotion, the universal respect for the freedom of the moral person.[4]

Kant lived a celibate life. His sexual abstinence was indicative of his general indifference to the role of pleasure in life. In the *Critique of Judgement*, he wrote that the value of life is "less than nothing" when it is measured according to the sum of pleasure.[5] The asceticism that pervaded Kant's outlook on the world and the conduct of his life reflects the Protestant adherence to monastic discipline in everyday life. Kant was deeply influenced by the Protestantism of the world in which he lived. Although he explicitly rejected elements of his Pietist upbringing, the dominant currents of ascetic Protestantism remained decisive for both his life and thought.

Kant's personal history brought him in close contact with the Pietist sect of the Reformation. Pietism was a form of Protestantism that intensified the ascetic tendencies of the Reformation, emerging in Germany as a reaction against the orthodoxy of the Lutheran church. However, in the Netherlands and England it was considered a Calvinist sect. Since the prominent German Pietists Spener, Francke, and Zinzendorf were strongly influenced by English and

Dutch Pietism,[6] there is an uneasy tension in German Pietism between both Lutheran and Calvinist elements. Because of the emotional nature of Pietism, its asceticism was perhaps weaker than that made possible by the thoroughly rational nature of Calvinism. But it was certainly more receptive to ascetic tendencies than was Orthodox Lutheranism. In Weber's view, the practical effect of the development of Pietism in Germany was the "penetration of methodically controlled and supervised, thus of ascetic, conduct into the non-Calvinistic denominations."[7]

Kant's Pietist religious and educational training exposed him to both the Lutheran and Calvinist elements of Protestantism. His parents, particularly his mother, were religious people. His mother's spiritual advisor was Franz Albert Schultz, one of the leading figures of the Pietist movement of Germany at the time. Schultz was the director of a school called the Collegium Fridericianum, which Kant entered at the age of eight, remaining a pupil there for eight years, before he entered the university at Königsberg. During his early schooling he received, in addition to a thorough knowledge of Latin, a "pietistically colored religious instruction."[8] Although Kant later rejected many aspects of Pietism, he maintained a high respect for certain aspects of it. He wrote, "Even though the religious ideas of that time and the concepts of what they called virtue and piety were anything but clear and adequate, still they really got hold of the basic thing. You can say what you want about Pietism— the people who were serious about it were outstanding in a praiseworthy respect. They possess the highest thing men can possess, that calm, that serenity, that inner peace undisturbed by any passion."[9] On entering the University of Königsberg, Kant began his studies in the philosophy faculty, which included the study of mathematics and science. Königsberg was one of the Protestant universities of Germany, founded in 1544.[10] Schultz, who was also one of the most influential professors of theology at the university, helped keep Pietism alive in this period. Kant himself seemed to have had contradictory feelings about Pietism. He was much attracted by the rationalism of Christian Wolff, who sought to establish a complete system of philosophy on the basis of the modern sciences.[11] Wolff's rational approach to theology, in opposition to the subjective religious impulse of Pietism, led first to Wolff's expulsion from the Pietist university of Halle, but eventually to his rectorship of it. On the other hand, Kant retained certain sympathies with Pietism. When he petitioned Schultz for aid in seeking a university post, Schultz asked, "Do you fear God from your heart?" and Kant assured him that he did.[12]

In some respects, Kant sought to distance himself from the religious influences of his youth. German Pietism attempted to recover Luther's early teaching regarding the importance of faith rather than dogma. Thus Pietism led at times to an excess of emotionalism, an obsession with the internal dimensions of religious faith. In describing the oppressive school atmosphere that Kant later reacted against, Cassirer characterizes its pietist practice in the following way. It strove for "possession of the *whole* human being, of his opinions, and convictions, of his feeling, and his will. This scrutiny of the 'heart,' in the pietistic sense, was practiced incessantly. There was no inner stirring, be it ever so hidden, that could escape or elude this examination, and that perpetual supervision did not attempt to control."[13] Kant's criticism of Pietism was directed against this emphasis on internal feelings and the conception of piety as based on a personal relation to God.

Despite Kant's rejection of pietist practice, certain fundamental elements of Protestantism remained decisive for his thought. Paulsen regards Kant as the "finisher of what Luther had begun."[14] Luther had revolted against the confusion of religion and science in scholastic philosophy and attempted to free faith from knowledge and from all external authority. Kant's separation between reason and faith epitomizes this Protestant position. In the preface to the *Critique of Pure Reason*, Kant writes, "I have therefore found it necessary to deny knowledge, in order to make room for faith."[15] Moreover, Kant's treatment of practical reason, which emphasizes the individual relation to the moral law as opposed to the dominance of church authority, echoes the Protestant turn toward the inner man. Paulsen comments that Kant "placed morality on a Protestant basis—not works, but the disposition of the heart."[16]

Kant distanced himself from the formal practice of Christianity, and toward the end of his life his writings on religion brought him into conflict with the religious enthusiasts in the government. Yet his moral philosophy can be seen as the "translation of this Christianity from the religious language to the language of reflection: in place of God we have pure reason, instead of the ten commandments the moral law, and in place of heaven the intelligible world." [17] In Paulsen's view, Kant reflects the "true spirit" of Christianity. He writes, "Its depreciation of the world and its pomps and glories, its indifference to all external distinctions of culture and education, the absolute value that it places upon the good will, the fidelity with which one serves God and his neighbor, its insistence on the equality of all men before God—these are all characteristic of Kant's view of life." [18]

Although Kant criticized the ecclesiastical form of religion, his interpretation of religion on the basis of a rational morality stems from Protestant sources. His emphasis on the moral will, as opposed to the external act, echoes Luther's stress on faith versus works. Kant's notion of the autonomy of the moral person, according to which each individual stands in direct relation to the moral law, is reminiscent of the Protestant notion of the priesthood of all believers. In Luther's view, each individual stands in direct relation to God through his faith, unmediated by the dogma and hierarchy of the church. Moreover, Kant's denial of the value of pleasure reflects the ascetic discipline that so strongly characterized Calvinist strains of Protestantism. But his transposition of these religious tenets into a rational morality did not leave these values untouched. Kant's basic disagreement with the Pietism of his youth was its unbridled emotionalism and personalism. Insofar as Lutheranism originally led in the direction of an emotional faith, Kant distanced himself from it. The role of the will in Kant's moral theory reflects the "innerlichkeit" of Lutheranism, by pointing to the subject's inner relation to religion. But Kant's inner man distinguishes between acting according to inclination and acting according to duty. Obedience to the rational law, not the inner felt emotion, provides the inner bond of Kantian morality. Consequently, it is not the natural endowment of sensibility that forms the basis of original sin in Kant's philosophy of religion. Instead, he attributes the evil in human nature to an impurity of disposition that shows itself in the failure to make the law the only determining ground of the will. [19]

The effect of these religious elements in Kant's thought extends beyond his moral theory into his discussion of knowledge. Paulsen's suggestion that Kant completed the work of Luther by separating faith from reason is misleading if it implies that Kant's treatment of reason is free of ascetic tendencies. Kant's treatment of knowledge cannot be divorced from the practices that shaped his own orientation toward life. His theory of knowledge, morality, and beauty must be examined in the context of this ascetic ideology.

# 8

# KANT'S TREATMENT OF SENSIBILITY

KANT DEFINES SENSIBILITY IN THE FIRST CRITIQUE AS THE FACULTY through which objects are given to us. He writes, there are "two stems of human knowledge, namely *sensibility* and *understanding*. . . . Through the former, objects are given to us; through the latter, they are thought."[1] Sensibility, in this context, refers to intuition as the model of empirical apprehension. However, elsewhere Kant recognizes a broader notion of sensibility. In the Introduction to the *Metaphysics of Morals*, Kant characterizes sensibility in the following way: "On the one hand, it can be referred to an object as a means toward cognizing it . . . here sensibility, as the receptivity for a representation that is thought, is sense. On the other hand, the subjective element in our representations may be such that it cannot become a factor in cognition . . . in this case the receptivity for the representation is called feeling."[2] Despite Kant's recognition that empirical receptivity includes both sense experience and feeling (e.g., the subjective feeling of pleasure or pain), he adamantly rejects the latter as a component of knowledge. Whenever he mentions feelings in the *Critique*, he emphasizes their irrelevance to knowledge. For example, in the Transcendental Aesthetic, he excludes feeling and volition from intuition. He writes that "everything in our knowledge which belongs to intuition—feelings of pleasure and pain, and the will, not being knowledge, are excluded" (*CPR* B67). Later in the *Critique* he repeats that "feeling is not a faculty whereby we represent things, but lies outside our whole faculty of knowledge" (*CPR* A802/B830). Thus, sensibility, as a faculty of knowledge, is only a restricted portion of our sensible apparatus. This purified conception of sensibility reflects in part Kant's ascetic heritage, which leads him to distance large portions of sensible apprehension from contributing to knowledge. These restrictions are evident not only in his assumption that affective responses have no bearing on cognition, but also in his desensualization of sense experience and his conception of intuition as the mode of immediate apprehension.

In the *Critique of Pure Reason*, Kant identifies the cognitive portion of sensibility with intuition. In the opening passage of the Transcendental Aesthetic, Kant defines intuition in the following way: "In whatever manner and by whatever means a mode of knowledge may relate to objects, *intuition* is that through which it is in immediate relation to them. . . . But intuition takes place only in so far as the object is given to us" (*CPR* A19/B33).[3] Kant's claim that intuition stands in immediate relation to the given object suggests that sensibility provides the raw material for empirical knowledge, independent of any theoretical constraints. But Kant's theory of knowledge is not merely one in which categories of the understanding are imposed on natural sensibility. Kant does not treat intuition as immediate in an experiential sense, but only in an analytical sense. In referring to his method of analysis, Kant comments that his goal in the Transcendental Aesthetic is to "isolate sensibility" by taking away all other components of knowledge, including the contribution of the understanding and of sensation (*CPR* A22/B36). This method of isolation is modeled on the method of chemical reduction to which Kant compares his own "experiment of pure reason" (*CPR* Bxxi n.). But if intuition is an *isolated* form of sensibility, it cannot refer to the immediate apprehension of an object. Instead, intuition is itself structured by Kant's theory of perception.

By reducing sensibility to intuition in the first *Critique*, Kant implies that observation is primary for knowledge. Kant uses intuition, "Anschauung," to refer to our general capacity for being affected by objects. But the commonly used word for sense perception is "Empfindung." "Anschauung" means to look at or view; "Schau" is a view or exhibit. By choosing "Anschauung" as the general term for our receptivity, including our empirical sensations (Empfindungen), Kant suggests that looking at or viewing is paradigmatic for sense perception. The perceiver's relation to the object is that of a spectator.

Kant takes observation as fundamental for knowledge in general in order to achieve the exactness of knowledge promised by the scientific method. Implicit in this choice is a hostility toward the body. By emphasizing observation as the primary mode of knowledge, the perceiver achieves a distanced relation to his or her own body. In the act of looking we are less aware of our body than, for example, in the act of touching. In discussing the sense of sight in *Anthropology from a Pragmatic Point of View*, Kant writes: "The sense of sight, while not more indispensable than the sense of hearing, is, nevertheless, the noblest, since, among all the senses, it is farthest removed from the sense of touch. . . . Not only does sight have the greatest radius of perception in space, but it also receives its sense organ as being least involved. . . . Consequently, it comes nearer to being a pure intuition (the immediate idea of a given object without admixture of evident sensation)."[4] The virtue of sight is not only its range. Among all the senses, it is the one in which the body is least involved in perceptual awareness. For Kant, awareness of our physical involvement actually distorts knowledge of an object. He stresses the importance of excluding awareness of our senses in the following comment: "When the sensation, however, becomes so strong that the awareness of the activity of the organ becomes stronger than the awareness of the relation to an external object, then outer perceptions are changed into inner perceptions" (*Anthro* 19.43–44). Since inner perceptions contribute nothing to knowledge, one must distance bodily awareness from sensible apprehension in order to have knowledge of the external world.

Kant contrasts the sense of sight with the sense of touch, which is the "most limited condition of perception" (*Anthro* 19.43). The restricted nature of touch is due not only to its narrow spatial scope, but also to the involvement of the sense organ in this experience. Unlike sight, touch cannot be thoroughly purified of any "admixture of evident sensation." Touch contributes to knowledge only insofar as it is completely devoid of any pleasurable sensation. Kant describes it as follows: "The sense of touch lies in the fingertips and their nerve endings, and enables us to discover the form of a solid body by means of contact with its surface" (*Anthro* 17.41). In his view, touch only contributes to knowledge of the formal properties of an object. Since perceiving the texture of an object depends on our sensual awareness, it is excluded from the noetic dimension of sense experience.

Since the senses of taste and smell in no way provide knowledge of the spatio-temporal form of an object, they are considered completely non-noetic. Kant describes them as "subjective senses," in which "the idea obtained from them is more an idea of enjoyment, rather than the cognition of the external object" (*Anthro* 16.4). Kant thereby establishes an opposition between the idea of enjoyment and the cognition of the external object. He considers the subjective senses to be the "senses of pleasure," indicating that pleasure derives solely from the subject's relation to his sense organs, not to outer objects (*Anthro* 21.45). (It is appropriate to include here a comment about the gender of the Kantian subject. Although Kant ostensibly adopts the masculine form to refer to both male and female subjects, I follow his usage to highlight the non-neuter character of his thought.) Since pleasure is cut off from the perception of an external object, it becomes a completely self-related experience. In the first *Critique*, in speaking of taste and of colors, Kant remarks, "They are connected with the appearances only as effects accidentally added by the particular constitution of the sense organs. Accordingly, they are not *a priori* representations, but are grounded in sensation, and, indeed, in the case of taste, even upon feeling (pleasure and pain) as an effect of sensation" (*CPR* A29). The feelings of pleasure and pain (Lust and Unlust) are a secondary, subjective response to the primary perception of the object, which is devoid of pleasure. When Kant speaks of intuition as the "immediate" relation to the object, therefore, he is referring to perception in this primary sense. In other words, the cognitive portion of sensibility, to which Kant ascribes the immediate apprehension of an object, excludes the feeling of pleasure as a subjective interference with external sensation.

Kant's distinction between intuition and feeling implies that the primary experience of an object resides in an objective perception, which is contrasted with subjective feeling. But why does Kant assert this priority of objective, desensualized perception? This distancing of feeling from cognition entails a suppression of large portions of one's sensible apparatus from one's immediate apprehension of the world. Kant's analysis of sensibility posits a disengagement from the world, which cannot unquestioningly be accepted as the paradigm for knowledge.

Kant's exclusion of feeling from intuition has consequences not only for his analysis of perception, but for his treatment of both feeling and desire. In the *Anthropology*, Kant focuses attention not only on the cognitive, but also on these noncognitive dimensions of human existence. His discussion of human nature in the *Anthropology* is not merely an addendum to his picture of human knowledge. It provides the substantive correlate to his model of cognition. In the introduction to the *Anthropology*, Kant describes his project in the following way: "A systematic doctrine containing our knowledge of man (anthropology) can either be given from a physiological or a pragmatic point of view . . . pragmatic knowledge of man aims at what man makes, can, or should make of himself as a freely acting being" (*Anthro* 3). Thus, Kant's empirical characterization of human nature is based on his normative conception of man as a free, rational being. In seeking pragmatic knowledge of man, Kant begins with the human understanding. Kant's inquiry indicates that in order to gain knowledge, the subject must comport himself in a particular way. Kant's treatment of feelings shows the practical consequences of this posture. Kant's notion that affective responses have no bearing on cognition has become virtually a presupposition in subsequent philosophical thought; therefore, the more vividly one conveys the implications of Kant's view, the better one is able to critically evaluate it.

Emotion (Affekt) and passion (Leidenschaft) share, in Kant's view, certain disagreeable features. In the third book of the *Anthropology*, Kant writes, "To be subject to emotions and passions is probably always an illness of mind because both emotion and passion, exclude the sovereignty of reason" (*Anthro* 73.155). He repeatedly uses the metaphor of illness to describe these feelings. He writes, "Emotion works upon the health like a stroke of apoplexy; passion works like consumption or atrophy. Emotion is like an intoxicant which one has to sleep off, although it is still followed by a headache; but passion is looked upon as an illness having resulted from swallowing poison" (*Anthro* 74.157). Again, "Passion is regarded as an insanity which broods over an idea that is imbedding itself deeper and deeper" (*Anthro* 74.157). Finally, "Passion, on the other hand, no man wishes for himself. Who wants to have himself put in chains when he can be free?" (*Anthro* 74.157). In contrast to this unpleasant disturbance, Kant describes the Stoic ideal of apathy: "The principle of apathy, that is, that the prudent man must at no time be in a state of emotion, not even in that of sympathy with the woes of his best friend, is an entirely correct and sublime moral precept of the Stoic school because emotion makes one (more or less) blind" (*Anthro* 75.158). Thus, Kant explicitly identifies his hostility toward emotion with that which derives from an ascetic philosophical tradition.

Kant's antipathy to emotion extends not only to excessive displays of feeling, but to its essential features as well. As Kant defines it, "Emotion is surprise through sensation, whereby the composure of the mind (animus sui compos) is suspended" (*Anthro* 74.156). The conception of emotion as "surprise" suggests that feeling is superimposed on our normal condition, an event from which one must recover the way one sleeps off a drunken bout. Emotion, therefore, is a temporary state that has no continuity with our past or future awareness. Kant's definition of emotion as "surprise through sensation" implies that emotion is a response to something in the external world. In contrast with desire, it follows rather than precedes the sensation of an object (*Anthro* 80.172). Yet Kant elsewhere insists that emotion has no intrinsic relation to an external object. In his view, feeling "contains only the relation of a representation to the subject" (intro., *MM* 10). In other words, affective responses, though stimulated by sensation, are not determined by the character of the perceived object. Furthermore, since emotion is a disruption of our normal state, affect cannot be determined by our subjective state. Kant's conception of emotion deprives him of any means of providing either an objective or subjective explanation of affect. Emotion appears as a strictly arbitrary occurrence. Kant cannot give an account of why one responds with either joy or melancholy in a given situation. Thus, emotion, in Kant's view, can never be considered an appropriate response to a person or an event.

In emotion, according to Kant, the composure of the mind is disrupted. In referring to the "Fassung" of the mind, which literally means the grasping or seizing, Kant implies that our normal state is one in which reason has seized control. Since emotion and passion threaten the sovereignty of reason, they must be excluded from ordinary consciousness. Kant's demand for rational control echoes the Calvinist imperative to rationalize every moment of existence. For the Calvinist, one's natural state must be subjugated to a rational discipline, eliminating any trace of spontaneity. Similarly, Kant's principle of apathy and self-control implies that emotion must be completely repudiated by the rational man.

Despite Kant's ideal of apathy, he recognizes that the feelings of pleasure and pain are necessary for life. He writes, "Gratification is the feeling of advancement; pain is that of a hindrance of life. But the life (of the animal) is, as physicians have also noticed, a continuing play of the antagonism between these two feelings" (*Anthro* 60.131). Insofar as Kant acknowledges the necessity of emotion, however, he endorses pain as the more valuable feeling. He states, "Pain is the incentive to activity, and above all, in activity we feel that we are alive; without such a good, inertia would set in" (*Anthro* 60.132). Kant actually perceives strong feelings of joy to be life-threatening. He comments, "One can see from the death lists that more persons have lost their lives suddenly on account of exuberant joy than on account of sorrow" (*Anthro* 76.159).[5] In other words, Kant's ideal of apathy leads him to value the pained and melancholy disposition which characterizes his own nature as well.

Kant's splitting off of feeling from the perception of an object relegates feeling to a strictly subjective domain. In Kant's view, feeling is an inner state of consciousness that illumines nothing about the external world. His description of feeling as subjective and blind implies that it cannot express one's response to another person or thing. Nor can feeling reveal anything about the subject's own intentions. In the *Metaphysics of Morals*, Kant comments that feeling in no way contributes to knowledge, "not even the cognition of our own state" (intro., *MM* 9–10). Feeling is distanced not only from objective perception, but even from one's own state of self-awareness.

This treatment of emotion presents feelings in greatly modified form. For example, the definition of emotion as "surprise through sensation" cannot elucidate the meaning of certain feelings, such as anxiety. For Kant, the feeling of anxiety is circumscribed by the metaphor of an intoxicant. It appears as a harmful indulgence, which reveals nothing about one's relationship to self or other. The limitations of Kant's treatment of emotion are evident also in his discussion of the feeling of joy. Kant defines joy as that emotion "which motivates the subject to remain in the state in which he currently finds himself" (*Anthro* 76.159). According to this definition, joy appears as a wholly self-related experience. But this definition is thoroughly inadequate when considered in light of experiences that we might have, though Kant did not. Even if the self-conscious desire to sustain this feeling may be intrinsic to joy, this experience also extends beyond the boundaries of one's self-relation. For example, a mother (or father) may feel great joy when a child brings home his or her first drawing from school, whereas a visiting neighbor would not feel so moved. The mother's feeling is motivated by her involvement with the child who has drawn the picture. Her feeling of joy is not strictly self-related but derives from her particular relation to another person: her responsibility and love for the child.[6] The neighbor, who observes the same child and the same picture, but who does not share this mother-child bond, can remain indifferent. Furthermore, the mother's joy does not imply that she wants to remain in the state in which she currently finds herself. On the contrary, this situation is special because it is a precursor of the growing independence of the child, who will eventually outgrow this desire to bring home drawings. Indeed, implicit in the mother's joy is the knowledge that this condition will be superseded. Kant's general definition of emotion as "surprise through sensation" is likewise misleading for interpreting this experience. The mother's ordinary consciousness is not suspended in this joyful encounter. Rather, her normal state of mind, her recognition of herself as a mother, is the precondition for this emotion.

Kant's definition of emotion, furthermore, omits any role for sensuality. Surely, even the mother's joy has a sensual component. The child who hugs and kisses and cries is a physical presence for the mother. Sensual pleasure is even excluded from Kant's discussion of the feelings of pleasure and pain (Gefühle der Lust und Unlust). The pleasure provided by the senses is limited to playing games, watching a drama, reading a novel, and, the greatest pleasure in life of all, relaxation after work (*Anthro* 60.133). Kant speaks of work as a "troublesome occupation (unpleasant in itself and delightful only in its success), so that relaxation, through the mere disappearance of a long hardship, turns into sensible pleasure, that is, cheerfulness, because otherwise there would not be anything enjoyable" (*Anthro* 60.133). No doubt many a reader of the *Critique of Pure Reason* wished that Kant had taken a more positive pleasure from his work, for then the task of unraveling it might have been less arduous. The pleasure in all of these activities, according to Kant, derives from the play of opposing emotions. Even in his discussion of sensuous pleasure, where he defines gratification (Vergnügen) as a pleasure of sensation (*Anthro* 60.130), he adds that this feeling can also be explained by "the effect which the sensation of our physical condition has on the mind" (*Anthro* 60.131). By stressing the component of self-reflection in this experience, sensuous pleasure is distanced from the immediate apprehension of an object.

Thus, Kant's examination of emotion portrays the ideal man as a highly disciplined, apathetic creature who values pain above pleasure, whose greatest enjoyment consists in the relaxation following work, and who finds no place for love in his life. The *Anthropology* is a graphic picture, not only of Kant's own disposition, but of the consequences of his analysis of cognition. It reflects the turning away from pleasure and love that has characterized the ascetic tradition.

Kant's analysis of emotion presupposes an opposition between feeling and knowing. He treats emotion as a subjective effect that interferes with knowledge. But emotion is also a means of apprehending persons and things. If, for example, a person gives me something, my feelings of warmth and appreciation are an appropriate response to this act. The feeling of warmth is not an irrational disturbance of a pure intuition but is itself a mode of recognition. Kant's exclusion of emotion and pleasure from intuition reflects the ascetic commitment to purify reason from sensuous existence. Thus, Kant's conception of rationality is not defined by purely rational interests but may be motivated by the presuppositions about the body inherent in this ascetic tradition. In other words, one must call into question Kant's claim to achieve pure truth, undistorted by emotion. His restriction of the cognitive portion of sensibility to intuition itself expresses an interest in selecting from and modifying the real.

Although Kant treats emotion as irrational because it distorts "objective" perception, one must question whether rationality is best defined by the parameters of a purified, desiccated intuition. One might consider rationality, instead, as that which articulates one's experience. Emotions that express one's intentions, or one's recognition of another, are rational for us in a way in which Kant's notion of intuition is not. The restricted form of sensibility that Kant includes in intuition may itself be experienced as an irrational violation of our sensible apprehension.

Like feeling, desire in Kant's analysis is excluded from immediate apprehension. In Kant's definition, "Desire is the power of the subject to determine itself through the representation of something future as an effect of its idea."[7] Desire, according to Kant, is a mode of self-determination. He comments that there is a subjective possibility of having a desire that "precedes the representation of its object" (*Anthro* 80.172). This possibility exists because desire is not a response to an object but an impulse to gain possession of one. What the subject seeks in the object of desire is the satisfaction of his own power of determination. Since desire is not a response to the presence of an existing object, but is oriented solely toward a future one, the object of desire appears to the subject as a mere idea and is thus wholly desensualized. When this object is finally achieved, the subject seeks a new object in order to prove to himself his capacity for self-determination. Because the desiring subject is exclusively concerned with his own power of representation, desire cannot serve as a mode of recognition of another person. By contrast, for Hegel, a desiring relation to another becomes the vehicle for the human struggle for recognition.

Since desire in Kant's view cannot contribute to the recognition of persons, sexual desire is viewed as reducing persons to objects. In sexual passion, according to Kant, one uses another person in order to satisfy one's natural instincts. Desire is not directed toward the loved one as a person with a consciousness and a will, but only as an object of gratification. Kant writes, "When love has been satisfied (by indulgence), the desire, at least with regard to the very person involved, ceases altogether" (*Anthro* 80.173). Kant views erotic desire as fundamentally opposed to human dignity; it debases another person as an object for one's own uses. In the *Lectures on Ethics*, Kant comments, "There is no way in which a human being can be made an Object of indulgence for another except through sexual impulse."[8] He continues,

> Sexual love makes of the loved person an Object of appetite; as soon as that appetite has been stilled, the person is cast aside as one casts away a lemon which has been sucked dry. . . . Taken by itself it is a degradation of human nature; for as soon as a person becomes an Object of appetite for another, all motives of moral relationship cease to function, because as an Object of appetite for another a person becomes a thing and can be treated and used as such by every one. This is the only case in which a human being is designed by nature as the Object of another's enjoyment. Sexual desire is at the root of it; and that is why we are ashamed of it, and why all strict moralists, and those who had pretensions to be regarded as saints, sought to suppress and extirpate it. (*LE* 163–64)

Since sexual desire is objectifying, the only vehicle for "true human love" is "practical love," which is dictated by the moral law.[9] Love that arises from feeling or inclination is "pathological" because it cannot be commanded by law. Human love, therefore, is not only desexualized, but it also "admits of no distinction between types of persons, or between young and old" (*LE* 163). This conception of love means that we will have the same love toward our intimate friends as toward a stranger or enemy. Since one can only love the person as a moral agent, according to Kant, one does not love his or her generosity or stubbornness or loyalty. And since sexual love is objectifying, there is no place in Kant's system for love of persons with empirical qualities. No wonder Charlotte von Schiller said of Kant that since he was not able to feel love, there was something defective in his nature.[10]

Kant considers sexual desire to be an instinct that serves "nature's end" and not "what we have devised ourselves as its end" (*Anthro* 219). By defining sexuality as strictly natural, the historical circumstances determining sexual relations appear to be natural phenomena. For example, Kant asserts woman's character, in contrast to man's, to be wholly defined by natural needs. Woman's lack of self-determination, in his view, is intrinsic to her nature. He writes, "Nature was concerned about the preservation of the embryo and implanted fear into the woman's character, a fear of physical injury and a timidity towards similar dangers. On the basis of this weakness, the woman legitimately asks for masculine protection" (*Anthro* 219). Because of their natural fear and timidity, women are also viewed as unsuited for scholarly work. Kant mockingly describes the scholarly women who "use their books somewhat like a watch, that is, they wear the watch so it can be noticed that they have one, although it is usually broken or does not show the correct time" (*Anthro* 221). Kant's remarks on women in the *Anthropology* echo his sentiments in *Observations on the Feeling of the Beautiful and the Sublime*. In that early work, Kant notes, "A woman who has a head full of Greek, like Mme. Dacier, or carries on fundamental controversies about mechanics, like the Marquise de Châtelet, might as well even have a beard, for perhaps that would express more obviously the mien of profundity for which she strives."[11] In Kant's view, women's philosophy is "not to reason, but to sense." And he adds, "I hardly believe that the fair sex is capable of principles."[12] No wonder that under these conditions the woman "makes no secret in wishing that she might rather be a man, so that she could give larger and freer latitude to her inclinations; no man, however, would want to be a woman" (*Anthro* 222).

In Kant's view, matrimony is the only solution to the inevitable objectification and degradation involved in sexual desire. Kant writes, "If I have the right over the whole person, I have also the right over the part and so I have the right to use that person's *organa sexualia* for the satisfaction of sexual desire. But how am I to obtain these rights over the whole person? Only by giving that person the same rights over the whole of myself. This happens only in marriage . . . each of them undertaking to surrender the whole of their person to the other with a complete right of disposal over it" (*LE* 167). Sexual gratification can be legitimately gained only if two individuals each have the "right of disposal" over the other's person. Kant treats sexuality as residing solely in the sexual organs, to which one must gain access. It is a "part" of a person the way shoes are a part of one's wardrobe. In Kant's view, sexual desire does not pervade the sensibility and relationships of an individual but can be neatly compartmentalized in the organs of the lower body. Although Kant recognizes sexuality as part of the totality of the person, he does not consider it intrinsic to one's humanity. For example, the desire that a man has for a woman "is not directed towards her because she is a human being, but because she is a woman" (*LE* 164). Thus, Kant separates out woman's sexual identity from her qualities as a human being.

Kant's alienation of sexuality from personhood signifies a fearful and defensive attitude toward erotic existence. His discomfort is so strong that he can scarcely bring himself to discuss it in his native tongue. For example, when Kant addresses "crimina carnis," which include "every form of sexual indulgence except in marriage," he has recourse to nineteen different Latin phrases on one page (*LE* 169). Kant reluctantly admits, "It is true that without it [sexual desire] a man would be incomplete; he would rightly believe that he lacked the necessary organs" (*LE* 164). Nonetheless, moralists "sought to suppress these inclinations because they degraded mankind" (*LE* 164).

Kant argues that the suppression of sexuality is a legitimate response to the objectification implicit in sexual desire. But his treatment of sensibility itself establishes the conditions for this objectification. By distancing desire from sensible apprehension of persons, Kant precludes it from serving as a vehicle for human relationships. Kant's hostility toward sexuality echoes that of the Christian ascetics, who rejected sexuality as a means of expressing love. But rather than accepting this ascetic suppression of sexuality as necessary for human dignity, one should question the operation Kant performs on sensibility. By distancing feeling and desire from immediate apprehension, he creates the conditions for the conception of emotion as irrational, and of erotic desire as objectifying.

Kant's commitment to the suppression of sexuality echoes the ascetic quest to escape embodiment and sensuality. Ascetic self-denial offers a means to control those factors of existence that appear threatening: the uncertainty of life and the promise of mortality implicit in sexual activity. Kant carries this ascetic impulse to his analysis of the transcendental conditions of knowledge, which exist prior to and independently of any particular human experience. These transcendental conditions provide an unchanging certainty and immortality in the system of truth that is not possible in human life itself.

But if Kant's theory of knowledge is built on this distancing of life and on a suppression of erotic factors of existence, it cannot support its claim to arise from a pure interest in knowledge, free of empirical motive. On the contrary, Kant's emphasis on purity in his analysis of cognition expresses a will to exclude certain things from the purview of cognition. This mode of knowledge does not express pure truth, in contrast to the distortions threatened by feeling and desire. Rather, Kant's exclusion of large portions of sensibility from contributing to knowledge reflects a disengagement from the world, which is itself a form of defense and control.

# 9

# KANT'S FETISHISM
# OF OBJECTIVITY

KANT'S ASCETIC COMMITMENT MANIFESTS ITSELF NOT ONLY IN HIS
desensualization of sensibility, but also in his analysis of objective
knowledge in terms of pure concepts of the understanding. Although the notion that the forms of thought are pure reflects the
historical attempt of asceticism to filter sensuality out of reason,
the specific function of the categories in Kant's system is linked
with social developments in eighteenth-century German society. In
particular, Kant's view of the "spontaneity" of the human understanding corresponds to the growth of new forms of human activity
in the world of work. Consequently, Kantian objectivity is not
merely a *theory* of knowledge, but in a broad sense it can be seen
as part of a social practice. The paradigm of objectivity not only
reflects an ascetic suppression of sensuality, but it also justifies the
particular form of suppression that developed in the emerging system of commodity production and exchange.

Kant's discussion of objective knowledge in the *Critique of Pure Reason* presents a description of human activity that parallels to a remarkable extent the phenomenon of fetishism later described by Marx in *Capital*. Marx's analysis of fetishism focuses on the commodity relation, which dominates capitalist society. Marx defines a commodity as a thing whose social value has absolutely no connection with its physical properties.[1] On the one hand, the commodity is a real, material thing that is produced by human labor. But on the other hand, in the nexus of economic relations, it is primarily an object of exchange whose value is completely independent of its use.

Commodity fetishism refers to the phenomenon in which the products of human labor appear to individuals not as what they immediately are, as products of labor, but appear instead as independent objects. Although created by human activity, commodities appear to individual producers as themselves rulers over the human world. In *Capital*, Marx characterizes the fetishism of commodities as follows: "There [with commodities] it is a definite social relation between men, that assumes, in their eyes, the fantastic form of a relation between things. In order, therefore, to find an analogy, we must have recourse to the mist-enveloped regions of the religious world. In that world, the productions of the human brain appear as independent beings endowed with life, and entering into relation both with one another and the human race."[2] In this situation, human beings become alienated from their own laboring activity. With the movement of commodities in the marketplace, a world of objects springs into being that appears to individuals as independent of human activity and as governed by laws that are given and immutable. At the same time, human labor itself becomes a commodity to be exchanged in the marketplace.[3]

A twofold process of abstraction takes place in commodity fetishism. The object itself, in order to be exchanged, must be reduced to a common standard by which its value in this system can be measured. Real, material objects become formalized according to abstract, universal criteria. Thus, qualitatively different objects can be treated in the marketplace as quantitatively comparable things. The human labor that produces the objects is also abstracted from its qualitative character. Labor is no longer defined by the sensuous, idiosyncratic character of the human personality, as it was in precapitalist economies. Instead, human activity is essentially defined by the labor time that provides the ground for the quantitative equality between commodities. The labor time required to produce the commodity becomes the measure of its value in this system of exchange. The object no longer stands in an immediate relation to the worker; it is neither an expression of one's personality nor a means of satisfying one's needs. Instead, it appears as an alien thing defined solely in terms of its exchange value.

The abstractness that characterizes both the commodity and the human labor that produces the commodity also determines the social relations between individuals. The individual producer encounters other producers through the act of exchange. Thus, individuals experience their social existence as a relation between these products. One's relation to other individual producers appears as a secondary, indirect result of the primary exchange-relation between things. Commodity exchange becomes the medium for all social relations. Marx comments that the "social character of labour appears to us to be an objective character of the products themselves."[4] An inversion occurs in the workers' perception of their experience in the marketplace. Instead of seeing their own activity and their relation with other individuals as primary and the products of human labor as secondary, mediating agents, the primary relation appears to be this exchange of products. Commodities appear to be what they in one sense are: abstract and alien creatures, acting independently of human will, foresight, and action.[5]

This dominance of the commodity relation results in an "objectification" of both the worker and the thing.[6] In order to enter the system of exchange, workers must treat their own labor as a commodity, which can be bought and sold. Their labor is their only possession; therefore, they themselves become objects of exchange in the marketplace. This process of self-objectification is based on the denial of those "irrational," "subjective" human qualities that interfere with the rationalization of labor.[7] Moreover, the sensuous qualities of the object are irrelevant to the fluctuations of value that take place in exchange relations. Through this process of objectification, not only do the relations between individuals become hidden in the commodity relation, but the relations between individuals and objects also become subsumed under the commodity form. The objects that should gratify human needs become alienated from this purpose.[8] To the reified mind of the worker, objectification appears as the authentic and immediate form of existence. No attempt is made to uncover the historical development of these forms or to transform them, since they are taken to be natural, immutable, and eternal.

This reification of relations between individuals and things is reflected in the philosophical thought of the modern period. Thinkers such as Kant take this reified existence as the only possible one and show no interest in the "birth and death" of the material conditions or in the corresponding genesis of prevailing forms of thought.[9] Kant explicitly disavows the relevance of historical changes to philosophical thought. This judgment is echoed in the philosophical tradition since Kant, which largely accepts his theory of objectivity as describing the essence of knowledge, which is free of any associations with empirical practices. Kant himself claims to have discovered the "one true system of philosophy."[10] Philosophical knowledge, as he declares in the *Metaphysical Elements of Justice*, itself has no history:

> It sounds arrogant, egotistical, and to those who have not yet renounced their old system, disparaging, to assert that before the critical philosophy arose there was no philosophy at all. . . . But objectively, inasmuch as there can be only one human reason, so likewise there cannot be many philosophies; that is, only one true system of philosophy based on principles is possible, however variously and often contradictorily men have philosophized over one and the same proposition. . . . Therefore, when the critical philosophy announces that it is a philosophy prior to which there was never any philosophy at all, it is doing nothing but what anyone who constructs a plan has done, will do, and indeed must do. (*MJ* 5–6)

Since philosophy has no history, in Kant's view, it remains unaffected by the particular practices of a society. But in order to have knowledge, the subject must distance himself from a multitude of sensuous, erotic, and emotional concerns. This practice of knowing reflects an ascetic discipline that philosophy has inherited from both Greek and Christian sources. Moreover, this abstraction of man from his immediate nature is expedient for a society based on the production of commodities, with the corresponding abstraction of both persons and things. Marx observes, "And for a society based upon the production of commodities, in which the producers in general enter into social relations with one another by treating their products as commodities and values, whereby they reduce their individual private labor to the standard of homogeneous human labor—for such a society, Christianity, with its *cultus* of abstract man, more especially in its bourgeois developments, Protestantism, Deism, etc., is the most fitting form of religion."[11] The detachment of the ascetic religious and philosophical devotee has much in common with the alienation of the individual in capitalist society. This similarity suggests that far from being removed from history, the philosophical view that becomes preeminent in a given period is the one best suited to the needs of social existence.

Kant has been one of the foremost thinkers in the modern philosophical tradition to stress the human contribution to knowledge through the spontaneous activity of human understanding. Nevertheless, his analysis of human activity reflects on the level of cognition the alienation of individuals from their activity in a society built on commodity relations. Kant claims that knowledge arises from two sources: the "receptivity of impressions" and the "spontaneity of concepts."[12] Through sensibility, the human subject receives impressions of the given, sensuous world. In contrast to this faculty of passive receptivity, the understanding actively brings forth its representations spontaneously from itself, independent of external impressions.[13] Knowledge is possible only insofar as the active component of knowledge is brought to bear on the sensuous content provided by sensibility. Thus, the human mind can only know objects of its own creation. As Kant writes in the preface to the second edition of the *Critique*, "Reason has insight only into that which it produces after a plan of its own" (*CPR* Bxiii). He later comments that Hume's great error was in failing to see that the understanding might itself "be the author of the experience in which its objects are found" (*CPR* B127). The understanding does not create the world insofar as the existence of objects is concerned, but it does determine objects to the degree that they can be known by us (*CPR* A93/B125–26).

Although Kant claims that the understanding is the author of experience, its creative activity is depicted in reified form. Kant's analysis of cognition embodies the contradiction between one's productive activity and one's experience of the objects of one's labor as alien, independent beings—the process Marx describes as fetishistic. For Kant the spontaneity of the understanding does not refer to the creative thought process of the empirical knower but to the formal conditions for the possibility of knowledge. The activity of thinking is abstracted from the qualitative, personal characteristics of individuals and analyzed instead in terms of the universal conditions of knowledge. All thinking subjects are reduced to an abstract standard of commensurability, and the cognitive world is distanced from the immediate experience of the individual thinker.

This notion that Kant's philosophy articulates the reified conditions of existence draws in part from Lucien Goldmann's discussion of the relation of great works of art or philosophy to social life. Goldmann views great creative works as those that coherently express on an imaginative or conceptual plane the self-understanding of a social class or group.[14] For example, he views Pascal as providing the conceptual prototype of Jansenism in seventeenth-century France. From this point of view, it appears that works become seminal or paradigmatic to the extent to which they articulate the social experience of the group. In other words, Kant's stature in the history of philosophy attests to the proximity of his views to the experience of individuals in modern bourgeois society. His epistemology, which reduces both subject and object to formally identical conditions, would appeal to the social group that demanded an abstract equivalence of persons and things in economic life. Kant's views about knowledge appear to be self-evident because he has systematized the "necessary conditions" of experience in a society characterized by commodity relations. In other words, the "experience" Kant undertakes to analyze is neither a neutral world of common sense nor simply a world of scientific objects. It refers to an "experience" that is fitting to a world of manufacture and exchange, in which science has become prominent because of its ideological and technological contribution to the system of production.

Although Kant views human activity as essential to knowledge, this activity is at the same time reduced to a very limited function. The understanding cannot create the sensuous content of the phenomenal world but can only combine the manifold of impressions given through intuition. The representations given through intuition remain an unconnected medley of impressions, unless they are united in an object through the transcendental unity of apperception.[15] Kant writes, "It must be possible for the 'I think' to accompany all my representations, for otherwise something would be represented in me which could not be thought at all, and that is equivalent to saying that the representation would be impossible, or at least would be nothing to me" (*CPR* B131).

The activity of the understanding, therefore, is explicitly limited to combining the disparate representations that are already given through intuition. The division of labor between intuition and understanding suggests, on the one hand, that what is given through the senses is originally lacking in unity. There is no organic or intrinsic connection between these various representations. They appear instead as totally unrelated impressions that attain integration and coherence only through the unifying function of the understanding. The only common feature of these representations is their capacity to be conjoined through the "I think" of apperception (*CPR* B131). Therefore, the unity of the object that is established expresses no intrinsic relatedness between representations but appears as external to the content of representations themselves. The capacity to think something as formally belonging to me appears as a tag, which can be attached to any impression. All possible impressions become equal and exchangeable in the face of a possible relation to the "I think." Just as the disparate representations are essentially unrelated and indifferent to each other, so the self-consciousness, which is the source of this possible unity, remains essentially indifferent to the content of these representations. The consciousness that combines these impressions in no way develops or changes through the act of unifying. The same, abstract "I think" unites this set of impressions as any other impressions. The self-consciousness implicit in the unity of apperception remains impervious to the content of anything that is known.

The disparate and fragmented nature of the given denies that there are any natural or organic bonds in sense impressions. The opposition between the fragmented nature of the sensible and the unifying function of the understanding parallels the opposition established within the object through commodity production. From the point of view of the commodity, the sensible qualities of an object appear as fragmented and irrational. Its rational unity is established only through the activity of labor. The natural bonds of the object are sundered in order to reestablish its identity in terms of a formal, universal measure. Labor, abstracted from its immediate, sensuous character, provides the foundation for the identity of the object qua commodity. Similarly, in Kant's epistemology, the formal "I think" establishes through the act of reflection the unity of the sensible qua object. Natural bonds within the object are denied in order to reestablish its identity in terms of the formal conditions of objectivity.

At the same time, this split between the given content of intuition and the unity provided by understanding implies that reflective consciousness can only arrange and manipulate what is given through intuition. The activity of human understanding in no sense extends to the determination of the content of sense experience. Therefore, human activity is merely theoretical and is effectively confined to contemplating the material conditions of existence. This contemplative stance mirrors the experience of the worker whose activity is limited to conforming to the preexisting demands of the machine being served.[16] The unifying function of consciousness, like the activity of the worker, is constrained to accept the preexisting conditions of empirical existence, which appear as fragmented and irrational.

Despite the restricted nature of human activity, Kant conceives of an alternative condition that transcends these limitations. He refers to an understanding that could "supply to itself the manifold of intuition—an understanding, that is to say, through whose representation the objects of the representation should at the same time exist" (*CPR* B139). The self-consciousness of such an understanding would not be limited to the act of combining, but would create and determine the material aspect of existence. Yet this creative function of reflection is projected solely onto a nonhuman, divine understanding. Like the move of fetishistic consciousness described by Marx, this human potentiality is attributed to a nonhuman force. Moreover, although Kant conceives of the possibility of substantive acts of creation, this activity could belong only to an "understanding." He cannot conceive of any other activity than that of reflection.

Not only is the activity of the human understanding merely contemplative, but also the "I think," which performs the unifying function for consciousness, is solely an abstract, universal condition of reflection. Kant remarks that the synthetic act of the understanding is "one, and must apply equally for all combinations" (*KRV* B130, my translation). In other words, the unifying activity of reflection applies equally to all representations within a single self-consciousness. But when Kant speaks of the conditions of the "Allgemeinen," the general or universal consciousness, he refers not only to what all representations must have in common to be united by one self-consciousness. He also includes the conditions that all self-consciousnesses must have in common. The German word "Allgemeinen" means both that which is shared and that which is universal. For the representations to belong to one self-consciousness, they must all have something in common, namely their association with the "I think." And what they thus share in common becomes the universal, defining feature of consciousness.

Kant explicitly differentiates this universal condition of consciousness from the empirical consciousness of an individual. He describes the latter in the following way: "For the empirical consciousness, which accompanies different representations, is in itself diverse and without relation to the identity of the subject" (*CPR* B133). Empirical consciousness, in Kant's view, cannot provide the unity by which I can call any representations "mine." Taken alone, empirical consciousness is as "many-colored and diverse a self as I have representations of which I am conscious to myself" (*CPR* B134).

Therefore, although human activity is the necessary condition for experience, in Kant's view this activity is not a function of the particular subject, whose feelings and history inform conscious activity. Rather activity is located in the abstract and universal form of consciousness, the "I think," which is empty of all content. Kant's analysis of the knowing consciousness echoes the conditions of reification that Marx and Lukács investigate. In Kant's system, the essential features of consciousness become reduced to the formal condition "I think," which establishes an equivalence between all subjects. Consciousness, therefore, becomes an interchangeable unit. My experience in knowing an object is identical with yours. All personal attributes, emotions, desires, and interests are irrelevant to the formal conditions of knowledge.

This abstract equivalence among diverse consciousnesses mirrors the quantitative equivalence of labor in a market economy. As Lukács writes, the value of labor resides in the "abstract, equal, comparable labor of the worker."[17] Only if labor is commensurable can it provide the basis for the exchange of the products of labor. Labor, therefore, becomes reduced to a formal equivalence, measured by a wage, in which all subjective attributes of the laborer are eliminated. Any laborer operating a particular machine must perform the same actions, regardless of whether the worker is black or white, male or female. Since the laboring activity is transformed into an interchangeable commodity, laborers experience their own labor as an alien activity. Work does not satisfy personal goals or gratify personal wants but exists in the dimension of the workers' lives in which they live for a wage, and not for themselves. The formal equality of abstract labor, therefore, creates a situation in which workers experience a split between their work and their personality. An analogous split is evident in the opposition Kant draws between the productive activity of formal consciousness and the empirical consciousness of the individual. Creative activity is not an outgrowth of one's personality but derives from the universal "I think." Like the reified consciousness of the worker, in which one's own activity appears as alien, the thinker in Kant's analysis is estranged from his own thought.

Furthermore, the thinker has sundered all immediate bonds with other individuals. The isolation of the thinking consciousness echoes the disintegration of natural bonds between individuals in the marketplace. The workers' relations with others are no longer determined by family, religious, or community ties but solely by their relation to the objects of production. Individuals come into contact with one another primarily through the exchange of commodities (including their labor power). The severed bonds between individuals are reestablished through the medium of exchange. Kant's analysis of the knowing consciousness reflects this social atomism of market society. As Goldmann observes, the "I" that thinks is not part of an organic community. He writes, "That it could never pass from the *I* to the *we*, that in spite of Kant's genius it always remained within the framework of bourgeois individualist thought, these are the ultimate limits of Kant's thought."[18] The subject of knowledge, in Kant's view, is the solitary "I" that conforms to the universal conditions of self-consciousness. This "I" constitutes the unity of the object of knowledge. Kant claims, "It is the unity of consciousness that alone constitutes the relation of representations to an object and therefore their objective validity and the fact that they are modes of knowledge" (*CPR* B137). Insofar as the "I think" in all consciousness "is one and the same" (*CPR* B132), all individuals stand in an identical relation with the object. Since the unity of consciousness constitutes the unity of the object, and since all consciousnesses are identical in this relation, the object that is thereby unified is valid for all thinkers. Knowledge of the object, therefore, can claim to have objective validity. Thus, the individual consciousness comes into relation with another only by virtue of sharing the identical relation with the object of knowledge. Like the situation of exchange, the relations between individuals are mediated by their relations with things.

But the reification generated by commodity relations does not arise simply from the fact that relations between human beings are mediated by the products of their labor. In fact, as Marx learned from Hegel, the "objectification" of consciousness through productive activity is necessary for the development of self-consciousness. However, in fetishistic consciousness, one's own activity disappears from view. The workers cannot see their own role in producing the objects of exchange; production and exchange appear instead as ordered by objective laws. Similarly, in Kant's account, the subject's capacity to combine the representations into an object becomes concealed from him. Kant claims, at one point, that the representations "are combined *in the object*, no matter what the state of the subject may be" (*CPR* B142). The subject, through the unity of consciousness, provides the foundation for the unity of the object. But this constituting activity is not immediately experienced by the subject. It is only revealed through a transcendental analysis of experience.[19] As the condition of all possible experience, which precedes any particular perception, this constituting activity appears to the subject not as an expression of his subjectivity but as an objectively given, external force. Thus, although for Kant the subject constitutes the objective world insofar as it can be known, this activity appears only in alienated form.

The subject's self-estrangement is explicit in the "Refutation of Idealism," where Kant denies that the subject has any immediate experience of himself. Kant argues that the "I think" or "I am" that immediately accompanies all experience is merely an empty, "intellectual" (*CPR* B178) representation that should not be confused with real knowledge of oneself. Kant writes, "Certainly, the representation 'I am,' which expresses the consciousness that can accompany all thought, immediately includes the existence of a subject, but it does not so include any *knowledge* of that subject, and therefore also no empirical knowledge, that is, no experience of it" (*CPR* B277). The subject, therefore, is deprived of any immediate experience of himself. Knowledge of oneself is possible, Kant argues, only on the basis of knowledge of external objects, which provide the permanent standard against which the subject can measure himself. Kant writes, "Inner experience is itself possible only mediately, only through outer experience" (*CPR* B277). Therefore, the subject's self-experience is mediated by the perception of this "permanent" standard through "a thing outside" him (*CPR* B275). The self-knowledge that is deduced from the perception of objects itself bears the stamp of the fixity that characterizes the external object. Instead of experiencing himself as the creator of the objective world, the subject finds his own empirical character to be shaped by the object. As in the fetishism of commodities, an inversion takes place in which the subject no longer sees himself as the ruler of the object world, but the objects themselves appear to regulate human life.

The reification of the thinker is evinced not only in the formal character of apperception but also in the categories that are derived from this unity of consciousness. Kant defines the categories as "pure concepts of the understanding" that apply "a priori to objects" (*CPR* A79/B105). These a priori concepts are not derived from experience but exist prior to and independent of any experience.[20] Kant's insistence on the a priori character of the concepts implies that the forms of thought, by which one unites the sensuous manifold, are indifferent to the sensible content of experience. The same forms of thought are universally applicable to all sensible impressions. This rigidity of the form of thought in relation to the matter of experience expresses the relation between form and content in the production of commodities. The formal character of labor, defined by its wage, is indifferent to the immediate, sensuous nature of the object produced by its labor.

The a priori character of the categories implies that they are eternal forms of thought. They are not derived from experience, yet they apply necessarily to all objects of experience. Since the concepts, in Kant's view, are universally valid, they themselves have no history. The pure concepts that are now valid must be valid at all future points. The activity of reflection undergoes no change but constantly repeats the same patterns of thought. Marcuse argues that this emphasis on the a priori character of the forms of thought effectively denies the possibility of any future activity.[21] Future thought is confined to repeating the present form of reflection, thereby precluding any change in consciousness. Thus, reasons's claims for a priori validity merely "freezes" the past relations between subjects and objects by defining them as eternally valid. The temporal character of already entrenched relations, which are reflected in the forms of thought, becomes concealed from the thinker. These relations appear as having no past, as being outside of history.

Kant defines the purity of these concepts as meaning "there is no admixture of anything empirical" (*CPR* B3). Since the categories have no sensuous content, the "combination" that takes place through the categories is wholly an "act of spontaneity" of the understanding (*CPR* B130). Kant writes, "Of all representations combination is the only one which cannot be given through objects. Being an act of the self-activity of the subject, it cannot be executed save by the subject itself" (*CPR* B130). The categories embody, in Kant's eyes, free human activity. But this "spontaneity" suggests only a very limited form of freedom. Although the understanding freely brings forth the categories, the categories provide the unalterable "rules" (*CPR* B145) by which the understanding can know anything at all. The freedom of the understanding in producing concepts is much the same as the freedom of laborers in producing material goods. Individuals are free to sell their labor, according to the constraints of the laws of supply and demand. Their free activity, therefore, consists merely in subjugating themselves to these apparently objective, pre-given laws of capital. Similarly, in Kant's discussion of knowledge, any real, spontaneous activity of the subject is annihilated by its subordination to the a priori laws of thought.

Through the pure a priori categories, therefore, human reflection acquires a "phantom objectivity."[22] Although the categories are ultimately grounded in the subjective unity of consciousness and apply to the objective world only insofar as it is a world of appearance for us, not as it is itself, at the same time they appear as an objectively given system to which the individual's thought must conform. Kant refers to the categories as a "possession" (Besitz) (*CPR* A87/B119) that must be explained. The metaphor of possession, or property, indicates that pure knowledge has an objective, independent character to which the knower must lay claim. The categories do not express the particular features of an individual's thoughts, but stand at a distance from the subjective character of the knower. The categories provide the formal currency of exchange by which common experience among individuals is possible.

Because the categories are "a priori conditions of possible experience" (*CPR* A95), they have universal applicability to objects of experience. The categories provide the form necessary for all possible experience. Kant writes, "The objective validity of the categories as a priori concepts rests, therefore, on the fact that, so far as the form of thought is concerned, through them alone does experience become possible" (*CPR* A93/B126). In Kant's view, the possibility of objective knowledge rests on our sharing these rules of thought. The sensuous content of the object known appears immediately as fragmented and chaotic; by itself it is incapable of providing the grounds of common experience. The common bond provided by knowledge, on the basis of which communication is possible, derives alone from these universal forms of thought.

This picture of knowledge—in which the forms of thought furnish the universal rules to order the fragmented content of sense experience—portrays on a cognitive level the condition of individuals in bourgeois society, in which individuals are united only on the basis of an abstract universal bond.[23] Concrete interests or desires are considered peculiar to the isolated individual. Insofar as desires are shared, they lead to turmoil and competition, which must be regulated by formal laws. The universality of individual experience, in this context, refers to the subordination of all individuals to formal conditions of social existence, such as laws concerning property. The abstract character of what is common is a feature, in Weber's terms, of an "associative" rather than a "communal" society.[24] In such a world, individual interests are determined independently of their identity as members of a social group. In contrast, communal bonds exist when individual interests express the shared goals of a social group. The universality of individuals in a communal group is based on precisely that common content of experience that Kant treats merely as a source of disorder. The epistemological problem for Kant, therefore, is how individuals who are fundamentally atomistic will arrive at identical results in their thought.[25]

In the categories, thought becomes rigidified into a fixed form, which appears as objective and independent of an individual's actual thinking. Although Kant insists on the indifference of the forms of thought to the sensuous content in his effort to preserve the purity and universality of the concepts, this strict separation itself reflects the material conditions of bourgeois society. The sharp split between form and content reduces thought to rigid patterns that appear as objective and independent of the thinker, like the apparently independent forces that rule workers' labor in the marketplace.

Just as the activity of the knower becomes alienated from the authentic needs and desires of the individual, so the product of this activity, the object of knowledge, bears the stamp of this alienation. The objects of knowledge, according to Kant, are constituted by the pure forms of thought in conjunction with the pure forms of intuition. In the Transcendental Deduction, Kant argues that the categories can have objective validity for objects of knowledge because they are the necessary condition for the experience of an object. He writes, "The representation is a priori determinant of the object, if it be the case that only through the representation is it possible to know anything as an object" (*CPR* A92/B125). The categories, therefore, convey the alienating features of the subject's activity to the objects of knowledge that they determine.

In the Transcendental Deduction, Kant poses the following question: "The question now arises whether a priori concepts do not serve as antecedent conditions under which alone anything can be, if not intuited, yet thought as object in general" (*CPR* A93/B126). The categories apply to the concepts of objects in general, which underlie all empirical knowledge (*CPR* A93/B126). The particular objects of experience, therefore, must conform to the abstract concept of an object in general. Kant elsewhere refers to this concept of an object in general as the transcendental object (*CPR* A251), which serves as the "correlate" of the unity of apperception (*CPR* A250). The underlying form of all objects of experience, therefore, mirrors the intrinsic unity of the subject. The unity of apperception presents a picture of diverse thinkers as possessing a uniform, quantitatively equivalent and exchangeable form of consciousness. Similarly, diverse objects share this "concept of something in general." Since all objects are defined essentially by this abstract feature, they too become equivalent and exchangeable. As in the marketplace, the abstract character of human activity, which suppresses the subjective, sensuous dimension of human personality, indelibly marks the products of its activity.

In commodity production, labor must conform to preestablished patterns of behavior. Kant's discussion of the categories reflects the fixity of these rules of behavior. If making is always done in the same way, then the thing that is made is likewise always identical. In fact, labor is rationalized and systematized in the marketplace precisely in order to produce identical commodities. Similarly, if thought always follows the same rules and patterns, then the object of thought, constituted by these rules, is always identical. All objects are known in exactly the same way, and hence become equivalent and exchangeable. Furthermore, future objects will always be known in exactly the same way. If the forms of thought themselves are denied any history and development, as occurs with Kant's insistence on the a priori character of the categories, then the fundamental character of objects that are thereby known must also be without history. The object world, which claims to be founded on a priori, atemporal conditions, seems impervious to critical examination. Just as the commodity appears to both producers and consumers as a given, inalienable feature of objective existence, so the abstract, formal character of objects in Kant's thought appears to the thinker as the necessary condition of knowledge.

Given the formal and unchanging character of objects of possible knowledge, they appear to the knower not in fact as objects that one has created but as alien, independent things. On the one hand, Kant stresses the creative role of the human mind in constituting objects of knowledge. An object is distinguished from any other representation because the former "stands under a rule" (*CPR* A191/B236) that is supplied by the understanding. Kant writes, "As mere representations, they are subject to no law of connection save that which the connecting faculty prescribes" (*CPR* B164). On the other hand, although we provide the form through which it is possible to experience an object (*CPR* A93/B126), the object that is thereby constituted is as alienated from the subject as is this constituting activity itself. As cited above, Kant notes that objective representations are "combined in the object, no matter what the state of the subject may be" (*CPR* 142). The object of knowledge, therefore, takes on a character that is completely independent of the particular condition of the subject. Like the commodity's detachment from the personality of the laborer, the object of knowledge bears no relation to the specific nature of the knower. Not only are all objects known in exactly the same way by the individual thinker, but all thinkers know each object in the same way as every other thinker. As with commodities, objects of knowledge can in no way express or gratify the particular needs or desires of the individual.[26]

Thus, although the rules of human understanding order impressions into objects, these rules appear to the knower as objective "laws" (*CPR* A126) comparable to the "laws" of the marketplace, which regulate the rise and fall of prices. The laws of the understanding are "universal and necessary" (*CPR* A111); they determine the concept of "nature in general," to which all empirical laws of nature are subject (*CPR* B165).

Not only are the objects of thought alienated from the knower, appearing as given and independent entities; like commodities they are also alienated from their own immediate, sensuous nature. Kant distinguishes between the object as appearance and the thing-in-itself. In order for the object to enter the system of human knowledge, it must conform to the pure forms of sensibility and understanding. In the preface to the second edition of the *Critique of Pure Reason*, Kant argues that all previous philosophy has attempted to make knowledge conform to the objects. Like Copernicus, he intends to reverse this relation. His transformation assumes that "the objects, or what is the same thing, that the experience in which alone, as given objects, they can be known, conform to the concepts" (*CPR* Bxvii). But in viewing the objects of knowledge as conforming to our concepts, we forsake knowledge of objects in themselves. Kant writes, "A priori knowledge of reason . . . has to do only with appearances, and must leave the thing in itself as indeed real per se, but as not known by us" (*CPR* Bxx). The object of knowledge is produced by formal, unchanging rules, which leave unknown the "true correlate of sensibility" (*CPR* A30/B45).

Marxist theoreticians such as György Lukács and Lucien Goldmann agree that Kant's treatment of the object of knowledge reflects the formalization of the object and its alienation from human activity that characterizes the commodity in capitalist society. However, for Lukács the thing-in-itself poses the problem of the relation of form to an "irrational" content that is not reducible to a formal system. In his view, the thing-in-itself, which lies outside the ken of human understanding, refers to the "facticity" or content of existence that cannot be deduced from rational forms.[27] For Goldmann, the notion of the thing-in-itself suggests that Kant, despite his reified system of knowledge, retained a vision of knowledge that would transcend the bounds of contemporary existence.[28] Both Lukács and Goldmann suggest that the concept of the thing-in-itself contains the germs of a critical transcendence on Kant's part. Although Kant's exclusion of the real from knowledge gives testimony to the alienating conditions of his system, he at the same time recognizes the limitations intrinsic to objectivity. By preserving the notion of a thing unconstructed by the reified conditions of existence, Kant, unlike the rationalists, offers a critical perspective to this totally rationalized system of life and thought.

But this interpretation is misguided in assuming precisely that which Kant is at pains, especially in the second edition of the *Critique*, to deny. The alienation of the object in Kant's system lies not only in its exclusion of the real, sensuous content, represented by the thing-in-itself; this alienation penetrates into the thing-in-itself as well. In Kant's view, the concept of a thing-in-itself is merely a logical concept, derived from his analysis of phenomena. It refers merely to the "negative" sense of something as "not an object of our sensible intuition" (*CPR* B307). In no way does it assert the "positive" existence of a "noumenon" (*CPR* B307). Kant writes, "The problematic thought which leaves open a place for them [intelligible objects] serves only, like an empty space, for the limitation of empirical principles, without itself containing or revealing any other object of knowledge beyond the sphere of these principles" (*CPR* A259–60/B315). Rather than pointing to the immediate, sensuous existence of a thing, the notion of the thing-in-itself absolutely denies the possibility of such an experience. As such, it reaffirms the conditions of objective existence as given and unalterable.[29]

Kant has generally been viewed as attempting to provide a philosophical foundation for Newtonian science. For example, Norman Kemp Smith writes of Kant as follows in his *Commentary*: "The absolute sufficiency of the Newtonian physics is a presupposition of all his utterances on this theme. Newton, he believes, has determined in a quite final manner the principles, methods and limits of scientific investigation. For though Kant himself imposes upon science a further limitation, namely to appearances, he conceives himself, in so doing, not as weakening Newton's natural philosophy, but as securing it against all possible objections."[30] And Ewing writes in his *Commentary* to the first *Critique* that one of its main purposes was "the provision of a philosophical basis for science . . . the science which he had most in mind was Newtonian physics."[31] How is an analysis of Kant's theory of objectivity as fetishistic justifiable? One might object that such an explanation ignores the paramount role of science in Kant's own worldview.[32]

The interpretation offered here in no sense denies Kant's relation to Newtonian science. But the scientific model must itself be understood in relation to the social world in which it operates. Both the theory of science and its object of study are shaped by social processes. The fact that the goals and methods of science appear to be independent of human intervention is itself part of this historical process. Max Horkheimer writes of science as follows: "For science, too, is determined in the scope and direction of its work not by its own tendencies alone but, in the last analysis by the necessities of social life as well."[33] However, science has often failed to grasp its relation to social reality, creating limitations in its effectiveness in solving social problems as well as in the development of scientific concepts themselves.

Kant's treatment of objectivity similarly refuses to see its relation to the social world. Kant's epistemology posits objectively given, immutable laws of nature; it treats the subject, the generator of knowledge, as an abstract, universal "I," divorced from all social relations; it makes objects into quantitatively equivalent things, in which the immediate, sensuous qualities are suppressed; and it assumes an unchanging relation between the individual knower and the object of knowledge. These same features are evident in the Newtonian conception of science: the eternal laws of nature; the formal properties of the object of knowledge; and the abstraction of the scientific investigator, who puts aside all personal interests and desires to investigate the object according to the predefined methods of scientific inquiry. These scientific categories take on a fixity because of the refusal to examine their relation to the dynamic movement of events. Moreover, the rigidity of these concepts both narrows the scope of scientific inquiry and precludes an understanding of the interrelation between different areas that science does study. Lukács comments on the formalism operative in science and philosophy in the following passage: "Thus philosophy stands in the same relation to the special sciences as they do with respect to empirical reality. The formalistic conceptualization of the special sciences becomes for philosophy an immutably given substratum and thus signals the final and despairing renunciation of every attempt to cast light on the reification that lies at the root of this formalism."[34] In the methodically purified world of science,[35] the reified world is taken to be the only possible one. Although science seeks to be critical in every step, it fails to critically examine how its own tasks are set. Insofar as science fails to grasp the relation of its own existence and tasks to that of the social world—indeed, is debarred from grasping these connections, because of the abstract and formalistic nature of its system[36]—science is part of the ideological apparatus of a society. But science does not operate merely on the level of ideas. It is also one of the productive forces of society.[37] Therefore, science shares the fate of other productive activities: it results in an increasing technological control over the details of social life but a decreasing control over the goals of society as a whole.[38] The control made possible by scientific knowledge is confined to manipulating the elements of a system. Like the worker's experience in confronting the machine, the scientist's activity is reduced to the level of contemplation.

Thus, the scientific system with which Kant identified himself is grounded in fetishistic relations between persons and things. The scientific investigators displace themselves from any social context and present their discoveries as lawful relations between objects. Human beings, in this scientific domain, become alienated from the objects of their inquiries. Objects of nature become merely a substratum to be dominated by scientific knowledge. By validating these relations as eternal and necessary, science raises social conditions to the level of universal truths.[39]

# 10

# MORALITY AND FETISHISM

THE FETISHISTIC QUALITIES OF KANT'S THEORY OF KNOWLEDGE
are evident in the alienation of the knower from himself and in the
objectification of the object of knowledge. But Kant's thought extended beyond the boundaries of pure reason to the domain of morality. Therefore, the question arises whether this critique of objectification in Kant's thought is guilty of importing into the domain of
knowledge criteria that are valid only in the moral sphere. Kant
distinguishes the moral world, as the realm of freedom, from the
phenomenal world, in which objects are ruled by laws of nature. Is
the subject's lack of freedom in the domain of cognition, which
concerns itself with the phenomenal world, compensated for by his
freedom in the moral realm?

Kant's moral theory, far from rectifying the loss of self experienced by the knower, reveals the same commitment to a fetishistic
worldview evident in his discussion of knowledge. The moral per-

son is alienated from concrete subjective qualities of existence. Moral action requires one to act purely out of duty, out of respect for the moral law. Sensuous inclinations, such as feelings of love and sympathy, can play no role in moral behavior. Although morality is the domain of personhood, relations between concrete individuals are no more evident here than in the system of objective knowledge. Persons, in Kant's view, are merely "examples" of the moral law. Kant writes as follows in the *Foundations of the Metaphysics of Morals*: "All respect for a person is only respect for the law (of righteousness, etc.) of which the person provides an example" (*Foundations* 18). All relations between persons are mediated by the objective laws of morality, just as the relations between knowers are mediated by the objective laws of thought.

Since morality contains the moral principles of real, existent men and women, it is not exempt from the fetishistic qualities that pervade this world. In speaking of the relation of principle to history, Marx writes:

> When we ask ourselves why a particular principle was manifested in the eleventh or in the eighteenth century rather than in any other, we are necessarily forced to examine minutely what men were like in the eleventh century, what they were like in the eighteenth . . . what were the relations between man and man which resulted from all these [material] conditions of existence. To get to the bottom of all these questions—what is this but to draw up the real, profane history of men in every century. . . . But the moment we present men as the actors and authors of their own history, we arrive—by a detour—at the real starting-point, because we have abandoned those eternal principles of which we spoke at the outset.[1]

Kant denies that morality begins with the real, profane history of the relations between human beings. In his view, moral principles are universally valid, independent of the content of any particular social situation. But the very formality of the Kantian moral law reflects the reification experienced by individuals in bourgeois society.

Just as workers in commodity production are marked by an abstraction from the immediate, sensuous qualities of their activity, so the agent in Kant's moral theory is likewise abstracted from his or her feelings, inclinations, and material interests in order to enter the "realm of ends." Only through the obedience of his will to the moral law is morally worthy behavior possible. Each agent, therefore, ruled by this universal law of morality, achieves an abstract equivalence with every other moral being.

In the *Foundations of the Metaphysics of Morals*, Kant describes moral actions as follows: "Thus the first proposition of morality is that to have moral worth an action must be done from duty" (*Foundations* 16). When an action is done from duty, it "wholly excludes the influence of inclination" (*Foundations* 17). Kant defines inclination as the "dependence of the faculty of desire on sensations . . . and inclination always indicates a need" (*Foundations* 30 n.). Thus, for an action to have moral worth, it must be wholly free from any sensuous influence. In Kant's view, if an individual derives inner satisfaction in spreading joy, his action has no moral worth (*Foundations* 14).[2] Since sympathy is an inclination, it cannot be the basis of any moral action. Love, as an emotion, also comes under the rubric of "inclination." Such love cannot be commanded and is therefore considered "pathological" (*Foundations* 16). Kant distinguishes moral from pathological love as follows: "But beneficence from duty, when no inclination impels it and even when it is opposed by a natural and unconquerable aversion, is practical love, not pathological love; it resides in the will and not in the propensities of feeling, in principles of action and not in tender sympathy, and it alone can be commanded" (*Foundations* 16). Kant identifies his exclusion of inclination from the determination of moral will with the Stoic conception of morality. In the *Anthropology*, Kant writes, "The principle of apathy, that is, that the prudent man must at no time be in a state of emotion, not even in that of sympathy with the woes of his best friend, is an entirely correct and sublime moral precept of the Stoic school" (*Anthro* 75.158). As an example of genuine moral behavior, Kant describes one who is insensible to the needs of others. He writes,

> Furthermore, if nature has put little sympathy in the heart of a man, and if he, though an honest man, is by temperament cold and indifferent to the sufferings of others, perhaps because he is

provided with special gifts of patience and fortitude and expects
or even requires that others should have the same—and such a
man would certainly not be the meanest product of nature—
would not he find in himself a source from which to give himself a
far higher worth than he could have got by having a good-natured
temperament? (*Foundations* 14–15)

Thus, the morally worthy character, who may well be cold-tempered
and indifferent, acts strictly out of "respect for law" (*Foundations*
16), excluding any "pathological interest" in the object of his
action.

Since feeling and inclination cannot motivate moral behavior,
the moral agent becomes detached from these sensuous components of existence. Feelings cannot be commanded by the moral
law; thus, they appear to Kant only as irrational interferences with
moral duty. To attempt to make the principles of duty "more ac-
cordant" with our wishes and inclinations is equivalent, in Kant's
view, to "corrupting" the "purity and strictness" of these "stern
laws of duty" (*Foundations* 21). Moral behavior is most clearly evident when inclinations run counter to the act that is commanded,
because this conflict insures that inclinations have no influence on
our action. Kant writes, "The sublimity and intrinsic worth of the
command is the better shown in a duty the fewer subjective causes
there are for it and the more there are against it" (*Foundations* 43).
Thus, in his discussion of moral action, Kant refers to a man whose
mind is so clouded by his own sorrow that all sympathy with others
is extinguished. Kant comments that if such a man were to "tear
himself, unsolicited by inclination, out of this dead insensibility
and to perform this action only from duty and without inclination—
then for the first time his action has genuine moral worth" (*Foundations* 14).

Therefore, in order to act purely out of respect for the moral law,
one must put aside all of one's empirical inclinations. Feelings of
love, sympathy, and caring are morally irrelevant, merely interfer-
ing with one's capacity to act solely out of duty.[3] Since feelings play
no role in moral personality, the moral person can in no sense be
viewed as the total person. In the *Metaphysics of Morals*, Kant defines moral personality as "the freedom of a rational being under

moral laws" (intro., *MM* 23). By contrast, he defines the psychological personality as the "capacity to be conscious of the identity of one's self in the various conditions of existence (intro., *MM* 23). Since the moral personality is defined as a strictly rational being, it has no affective dimension. Kant's prescription for morality, therefore, demands an alienation of the individual from his immediate sensuous existence. The separation between feelings and moral personality results in a fragmentation of the subject. This split within the subject in the moral domain recalls the division between the cognitive and the sensuous subject in Kant's discussion of knowledge.[4]

Moral action, in Kant's view, is regulated by the universal law of morality, just as the worker's productive activity is regulated by the apparently universal and unchanging laws of the marketplace. In the *Foundations*, Kant writes, "Since I have robbed the will of all impulses which could come to it from obedience to any law, nothing remains to serve as a principle of the will except universal conformity of its action to law as such" (*Foundations* 18). The universal validity of the moral law derives from its purely formal character. It cannot be reduced to any particular law, for such a law would always have a particular object in view. Thus the moral law can only be the mere form of law: The principle of one's action should serve as a universal law. Kant encapsulates this view in the categorical imperative: "I should never act in such a way that I could not also will that my maxim should be a universal law" (*Foundations* 18).

The formality and universality of the moral law establish an equivalence between moral agents. The form of the moral act is identical in every situation and for every individual.[5] Since the moral worth of actions is determined strictly by one's obedience to the law, to act morally means that all individuals perform an identical moral act. The actual content of one's choice is irrelevant to its moral character. For example, a lie told to save a friend's life is as heinous as one told to conceal one's own criminal activity. Like the workers in the marketplace who share an identical relation to the products of their labor, the qualitative features of individuals' relations to other persons are suppressed in Kant's moral theory. Rules of moral behavior are defined in advance by the categorical imperative, and moral action consists in a repetition of this formal law.

The imperative that one act strictly out of respect for the "conception of the law in itself" (*Foundations* 17) implies that the unchanging form of law that determines the morality of an action is indifferent to the particular, concrete content of that action. The formalism of Kantian ethics presumes that the principles of morality are independent of the particular society in which they are operative. Despite the universal, formal nature of the categorical imperative, the specific content that Kant gives to it is borrowed from bourgeois society. Lukács writes, "The moment this ethic attempts to make itself concrete, i.e., to test its strength on concrete problems, it is forced to *borrow* the elements of content of these particular actions from the world of phenomena and from the conceptual systems that assimilate them and absorb their contingency."[6] For example, Kant considers the dilemma of a man who is forced by need to borrow money, knowing he cannot repay it within the promised time (*Foundations* 40). In Kant's view, it is immoral for the man to borrow money because he could never will his maxim to be a universal law. If the man were to lie in order to obtain a loan, his action would be equivalent to willing a universal law to lie, which would destroy the institution of promise-keeping on which his own lie depends. Kant writes, "I immediately see that I could will the lie but not a universal law to lie. For with such a law there would be no promises at all, inasmuch as it would be futile to make a pretense of my intention in regard to future actions to those who would not believe this pretense or—if they overhastily did so— who would pay me back in my own coin. Thus my maxim would necessarily destroy itself as soon as it was made a universal law" (*Foundations* 19). In Kant's view, the act of lying, and every action contravening ethical norms, contains a self-contradiction.[7] But if the man borrowed money under these circumstances, would he violate primarily the formal principle of promise-keeping, or the specific institution of loan-repayment? If there were no need to repay the loan in an amount of time incommensurate with the man's capabilities, there would be no need to violate a promise. In other examples Kant considers the moral dimension of whether a shopkeeper should be honest and whether one should embezzle a bank deposit. Thus, the moral dilemmas he examines draw heavily from the financial relations that exist in a market society.

Although Kant claims to derive moral principles that are independent of society, these same principles lead him to assert the inviolability of the existing order of law. In the *Metaphysical Elements of Justice* he refers to the practical principle of reason "that one ought to obey the legislative authority that now exists, regardless of its origin" (*MJ* 85), and he adds, there can be "no legitimate resistance of the people to the legislative chief of the state . . ." (*MJ* 86). The legitimacy of positive law, in Kant's view, is ultimately grounded in the law-giving capacity of the will of the people (*MJ* 78). Therefore, positive law has the same status as the moral laws that we prescribe for ourselves. In the introduction to the *Metaphysics of Morals*, Kant defines the moral person as "subject to no laws other than those which he (either alone or at least together with others) gives to himself" (intro, *MM* 23). Kant describes the legislative will of people in the same vein: "Each decides the same for all and all decide the same for each . . ." (*MJ* 78). Since the legislative authority of positive law is grounded in the law-giving form of the will, the particular laws obtaining in a society are considered morally binding.

Not only does the moral law, in Kant's analysis, borrow its content from bourgeois society; the very formalism of the moral law reflects the phenomenon of reification. Moral personality, in Kant's view, refers to the freedom of a rational being under moral laws. Since the moral person is subject to no laws other than those that he gives himself, moral laws are self-legislated and ultimately grounded in the law-giving capacity of the human will. Like the laws of human understanding, therefore, the laws of morality are humanly created. However, the moral law is also an "objective principle" (*Foundations* 17 n.) that excludes the subjective influence of feeling and inclination. The law binds us "a priori and unconditionally by means of our own reason" (intro., *MM* 27). Thus, although the moral law is grounded in the human will, it appears to the moral agent as an objectively given principle that is legitimated independently of his own activity. In the mind of the moral agent, as in the reified mind of the worker in the marketplace, he is not the authentic master of his own activity. He appears to himself not as the author of the law itself but as the author of the "obligation imposed by the law" (intro., *MM* 27). Moral action is reduced to making his will conform to this preestablished law, which is universal and necessary.

The formalism of the moral law, which commands us to act out of respect for law as such, serves ultimately as a justification of authority in general. In Marcuse's words, the imperative of the universal law "justifies not only the authority of the actual system of 'governments' but also authority in general as a social necessity. . . . This is the highest rationalization of social authority within bourgeois philosophy."[8] Respect for law as such, independent of its content, is instilled in individuals. By accepting this universal respect for law, one abrogates the right to distinguish between just and unjust laws. Moreover, individuals are taught to internalize this law-giving authority. The identification of the individual with authority in Kant's moral theory speaks to the bourgeois class that identifies itself with the authority of the state. Whereas both the working and the property-owning classes are subject to the reification that pervades capitalist society, they each have a different relation to their social conditions. Marx writes, "The property-owning class and the class of the proletariat represent the same human self-alienation. But the former feels at home in this self-alienation and feels itself confirmed by it; it recognizes alienation as its own instrument and in it it possesses the semblance of a human existence. The latter feels itself destroyed by this alienation and sees in it its own impotence and the reality of an inhuman existence."[9] The individual's identification with the law, in Kant's system, implies that he feels at home in this system of law. The moral person, therefore, deprives himself of the right of criticism and resistance, which would be possible if authority were viewed as an external power.[10]

Since Kant defines moral behavior as the determination by the will to obey the moral law, moral worth derives entirely from the inner form of the act. This stress on the inner act implies that reification reaches into the heart of the moral agent. Motives and intentions must themselves be regulated to accord with the universal law. The formal character of the law stamps not only the external behavior of the individual, but it also becomes the standard by which all internal events are evaluated. Kant's analysis of the motive for rational behavior suggests that every moment of existence must come under the watchful scrutiny of the rational law, and reification becomes totalizing. This rationalization of moral consciousness in Kant's theory also expresses the intensification of monastic discipline that typifies ascetic Protestantism.

Kant's concern with the inner form of the act bespeaks at the same time an explicit indifference to the consequence of the act. Kant writes of the good will as follows: "Usefulness or fruitlessness can neither diminish nor augment this worth" (*Foundations* 10). Since moral freedom is limited to the self-determination of the will, it is unconcerned with the events in the external world. The freedom to determine the will is transcendental and therefore neither results from any external liberation nor is hampered by external restrictions. The moral law insures liberation of the will from empirical determinations. However, this liberation of the will can coexist with any kind of external unfreedom.[11] Since moral freedom is defined by the internal determination of the will, it is indifferent to restrictions placed on freedom in the external, phenomenal world. Consequently, the external realm retains the necessity with which Kant characterized it in the first *Critique*, and the apparently objective laws of bourgeois society remain impervious to moral consciousness. Although moral philosophy for Kant is the realm of practical action (Handlung), action is limited to the individual's adopting a standpoint from which to judge his own behavior.[12] The man debating his doubtful prospects for acquiring a loan must either judge himself as moral, and not seek the loan, or he must judge himself as immoral if he seeks it, knowing he will be unable to repay the money in the stated time. However, he does not call into question the circumstances that create his dilemma. His action is limited to contemplating the absoluteness of the moral law and the inevitability of the external constraints, and in adjusting himself to these necessities.

Kant's moral theory echoes the social phenomenon of objectification, in which relations between persons appear as exclusively mediated by the objective laws of exchange. The immediate social bonds between individuals disappear from view, in Kant's theory, as they become regulated exclusively by the objective law of morality. Moral relations between individuals are only a mediated result of the objective moral law. The primary object of moral action is respect for the law. In the *Foundations*, Kant writes, "The only object of respect is the law. . . . All respect for a person is only respect for the law (of righteousness, etc.,) of which the person provides an example" (*Foundations* 18 n.). Other persons become objects of moral interest only indirectly, insofar as they embody the moral law. The "direct" moral relation occurs beween the moral law and the individual will that it determines (*Foundations* 17 n.).

Thus, Kantian morality results in a rationalization and objectification of individuals. An individual is a moral "person" only insofar as he embodies the attributes of the objective moral law, which is rational and universally binding. Through the "direct determination of the will by the law," the moral agent becomes reduced to a subject in whom all other influences, including inclinations and feelings, have been eradicated. Moral relations between individuals, therefore, presuppose a mutual condition of alienation. Like the reified relations produced in the marketplace, the natural bonds of love, sympathy, and caring between individuals disintegrate as the basis for moral relations. Instead, these sensuous feelings are displaced by the rationalized relations deduced from the moral law.

Just as the rationalization of relations in the marketplace results in atomization, in which individuals appear to share only their formal identity as producers of commodities, so the atomization of the social subject is affirmed in the moral sphere. The moral subject is an "I" who is not part of the "we,"[13] a being who shares no common material interests with any other subjects, but only their formally identical nature as rational agents under moral laws. Kant's valorization of the Stoic ethic, which allows no feelings of sympathy to disrupt the mind's composure, makes normative the isolation experienced by the individual in bourgeois society.[14] Ultimately, Kant denies that the moral subject is a social subject related to others by passions and interests. Moreover, the absoluteness of the moral law, combined with Kant's endorsement of existing laws, leads to a confirmation of the basic values of this society. According to the categorical imperative, under no circumstances would a man be able to morally justify an act of theft, even if it was necessary to obtain medicine that would save a person's life. By stealing from the druggist, the man would be treating him merely as a means rather than as an end. But this formal respect for persons as "ends" accords, at the same time, with the valuation of property over life.[15]

The dilemmas of whether to steal medicine or deceitfully borrow money indicate that moral problems reflect the contradictions of a society which pits universal respect for personhood against the concrete needs of human life. In bourgeois society, the abstract respect for personhood can undermine the possibility of sustaining concrete moral relations, just as abstract freedom can coexist with conditions that undermine individuals' ability to exercise their freedom.

Thus, although Kant turns to morality in order to account for moral personality, freedom, and self-determination, his analysis of moral relations reflects the same conditions of objectification that mark his analysis of knowledge. Although he aims to radically separate the sphere of freedom from the sphere of necessity and the noumenal self from the phenomenal self, he fails to counter the reified relations of the phenomenal world.[16] Kant's analysis of the formal and universal conditions of morality, rather than providing the criterion by which reification can be criticized, endorses as normative these alienating relations.[17]

## 11

# THE AESTHETIC DIMENSION: TRANSCENDENCE OR REIFICATION?

Kant's treatment of aesthetic pleasure in our experience of art and of nature appears, at first, to provide an escape from objectification in the cognitive and moral spheres. Aesthetic judgment articulates feelings, which are excluded both from contributing to knowledge and from serving as a motive for moral behavior. Whereas the cognitive sphere is concerned with the objective concept of nature, and the moral sphere is concerned with the objective concept of freedom, the aesthetic sphere pertains to the relation of a representation *to the subject*. Kant writes, "That which in the representation of an Object is merely subjective, i.e., which indicates its reference to the subject, not to the object, is its aesthetical character . . ."[1] Through the aesthetic realm, therefore, Kant attempts to bring the subject back into the analysis of experience, to resituate nature in relation to subjective purposes that are omitted from the scientific analysis of nature, and to explore the playful possibilities of human apprehension in contrast to the law-bound work of cognition.

However, there is a tension within Kant's own attempts to understand feelings. On the one hand, aesthetic feelings promise a gratification excluded from cognition and morality; on the other hand, Kant's analysis of aesthetic pleasure is unable to transcend his own objectifying categories. The aesthetic satisfaction that Kant describes in the *Critique of Judgement* is a very attenuated form of gratification. He considers the feeling of pleasure to be the consciousness of purposiveness, through which we experience objects as if they were designed for our purposes. Since pleasure is the consciousness of the mere form of purposiveness, it is completely desensualized. Far from liberating the subject from the reified dimension of objectivity, Kant's conception of pleasure offers only an illusory form of gratification. This deceptive gratification itself serves the purposes of a world that, having segregated out pleasure from work, must provide a mechanism by which feelings can be rationalized and controlled.

In the preface to the *Critique of Judgement*, Kant announces his intentions as follows: "Whether now the Judgement . . . has also principles a priori for itself; whether these are constitutive or merely regulative (thus indicating no special realm); and whether they give a rule a priori to the feeling of pleasure and pain . . . these are the questions with which the present Critique of Judgement is concerned" (*CJ* 2–3). Kant is concerned to discover the constitutive, a priori principle of the feeling of pleasure and pain in our experience of beautiful objects in nature and in art. He discovers this "constitutive principle" (*CJ* intro., 9.41) of pleasure in the concept of purposiveness. The purposiveness of an object consists in our experiencing it as if it were created for our own purposes. This experience occurs when the representation of an object accords with the harmony of our cognitive faculties. Kant describes this harmony of the faculties in the following passage: "For that apprehension of forms in the Imagination can never take place without the reflective Judgement, though undesignedly, at least comparing them with its faculty of referring intuitions to concepts. If now in this comparison the Imagination . . . is placed by means of a given representation undesignedly in agreement with the Understanding . . . and thus a feeling of pleasure is aroused, the object must then be regarded as purposive for the reflective Judgement" (*CJ* 7.32). The pleasure in the experience of a beautiful object, therefore, is grounded in the harmonious interplay of the imagination and the understanding when they are freed from the normal rule-bound work of cognition. This state of mind provides the ground for the universality and necessity of judgments of taste.

Despite Kant's claim that pleasure is "immediately" connected with the representation in aesthetic judgment (*CJ* 7.31), his treatment of pleasure indicates a highly mediated form of feeling. Pleasure, which is constituted by the principle of purposiveness, is distanced from the subject's immediate apprehension of an object. Although Kant distinguishes feeling as subjective, in contrast to objective concepts, he seeks to show that the feeling of pleasure should be universally shared. Kant describes the dilemma presented by aesthetic feeling as follows: "The strange and irregular thing is that although it is not an empirical concept, but a feeling of pleasure (consequently not a concept at all), through the judgement of taste it is attributed to everyone, and should be connected with the representation of the object, just as if it were the same as knowledge of the object's predicate."[2] Kant's task is to investigate how the subjective feeling of pleasure can be attributed to everyone, in order to justify his contention that taste, like knowledge, is universally valid. He finds the "key" to this problem in the universal structure of feeling. He distinguishes the aesthetic feeling of pleasure from "mere pleasantness in the sensation" (*CJ* 9.63). The latter, which is dependent on the sensation of the object, has merely "private validity" (*CJ* 9.63). In contrast, aesthetic satisfaction can have universal validity because it is grounded in a state of mind which is universally communicable. Kant writes as follows: "Hence, it is the universal communicability of the state of mind in the given representation, which underlies the judgement of taste as its subjective condition, and has the pleasure in the object as its consequence" (*KU* 9.286). Kant refers to this state of mind as the "feeling of the free play of the powers of representation" (*KU* 9.286). In Kant's view, this feeling of free play between the faculties is "valid for everyone," " . . . just as if it were a definite cognition" (*CJ* 9.65). This subjective state of mind is the ground of the feeling of aesthetic pleasure. Of this subjective state, Kant says, "It precedes the pleasure in the object and underlies this pleasure, by the harmony of the faculties of knowledge" (*KU* 9.287).

Thus, Kant considers the feeling of pleasure to refer to the mental state of the subject. He writes, "The consciousness of the mere formal purposiveness in the play of the subject's cognitive powers, in a representation through which an object is given, is the pleasure itself" (*CJ* 12.71). By considering pleasure in the beautiful to be a pleasure of mere reflection (*CJ* 39.168), Kant desensualizes feeling. For example, he distinguishes aesthetic satisfaction from the pleasant, which he defines as "that which pleases the senses in sensation" (*CJ* 3.48). The pleasant is a response to the object through sensation. Since this sensual gratification arouses a desire for the object, it is not indifferent to the existence of an object (*CJ* 3.50). The subject's interest in the object makes it impossible to consider the state of pleasantness as a universally valid condition (*CJ* 8.60). Kant contrasts this interested state with disinterest, which he considers to be the "first moment" in the judgment of the beautiful. He writes, "Every one must admit that a judgement about beauty, in which the least interest mingles, is very partial and is not a pure judgement of taste. We must not be in the least prejudiced in favour of the existence of things, but be quite indifferent in this respect, in order to play the judge of things of taste" (*CJ* 2.47–48). Since sensual gratification brings with it an interest in the object, it can play no role in aesthetic judgment.

Although the senses are not completely excluded from aesthetic judgment, they are involved only in a highly mediated fashion. The imagination serves the purposes of "gathering together the manifold of intuition" (*CJ* 9.64). The relation between the faculty of imagination, which gathers together the sensuous manifold, and the understanding provides the ground for the judgment of taste. Thus, sensation serves as the *occasion* (Anlass) for the judgment of taste (*KU* 9.288).

But the *ground* of the judgment of taste does not lie in this material of sensation—rather, it lies in the formal purposiveness evident in the harmonious play of the cognitive faculties. The representation of an object gives rise to a feeling of satisfaction when the formal relation among sensations coheres with the order, uniformity, design, and purposiveness of the understanding.[3] Therefore, the judgment of the beautiful is pure because "no empirical satisfaction is mingled with its determining ground" (*CJ* 14.73). It is a judgment regarding strictly the form of the object, not the material of sensation. Kant writes, "A pure judgement of taste has for its determining ground . . . no sensation as the material of the aesthetical judgement" (*CJ* 14.76). Kant refers to taste as "barbaric" that still requires "charms and emotions" for satisfaction (*CJ* 13.72).

Thus, the senses do not themselves provide gratification but merely serve as the occasion for the mind to reflect on the form of purposiveness in the representation of the object. It is the free play of the cognitive faculties that produces the feeling of pleasure in the harmony of the faculties. Consequently, the aesthetic feeling is not an immediate response to the sensation of the object itself, but it expresses the relation between the form of the object and the activity of the mind's faculties.

Sensations, for example of tone or color, themselves can be considered beautiful only insofar as they themselves are "pure," that is, only concerning their form (*CJ* 14.74). The charms of sensation, which concern their matter, can never add to the beautiful or be the determining ground of the judgment of taste. They are at best indulged in as "aliens," which may enhance our interest in the beautiful object (*CJ* 14.75).

For example, a rose is beautiful because of its form, not because of the sweetness of its smell, the luster of its color, or the softness of its touch. All of these qualities belong merely to the empirical satisfaction in the object, which leads us to judge the rose as pleasant but not as the source of a pleasure that is universally valid. A painting of a rose, likewise, is considered beautiful because of its "delineation" (*CJ* 14.75). In other words, the judgment of taste requires a filtering out of all the matter of sensation in order to contemplate the pure form of the object. Although one may still find the matter of sensation pleasant, it does not contribute to the judgment of beauty, except insofar as it highlights the object's form. Thus, aesthetic pleasure, according to Kant, must distance itself from any enjoyment of the sensual qualities of the object and substitute the reflective pleasure in the contemplation of form.

By filtering out sensation and interest from the judgment of the beautiful, Kant establishes the formal conditions of aesthetic pleasure. However, the universality of these conditions presupposes the subject's severing of ties both to the object and to himself. In aesthetic satisfaction, the subject is not concerned with the sensuous qualities of the object but only with the reference of the representation of the object "to the subject, and its feeling of pleasure or pain" (*CJ* 1.45). Kant's stress on the disinterested nature of pleasure indicates that the circumstances determining an object's existence are irrelevant to the feeling of pleasure. For example, he remarks that a palace is judged as beautiful, regardless of the sweat of the people wasted in its construction (*CJ* 2.47). If its form arouses the feeling of pleasure through the harmony of the cognitive faculties, one judges it as beautiful. Kant defines the beautiful object as that "whose form (not the matter of its representation, as sensation) . . . is judged as the ground of a pleasure in the representation of such an object" (*CJ* 7.32). The object of aesthetic pleasure is detached not only from its sensuous content but also from any moral concerns.[4] In Kant's discussion of the "purposiveness without purpose" of the aesthetic object, he explicitly eliminates the purposes of moral determinations from the realm of aesthetic judgment (*CJ* 11.69).

Thus, the beautiful object is alienated from its sensuous qualities and from the value embedded in its existence in the same way that the object in the marketplace is deprived of its immediate, qualitative character. The formal conditions by which an object is judged to be beautiful establish a quantitative equivalence between such objects. Since the condition for the judgment of the beautiful is the same for all objects, every object is experienced as beautiful in the same way, independent of the individual features that distinguish one object from another. Moreover, Kant's notion of disinterest implies that everyone experiences the beauty of an object, like a palace, in an identical fashion, whether one is the owner of the palace or a member of the awed masses. All individuals can equally enjoy the beautiful, since the feeling of pleasure derives solely from the internal harmony of the cognitive faculties. These formally equal conditions for aesthetic enjoyment conceal what is in reality an unequal access to the object. The equality in the contemplation of the beautiful, in Kant's theory, provides a substitute satisfaction for the inequality in the actual sensuous enjoyment of the object.[5] By insisting that all individuals share the same aesthetic experience, the formal concept of beauty becomes a means of subordinating individuals to the dominant cultural values, irrespective of differences in class, race, or sex.[6] Kant's theory creates, in the aesthetic sphere, a realm of unanimity that is in direct opposition to the conflicts and inequalities of the material world.

Not only is the object of aesthetic pleasure abstracted from its immediate sensuous existence, but the subject who contemplates the object must likewise abstract from his sensuous enjoyment. Kant denies that "charm or emotion" can interfere with the "pure," nonempirical judgment of taste (*CJ* 13.73). The pleasure is merely the consciousness of the "formal purposiveness in the play of the subject's cognitive powers . . ." (*CJ* 12.71). Thus, pleasure is cut off from the sensuous object and resides entirely in the interplay of the cognitive faculties. The harmony of the faculties provides the formal, universally valid conditions of aesthetic pleasure. Kant's attempt to discover the common structure of pleasure extends the universality that prevailed in cognition and morality to feelings in the aesthetic domain. Aesthetic feelings themselves, therefore, become subject to an imperative. Kant writes, "The judgement of taste requires the agreement of every one; and he who describes anything as beautiful claims that every one *ought* to give his approval to the object in question . . ." (*CJ* 19.92). Since the judgment is the reference of the representation to the subject's feeling of pleasure (*CJ* 1.45), to demand agreement in the judgment of the beautiful imposes an obligation on the subject's own feelings.

By establishing the universal conditions of the feeling of pleasure, Kant objectifies that aspect of sensibility that he insistently describes as subjective. Kant repeatedly characterizes the feeling of pleasure as analogous with cognition. For example, he maintains that the aesthetic feeling is attributed to everyone, "just as if it were the same as knowledge of the object's predicate" (*KU* 7.260). He later remarks that we speak of the beautiful "as if beauty were a characteristic of the object and the judgement logical (constituting a cognition of the Object by means of concepts of it) . . ." (*CJ* 6.56). Feeling, in the *Critique of Judgement*, imitates the work of cognition. Although Kant has distinguished the "free play" of the cognitive faculties in aesthetic judgment from the rule-bound work of cognition, in this free play the imagination happens to find itself in conformity with the lawfulness of the understanding (*CJ* 22.96). The law-giving activity of understanding is not suspended in its interplay with imagination. Rather, the understanding need not behave coercively because the imagination is freely in accord with this lawfulness. When imagination and feeling themselves are bound by lawful conditions, reification has entered the last preserve of the subjectivity of the individual.

Thus, Kant's treatment of pleasure ultimately depicts both the subject and object of aesthetic judgment in a fetishistic manner. Since Kant considers aesthetic enjoyment to be universally applicable, all particular qualities in the subject's experience of the beautiful must be suppressed. The subject becomes reduced to a form of consciousness equivalent to every other, each experiencing the beautiful in the same way. Since individuals stand in an identical relation to the object of judgment, aesthetic experience becomes interchangeable. The beautiful object, defined solely on the basis of its formal purposiveness is likewise divested of any immediate sensuous qualities. Through this regulation of the feeling of pleasure, Kant imports into the aesthetic sphere the ascetic paradigm that dominates his theory of knowledge and morality. Pleasure in the judgment of a beautiful object is pure, not empirical; it resides in the formal interplay of the cognitive faculties; and its universal validity has the status of an a priori principle (*CJ* 37.165). Pleasure is allowed within Kant's system of experience only insofar as it is subject to these constraints. This formalization of aesthetic pleasure is analogous to the legislation of feeling that develops in the marketplace. As in his theory of objectivity, Kant's treatment of aesthetic judgment articulates and elaborates an inherent dynamic of social conditions. Sensuous feelings are excluded from production as subjective interferences with the rationalized system of labor. The unsatisfied needs for sensual gratification pose a threat to the system of labor that requires their renunciation. Therefore, the marketplace, which segregates out pleasure from labor, must also provide a mechanism for controlling these needs. Adorno and Horkheimer argue that the realm of enjoyment in bourgeois society itself becomes a domain for regulation and profit making. They describe the aesthetic enjoyment that is made available to individuals in capitalist society as follows: "Amusement under late capitalism is the prolongation of work. It is sought after as an escape from the mechanized work process, and to recruit strength in order to be able to cope with it again. But at the same time mechanization has such power over a man's leisure and happiness, and so profoundly determines the manufacture of amusement goods, that his experiences are inevitably after-images of the work process itself."[7]

Thus, the rationalization of pleasure in the marketplace is constructed on a fundamental deception: it appears as if the needs for pleasure are genuinely gratified, for example, through entertainment. But instead of serving as an escape from the world of industry, the images of entertainment themselves reflect the standardized operations of the work process. Rather than offering a genuine alternative to the reification of the social world, these images reinforce individuals' resignation to a world in which they are deprived of satisfaction in their work and in their leisure. The "culture industry" that exists in the contemporary world has exaggerated the earlier tendency in capitalism to translate art into the sphere of consumption, and it has executed this project with greater sophistication and finesse. The result is a wholly unified culture, in which art no longer evokes the discrepancy between an individual's goals and social norms. Adorno and Horkheimer describe the "culture industry" that impresses its stamp on everything, writing, "The culture industry [is] no more than the achievement of standardization and mass production, sacrificing whatever involved a distinction between the logic of the work and that of the social system."[8] In such a world, art becomes primarily mass art. The individual is reduced to accepting whatever is offered by the culture industry; one has a choice merely among commodities produced for mass consumption, all of which are created by business interests. Differences between objects of pleasure are reduced to the differences, for example, between one film star or another. As the objects of pleasure become commodified, we are served up identical images of how to gratify our dreams. With the loss of qualitative differences in the objects of art and entertainment, the subject suffers a consequent loss of imagination to this standardized world. Yet above all, what is reinforced through these cultural images is the lack of gratification, the inability to translate dreams into reality. Adorno and Horkheimer describe the deception perpetrated by the images in movies, television, and radio as follows: "The culture industry perpetually cheats its consumers of what it perpetually promises . . . the promise, which is actually all the spectacle consists of, is illusory: all it actually confirms is that the real point will never be reached, that the diner must be satisfied with the menu. In front of the appetite stimulated by all those brilliant names and images there is finally set no more than a commendation of the depressing everyday world it sought to escape."[9] The images in entertainment symbolize not an escape from the reified world but the permanent unattainability of that existence that would truly gratify us.

The core of Kantian aesthetics anticipates this deceptive turn in culture. Feelings behave as if they were knowledge; beauty appears as if it were a quality of the object; and nature and art appear as if they were created to harmonize with our own subjective purposiveness. The promise of pleasure in the beautiful can only be sustained by these illusions, for feeling is not knowledge, beauty is not a quality of the object, and nature is not created for our own purposes. In Kant's thought, pleasure is sought through a turning away from existence and through the illusion of purposiveness.[10] This conception of beauty reinforces an ascetic paradigm, not only in excluding sensuousness from the beautiful, but also in ultimately treating pleasure as based on mere illusion.

Kant's aesthetic theory is concerned not only with beauty in art, but also with the aesthetic dimension of nature, both as an object of beauty and as a source of artistic creation. Initially, Kant's discussion of the purposiveness of nature in the *Critique of Judgement* seems to contrast with his treatment of nature in the first *Critique*. In the aesthetic experience of nature, all of nature's empirical laws appear as if they cohered into a higher unity, which harmonizes with our cognitive faculties. Kant writes of the purposiveness of nature as follows: "Nature is represented by means of this concept, as if an Understanding contained the ground of the unity of the manifold of its empirical laws" (*CJ* 4.19). Thus, the harmony of human understanding with nature is possible through the idea of a transcendent understanding that unites both man and nature under its rules.[11] This unity contrasts with the dominance of human understanding in relation to nature, when nature is viewed from a scientific perspective. In Kant's view, the universal laws of nature have their ground in our understanding, "which prescribes them to nature . . . ." (*CJ* 46.188). In the context of knowledge, human understanding dictates to nature the rules of its appearance.

Although in aesthetic judgment the conception of purposiveness offers an alternative to this scientific view of nature, Kant stresses that the aesthetic dimension does not challenge the scientific one. Kant writes, "The purposiveness, therefore, which precedes the cognition of an object . . . is that subjective [element] which cannot be an ingredient in cognition" (*CJ* 7.31). Scientific knowledge continues unimpeded by this aesthetic dimension, which appears as an addendum or as a sphere of play for the faculties when they have finished the serious work of cognition. By limiting purposiveness to the aesthetic perspective, Kant affirms at the same time the law-giving capacity of the human understanding in the scientific domain, through which nature remains subordinate to human rules.

Kant's discussion of the role of nature in artistic "talent" likewise appears to challenge the relation of man to nature implicit in the scientific paradigm. Kant writes, "Since talent as the innate productive faculty of the artist, belongs itself to Nature, we may express the matter thus: Genius is the innate mental disposition through which Nature gives the rule to Art" (*CJ* 46.188). In Kant's conception of genius, the artistic man stands in an immediate relation to nature: nature within him gives the rule to his art. This immediacy contrasts with the capacity of the human understanding to give the rules to nature in cognition. It suggests a unity between external nature and nature within us. This unity between human beings and the natural world provides the basis for art to reflect in an intentional form the purposiveness in nature.

Kant's claim that nature gives the rule to art suggests an openness of the human to the natural world. Human consciousness, in the form of genius, appears as an articulation of nature rather than as a dictatorial consciousness. The task of artistic production is to make in rational form the purposiveness found in natural beauty.

Kant writes of art, "The purposiveness in its form must seem to be as free from all constraint of arbitrary rules as if it were a product of mere nature" (*CJ* 45.187). Kant's discussion of genius suggests that nature provides not just the material to be formed by the productive consciousness, as occurs through scientific knowledge, but that it also provides the form, the purposiveness, to the human mind. But at the same time, this openness to nature occurs only insofar as nature is viewed as art. The natural world in which genius finds an affinity does not include nature as it is construed by cognition but refers solely to nature viewed as an aesthetic object.

Ultimately, Kant's conception of nature as giving the rule to art relies on a romantic depiction of nature that itself serves the purposes of a fetishistic world. The aesthetic perspective presents the picture of a harmonious existence with an uncorrupted nature as a healthy contrast to the mechanical system of production.[12] This romantic view suggests that a harmonious relation with nature can coexist with the alienated conditions of production, as if nature within us and nature without remain untouched by the conditions of social existence. This view of nature completely bypasses the social mediations, by means of which nature informs our sensibility and is itself transformed. Marx criticizes such a view of nature, in his comments on Feuerbach in *The German Ideology*, as follows:

> [Feuerbach] does not see how the sensuous world around him is not a thing given direct from all eternity, remaining ever the same, but the product of industry and of the state of society. . . . Even the objects of simplest "sensuous certainty" are only given to him through social development, industry and the commercial intercourse. The cherry-tree, like almost all fruit trees, was, as is well-known, only a few centuries ago transplanted by *commerce* into our zone, and therefore only by this action of a definite society in a definite age it has become "sensuous certainty" for Feuerbach.[13]

Kant, like Feuerbach, views nature in the aesthetic sphere as devoid of human impact. Nature is no more seen as re-created by human activity than the world of production is seen as created by human labor. Thus, cloaked under the garb of beauty, Kant's aesthetic treatment of nature reflects the loss of subjectivity experienced by the individual in the systems of labor and cognition.

Kant's theory of aesthetic pleasure expresses in germinal form the manner in which pleasure comes to be treated in bourgeois society. Aesthetic pleasure is sought in our society not just from the beautiful objects in nature and in art, but from commodities in general. Through the commodity form, the consumer has an aesthetic relation, in Kant's sense, to the object. The acquisition of the object in the marketplace, like the appreciation of the aesthetic object in Kant's system, is detached from any concern with the existence or morality of the process of production. The object, qua commodity, is defined by its formal properties through which it becomes equivalent to other commodities in the system of exchange. The object is abstracted from its sensuous qualities and from the specific uses that it serves. The pleasure that is sought in the commodity, therefore, lies not in its concrete existence, but in these formal, universally shared features. The consumer's attitude toward the existence of the particular object is one of indifference, like the disinterest of the aesthetic observer in the beautiful object. For example, although an article of clothing may genuinely serve useful functions of protection and warmth, the pleasure that is promised by the commodity lies not in the prospect of its warmth but in the promise that the commodity is the source of universal pleasure. Since all individuals are bound to find pleasure in this article, its acquisition holds the promise of universal acclaim.[14]

Therefore, pleasure is derived from the commodity character of the object, not from its immediate sensuous existence. Consequently, the possession of the concrete object can never provide gratification. The sweater in the store, qua commodity, may hold the promise of universal and necessary feelings of pleasure in all its beholders. Once it is acquired, however, it confronts the possessor merely as the particular, empirical object that it is. Since its sensuous nature was not what was sought in the commodity, the acquisition of the object can never fulfill its promise of pleasure. The sensuous gratification, which is genuinely possible in the possession of the object, is sacrificed in the quest for the object of universal pleasure. This frustration in the process of consumption is in fact required by the imperative of the market for ceaseless acquisition. Only if gratification constantly eludes us will we seek to acquire the endless stream of new commodities that are generated by the system of production.

In seeking pleasure in the commodity, we detach it from the context of its production. We are not concerned with how or why it is produced, but merely with its reference to ourselves and our own pleasure in it. The commodity's abstraction from its origin corresponds to the purposiveness without purpose of Kant's aesthetic object. According to Kant, pleasure in the object has nothing to do with the concept of the "internal or external possibility of the object by means of this or that cause" (*CJ* 11.69), but only with its reference to the feeling in the subject. The feeling of pleasure is not concerned with how the object is made, but treats the object as if it were free of all subjective and objective determinants, as if it were created solely for our pleasure. Similarly, a commodity like the sweater in the store is represented to us merely as the source of pleasure, irrespective of the money-making imperative of the industry that produces it. Thus, our aesthetic relation to the commodity, which treats the object as free of objective and subjective determinants, conceals the real forces that are operative in the marketplace.

Although we experience the aesthetic object as created exclusively for our pleasure, this experience coexists with the assumption of a transcendent, benevolent rationale that makes possible this harmony between the object and ourselves. Kant articulates this view in describing the concept of purposiveness as assuming that a will (not our own) would order the object according to a certain rule (*CJ* 10.68). In the world of commodities, although the object does not appear as the product of human purposes, it does appear that some formal purposiveness lies behind its promise of pleasure. This assumption of an indeterminate will or purposiveness is itself part of the ideology of the marketplace. Objects seem to fulfill a purpose provided by an independent rationale, which transcends the limits of human comprehension. This assumption of an indeterminate will leaves us open to manipulation by the "rationale" of the marketplace while hiding the role of human activity in these apparently nonhuman purposes.

Thus, the reification in the marketplace is reflected in the structure of the pleasure that it promises. Just as the object, qua commodity, is abstracted from its immediate sensuous character, and the subject, qua laborer, becomes a formally identical consciousness, alienated from his or her particular human qualities, so the commodity entices the consumer not by its sensuous existence, but only by the empty promise that the object exists for his or her pleasure. Since this construction of pleasure does not bring the subject sensuous gratification, the commodity appears to us as that which constantly titillates but never satisfies. The structure of pleasure in this reified world is one of frustration. The consequences of this aesthetic treatment of the object are recognized and validated by Kant. He emphasizes the "as if" quality of the concept of purposiveness: as if the object were created for our purposes. In actuality, this concept of aesthetic purposiveness is revealed in its true nature, as mere illusion.

Since commodities, including objects of art and nature that themselves become commodified, are unable to gratify our sensual feelings, the consumers experience a frustration comparable to that of the ascetic life. Ironically, commodity fetishism itself appears as a form of asceticism. The injurious results of such frustration have been noted by Freud, who wrote of sexual abstinence: "On the whole I have not gained the impression that sexual abstinence helps to shape energetic, self-reliant men of action, nor original thinkers, bold pioneers and reformers; for more often it produces 'good' weaklings who later become lost in the crowd that tends to follow painfully the initiative of strong characters."[15] Just as Freud suggests that sexual abstinence creates a submissive personality, so some thinkers suggest that the frustration and control of sensual satisfaction in our society promote individuals' submission to the status quo.[16] The reification of pleasure in the marketplace, which holds the promise of gratification, discourages us from seeking gratification outside the boundaries of the commodified world and thereby serves to maintain our subordination to the dominant rationale of this world.

**III**

CONCLUSION

## 12

# REIFICATION AND ASCETICISM

In exploring the significance of the prevailing interpretation of objectivity in Western philosophy, two central themes have
emerged: asceticism and fetishism. The inquiry into the exclusion
of eros from cognition has led back to philosophy's roots in ascetic
Greek religion. Here, the philosophical commitment to purity was
shown to reflect the ascetic denial of sexuality and the concomitant
exclusion of women from ascetic practices through which initiates
sought to escape the threat of death immanent in the life cycle itself. This genealogical investigation examined philosophical ideas
in the context of specific historical practices rather than in isolation
from the concerns of empirical existence. Through such an approach, philosophical claims to universal, necessary, and eternal
truths may be revealed instead as articulating the experience of a
particular group in a given historical epoch. By masking themselves as the source of universal truths, demands for purity have

concealed the particular social practices that they legitimate. To
the extent that the value of purity, which originally expressed ascetic beliefs, has been taken as a natural component of the philosophical enterprise, the philosophical demand for purity itself assumes an ideological function.

But what relevance does this quest for origins have for the modern philosophical tradition? If one discloses the meaning of purity
as it first appears in philosophical thought, can one conclude that
these parameters remain operative in the modern world? Is the concern for purity in Kant's concept of objectivity, for example, reflective of this original ascetic flight from death?

In Kantian philosophy, the demand for purity occurs in relation
to social practices that differ in fundamental respects from those of
early Greece. "Pure" reason reflects and idealizes the objectification that occurs in bourgeois society. Kant's systematic purification
divests both the subject and object of all immediate, sensuous,
qualitative features. It establishes the philosophical basis by
which persons and things mesh neatly with the rationalized system
of exchange. This historical transformation of philosophical concepts, which is manifest in Kant's concern with purity, is described
by Marcuse as follows: "It is not so much their content as it is their
position and function within philosophical systems which changes.
Once this is seen, it becomes clear that these very concepts provide a clearer indication of the historical transformation of philosophy than those whose contents are far closer to facticity."[1] This
study has attempted to uncover the historical significance of the
concept of purity in the Western philosophical tradition. In Platonic philosophy, purification seeks to establish a harmony between the individual soul and the cosmos through transcendence of
the phenomenal world. Purity characterizes the true forms of Being, which the philosophical soul strives to know. In Kantian philosophy, on the other hand, the forms of human intuition and
understanding become the incarnation of purity. Despite their origins in the human mind, these forms appear to man as objective
and independent of his existence. This dual nature of the pure
forms of thought reflects the duplicitous character of the commodity
structure, in which what is created by human labor appears as
existing prior to and independent of human activity. Purity in this

modern context no longer establishes a harmony between the soul and the forms of Being but signifies man's split from the world as it is given. A correlation between the subjective mind and objective forms is established not through the education of the soul toward harmony with the given forms of the world, but through the creation and control of these objective forms by man.

Thus, modern philosophy has become the purveyor of religious notions of purification; but the function of the religious notion of purity has thereby been transformed. Both Weber and Marx argue that Protestant practices bolstered commodity relations in bourgeois society. For example, in *The Protestant Ethic and the Spirit of Capitalism*, Weber proposes that ascetic Protestantism contributed to the intensification of work and the accumulation of resources necessary for the development of a capitalist economy. Marx also indicates a correspondence between religious and economic forms. He writes, "The religious world is but the reflex of the real world. And for a society based upon the production of commodities, Christianity with its *cultus* of abstract man, more especially in its bourgeois developments, Protestantism, Deism, etc., is the most fitting form of religion."[2] Whether religious practices serve as the precondition for economic relations or themselves reflect the abstract system of labor, religious and economic practices are interdependent components of the bourgeois world.

The demand for purification imposed by commodity relations also requires a form of sexual abstinence or control, like that demanded by the original ascetic impulse. All sensual elements of life become subjected to the rationalized system of production and exchange. But sensuality appears as dangerous not merely because, as in early Greek religion, it contained the threat of death immanent in the natural life cycle. Sensuality also poses a threat to the structures of capitalist society themselves. The system of commodity relations requires this rationalized, desensualized mode of existence in order to hold at bay its own demise.

This confluence between asceticism and commodity fetishism suggests that commodity fetishism itself is a modern form of asceticism. The original ascetic impulse contains the seeds of this contemporary mode of objectification. The quest for an eternal, unchanging system has led not to the salvation of the individual from a corrupted existence but has contributed instead to the rule of alienating forms of material life. Moreover, the historical link between asceticism and fetishism suggests that commodity fetishism preserves the repressed form of sexuality and the consequent hierarchical relations between the sexes that are requisite for the original ascetic project.[3]

The phenomenon of fetishism illuminates the dynamic implicit in earlier forms of asceticism just as, in Marx's view, bourgeois society provides insights into earlier social forms. In the 1857 introduction to the *Grundrisse*, Marx writes,

> Bourgeois society is the most developed and the most complex historic organization of production. The categories which express its relations, the comprehension of its structure, thereby also allow insights into the structure and the relations of production of all the vanished social formations out of whose ruins and elements it built itself up, whose partly still unconquered remnants are carried along within it, whose mere nuances have developed explicit significance within it, etc. Human anatomy contains a key to the anatomy of the ape. . . . The bourgeois economy thus supplies the key to the ancient, etc.[4]

In Marx's view, out of the full-blown development of modern social forms one can glean clues for understanding the dynamics of their historical antecedents. However, one cannot *identify* modern forms with earlier ones. Marx writes, "Although it is true, therefore, that the categories of bourgeois economics possess a truth for all other forms of society, this is to be taken only with a grain of salt. They can contain them in a developed, or stunted, or caricatured form, etc. but always with an essential difference."[5] The intricate relations between past and present forms cannot be deduced abstractly from the logical unfolding of the concept, as Hegel attempts, but only through an examination of the particular forms of social life.

Following Marx in this interpretation of historical change, one can view fetishistic consciousness as retaining the ascetic denial of sensuality in a mutated way. The practice of asceticism has been shown historically to contain a dialectic, which precipitates it into consequences opposite to those it seeks. Although it intends a flight from the world of materiality, from the prison of existence, in fact it creates the prison house from which the soul must flee. The body is not first of all given as a prison but only appears as such once it is divested of all value, of all significance in the world of human relations, of all possibility of serving as the bearer of human consciousness. Philosophers have imprisoned themselves in an existence that is suited to the reified relations of commodity exchange, in which the material world becomes devoid of personal meaning and value.

In the ascetic imperative manifest in fetishistic relations, a transformation of this original ascetic project appears. The early ascetics strove, by distancing themselves from sensuous existence, to escape the threat of death and thereby to achieve a form of immortality. The suppression of sensuous existence in the commodity system also provides a kind of immortality: the form of the commodity is universal and unchanging. But in reality one experiences not the immortality of existence but the obsolescence of the product and of the laborer. And whereas the original goal of the ascetic project was to achieve wisdom, the truth that is possible in a reified world is only a technical knowledge of the particular parts of the system, with no understanding of the whole.

Objectivity, as it is formulated in Kantian philosophy, not only reflects the reified existence in bourgeois society, but the Kantian objectification of both subjects and objects is also a manifestation of the ascetic denial of sensuality. But Kant's exclusion of feeling and sensuality from cognition, morality, and aesthetic enjoyment does not indicate that these facets of existence are in fact irrelevant to the Kantian project. Rather, the intensity with which pure rationality is pursued suggests an *interest* in denying the erotic component in knowledge, morality, and art.[6]

If the ascetic ideal consciousness were identical with real consciousness, then eros would be irrelevant to philosophical knowledge. Plato expresses the ascetic ideal in his vision of a soul purified of the phenomenal world, which achieves an identification with the pure forms of Being. In Kant, the ascetic ideal is sought through the faculty of pure reason, which is devoid of any interest save the pure interest in knowledge. Even the sensible components of knowledge are emptied of affective or sensual content. But the notion that the ascetic ideal consciousness can be incarnated is itself paradoxical. The contradiction between the purity sought by asceticism and the impurity of the phenomenal world is expressed through the constant philosophical tension between essence and existence. If ascetic consciousness seeks to reject the body, how can it exist in a body? Plato acknowledges this problem when he indicates that although the pure forms disclose the essence of being, this essence is graspable only after death, after the end of phenomenal existence. Therefore, the desire to attain an immortal truth that is not possible in temporal existence leads the Platonic philosopher to a love of death. The problem of the incarnation of pure consciousness is also evident in Kantian philosophy, in which pure forms of thought are constitutive of the phenomenal world only at the price of excluding noumenal reality from knowledge. Both solutions indicate that the ascetic ideal can only be realized by denying the "reality" of phenomenal existence.

In other words, asceticism is not descriptive of the absence of sensuousness in phenomenal reality; rather it is an ideal, a prescription for how one ought to behave. Thus, the imperative to deny erotic feelings does not imply that these feelings are truly absent but that they must be diverted or suppressed, so as not to appear in legitimate philosophical discourse. In Nietzsche's view, in seeking truth behind the world of appearance, ascetic philosophers have not only violated truth, but they have also violated their own sensibilities. But the ascetic philosopher or scientist has not divested himself of sensuality, as his emphasis on pure truth proclaims. Instead, he has displaced his sensual interests onto the hidden forms that he constructs. Thus, the philosophical view of pure and unchanging truth contains an erotic intent, which is hypocritically denied.[7] Within this purified realm of reflection, therefore, there remain the residual effects of suppression.

Since despite all philosophical attempts to the contrary, consciousness is incarnate, one must consider how erotic desire is formed in an objectified world. Of particular interest is the question whether the displacement of subjective capacities onto objects, as occurs in commodity fetishism, also represents a displacement of erotic interest from subjects to objects. This line of inquiry suggests that the powerful hold of commodity fetishism on consciousness, in which the subject experiences a loss of power to the commodities, is rooted in a reorientation of individuals' erotic desire exclusively toward objects.

Asceticism creates a tension within the subject, who is faced with the imperative to deny the demands of embodied existence. Ascetic objectivity both expresses this conflict and provides a means of resolving it. Since erotic feelings toward another person are explicitly prohibited, a substitute gratification is sought through the object. Freud's analysis of sexual fetishism offers an illuminating account of how an object can be substituted for a beloved person in the quest for sensual gratification.

Freud defines fetishism as a case in which "for the normal sexual object another is substituted which is related to it but which is totally unfit for the normal sexual aim."[8] In this aberrant development, sexual interest is directed toward an object, for example a body part, which is originally (or symbolically) associated with the person whom one loves. This object becomes endowed with certain magical qualities. In Freud's view, fetishistic feeling commonly plays a role in normal love relations. For example, the handkerchief of a loved one may seem to bear certain special powers that make it unique. However, an abnormal interest in the object occurs when the fetishized object becomes disengaged from the person and serves as a substitute for normal sexual aims.[9] The fetish itself becomes the sexual object. In sexual fetishism, one's interest in the object is fixed and rigid; no other object is as attractive, including the person with whom the fetish was originally associated.

Kant's account of the relation between the subject and object of knowledge displays a fetishistic interest in the object. Philosophical interest is not primarily focused on persons but on objects, which are detached from any relations with persons. Although this interest in detached objects has been assumed to be a natural component of the philosophical enterprise, one can view this notion of objectivity as a displacement of interest from persons to things. The object, through its disengagement from persons, seems to acquire magical properties. It becomes the sole locus of interest, permitting no deviations and variations. Kant defines the object of knowledge in terms that are universal and necessary, fixing in advance the only acceptable approach to the world of objects. Moreover, this unswerving focus on objectivity makes it impossible to adequately account for human relations. Kant's analysis of morality excludes all features of sensibility that constitute the relations between empirical individuals. This interest in the formal object does not coexist with an interest in persons in any but the most abstract sense. Instead, the structure of objectivity precludes a regard for the emotional and sensual components of human relationships. Persons are relevant to the philosophical enterprise only insofar as they themselves conform to the conditions of objectivity, either as phenomenal objects or as moral agents who typify the objective moral law.

According to Freud, this shift of interest from the subject to the object is a pathological one that occurs as a defensive reaction to the fear of loss. In his view, the fetishist fears the loss of the penis; the fetish provides a substitute that will preserve this threatened power in altered form. In his essay entitled "Fetishism," Freud depicts the boy's reaction to the sight of his mother's genitals. The child is forced to recognize the mother's lack, her castration, which holds an impending threat to his own precious organ. In one sense, the fetish is a refusal of reality. By providing the woman with a substitute that will preserve her organ intact, the boy not only denies the woman's loss, but denies the threat posed to his own organ. At the same time, however, the fetish serves as a constant reminder of this threat. The original perception is repressed, but not thereby lost. Instead, the energy necessary to maintain this denial of reality poses a constant demand on the subject. The fetish preserves both moments of this contradiction between reality and wish; it thereby mediates between the impending loss of power and its preservation in this symbolic form.

Of primary interest in Freud's analysis of fetishism is the individual's response to a threatened loss of power. Faced with a threat to one's potency or control, a substitute is created that preserves both moments of the threat. The substitute object serves both as a constant reminder of the danger and as a means of safeguarding against it. Similarly, the Kantian interest in objectivity can be viewed as a response to a threatened loss of power by the subject. Affective responses toward persons, as Kant stresses in his defense of the Stoic principle of apathy, jeopardizes the sovereignty of reason. Since one's feelings for others display one's own vulnerability and lack of control (Kant writes in the *Anthropology* that emotion makes us "blind"), they must be avoided at all cost. The obsessive concern with objectivity is a means of defending against this reminder of our own vulnerability, and it provides an alternative focus of interest. Kant's system of objective knowledge mediates the contradiction between a wished-for inviolability and the reality of human frailty and lack of omnipotence. Objectivity provides the structure through which the subject can maintain control by producing the constitutive conditions of knowledge. Yet at the same time, Kant's distinction between the phenomenal and noumenal serves as a reminder that this system is not, ultimately, what is real.

Two questions emerge from this reading of Kant. The first concerns the erotic significance of objectivity. Although there is a shift of philosophical interest from persons to objects, does this shift prove erotic intent? And if objectivity has an erotic import, does philosophical interest become reduced to sexual motivations? The second question concerns the social identity of the Kantian knower. Does the interest in objectivity express a defense that any subject would make against a threat to one's power? Or does this response articulate as universal and necessary a response that derives particularly from the masculine ascetic tradition?

Kant's emphasis on the subjective constitution of objects of experience provides a clue for interpreting the erotic meaning of objectivity. The subject in Kant's philosophy experiences objects through a process of purifying, distancing, and desensualizing. Since the object is itself a product of these ascetic operations, it becomes invested for the subject with the consequences of this erotic denial. Moreover, since ascetic norms can never be fully realized in phenomenal existence, they do not so much eliminate sensuality as create a repressed or distorted expression of erotic interest. Therefore the interest in the formal features of objects, manifested in Kant's discussion of objectivity, may itself be interpreted as a displacement of this forbidden erotic intent. Instead of seeking out the sensual qualities of persons and things, the objective knower substitutes an interest in detached, formalized objects that pose no threat to the demand for self-control. The object of knowledge itself becomes a sexual fetish by providing a substitute for interests that cannot be gratified in the realm of human relations.

Interpreting objectivity in the context of erotic interest is compatible with Merleau-Ponty's view of the subject as an embodied consciousness. Experience does not happen to an "inner state" of consciousness [10] that inhabits the body as a stranger and adds sexual interest to objects only on appropriate occasions. Instead, objects appear to us through erotic perceptions. Both sexual feelings and cognitive attitudes are part of the total structure of one's existence.

However, Merleau-Ponty's treatment of sexuality as a fundamental horizon of existence does not reduce consciousness to sexuality, as if the latter were a natural, given substratum of human nature. Instead, Merleau-Ponty stresses the intentional nature of sexuality. He describes the interdependency of sexuality and consciousness as follows: "Thus sexuality is not an autonomous cycle. It has internal links with the whole active and cognitive being. . . . Here we concur with the most lasting discoveries of psychoanalysis . . . [which led] to a discovery in sexuality of relations and attitudes which had previously been held to reside *in consciousness*. Thus the significance of psychoanalysis is less to make psychology biological than to discover a dialectical process in functions thought of as 'purely bodily,' and to reintegrate sexuality into the human being." [11] In other words, one's experience as a sexual being, one's sexual interests and pathologies, embody the desires and fears that shape the life of the individual. If one seeks to distance oneself from other persons, this detachment will shape one's sensuous perception. Such an individual encounters the world only as a spectator who views but does not touch or feel. This emphasis on vision expresses the erotic interest of the voyeur, whose gratification is derived solely from looking at the object of desire. This attitude also establishes a distance between the subject and his own body. Kant typifies this attitude of the spectator, who views his body as an object to which he has no primordial connection. Kant is justly infamous for his description of marriage, which treats the sexual organs as objects of exchange. In the *Metaphysics of Morals*, he writes, "Sexual community is the reciprocal use made by one human being of the sexual organs and faculties of another . . . marriage . . . [is] the union of two people of different sexes for the lifelong mutual possession of each other's sexual qualities." [12] In

Kant's view, sexuality is located exclusively in the genitals, which become as much an object to the subject as to the partner with whom one exchanges the rights of possession.

This treatment of the body as a detached object is suited both to a social practice built on exchange relations and to a scientific practice in which the body becomes an object of investigation and control. For example, in the third essay of *The Conflict of the Faculties*, Kant discusses in detail how to breathe through the nose rather than the mouth and how to swallow so as to preserve saliva. In Kant's view, one walks for the sake of proper digestion; one's every breath is taken with an eye to the consequences for one's head and throat.[13] These stratagems serve the health and longevity of the body with which, as Foucault notes, the eighteenth-century bourgeoisie were inordinately concerned.[14] This attitude is built on such a self-detachment that Kant, for example, was able to lose sight in one eye for three years without noticing it.[15] The ascetic detachment from the body contributed not to a disinterest in bodily matters but to a practice in which bodies became reduced to scientific objects.[16]

Thus, not only does the philosophical interest in objectivity reflect the reified relations of the marketplace, but this fetishism of objectivity must also be understood in the context of the shaping and deformation of erotic existence. In other words, these objectifying social relations themselves generate an alienating form of sexuality. Commodity fetishism can be viewed as a form of displaced eroticism.

The production and exchange of commodities is built on a process of desensualization in which persons and things in their multidimensionality become reduced to a minimal existence as objects. But this ascetic operation does not eliminate sensuality as a theme of existence. Just as the paradigm of objectivity involves a displacement of erotic interest from persons to things, so a similar displacement occurs in a world dominated by commodities. The over-valuation of commodities that characterizes bourgeois society occurs not merely in response to the propaganda of advertising. The social conditions of commodity fetishism generate a dynamic within individuals through which, in response to their deprivation, a substitute gratification is sought. Like the sexual fetishist in Freud's account, the producer of goods within a capitalist system experiences a threatened loss of power. Laborers are no longer the masters of their own activity, and their products no longer exist for their own use and discretion. Instead, the length of time required for productive activity and the type of the work performed is determined by the rise and fall of prices in the marketplace. But work is a form of sensuous human activity, as Marx notes in the *Theses on Feuerbach.* Consequently, when both the body and mind are made into instruments of labor,[17] the alienation experienced by workers in the domain of economic production has repercussions for their sensuous, erotic existence. A threat to one's power in the social world poses a threat to one's sexual being. Both Marcuse and Reich argue that alienated work requires an alienated, repressed sexuality. In *Eros and Civilization,* Marcuse claims that an organization of sexuality, delimiting it in terms of time (relegated to leisure) and space (oriented solely toward genital satisfaction), is necessary for the body to become an instrument in capitalist production. In his view, desexualization of the body is not necessary for the work of culture per se, as Freud believes. Rather, work becomes opposed to individual gratification only when its primary function is to maintain the domination of one social group over the whole of society. Reich also looks to sexuality in an attempt to broaden our understanding of the material conditions that are necessary for productive activity. He argues that a repressive sexuality, in which one is deprived of sexual gratification, produces an attitude of submission toward authority. Hence, sexual repression generates the psychological conditions for accepting a set of beliefs and practices that run counter to one's own interests.

Marcuse and Reich are two of the Marxist theoreticians who have begun to integrate sexuality into an analysis of bourgeois social relations. They point out that the suppression of sensuality in commodity production not only deprives workers of an ability to achieve sensual gratification through the objects they create, but that it also constricts their sensual feelings toward others in general. For example, in *Group Psychology and the Analysis of the Ego,* Freud discusses the potential erotic bond that can develop between workers. He writes as follows: "The libido props itself upon the satisfaction of the great vital needs, and chooses as its first objects the people who have a share in that process."[18] When erotic feelings toward others are restricted by the imperative to conform to uniform, interchangeable patterns of behavior, the repressed feelings take on a distorted form. As Freud writes in his essay, "Repression," affect that is repressed "proliferates in the dark, as it were, and takes on extreme forms of expression."[19] The repression of erotic bonds in productive activity leads one to turn to the commodity as a substitute. Since the process of making objects cannot gratify us, we seek gratification instead in objects that we buy. Commodities, therefore, become the recipients of these displaced erotic needs. By providing a substitute gratification, the commodity serves as a defense against the loss of satisfaction; yet, as a substitute, it is a constant reminder of this loss. The commodity itself becomes a sexual fetish, a rigid object that is detached from its original association with persons and that promises gratification only at the price of turning away from the world of human relations.

This turn to commodities for substitute gratification has consequences for the erotic component of relations between persons in general. In bourgeois society, the objectification of persons in the marketplace becomes paradigmatic for the structure of human relations in general. Therefore, the erotic relations between individuals, like social relations more generally, become mediated by these objects of exchange. Commodities become the vehicle for expressing sexual potency. For example, a large American car can become a symbol of sexual prowess. Even intimate bonds between individuals bear the stamp of this objectifying mechanism. True love is displayed through a diamond ring or a fur coat. The power of these objects lies not in their utilitarian purposes but in the way they serve as vehicles for expressing erotic interest. Not only is the object, qua commodity, detached from the particular features of a human relationship, but the erotic interest that is invested in this symbol is also abstracted from the immediate relation with another.

Advertising takes advantage of the role of commodities in mediating sexual relations. A beautiful woman draped over a car suggests the erotic properties inherent in the car: by buying the car, a man can vicariously draw to himself the sexual interest that the commodity carries. Sex sells cars and liquor not merely because advertising techniques add a sexual interest to commodities. Rather, advertising manipulates the erotic interest that is displaced onto the commodity through the dialectic of fetishism. The sensual interests that are denied in our immediate relations to persons and things find a substitute in the fixed form of the commodity. But, like the promise of satisfaction in Kant's aesthetic object, this gratification permanently eludes us. The car cannot provide, in any lasting sense, the sensual gratification with which the elusive images of advertising perpetually tantalize us.

Thus, the historical lineage that connects asceticism and fetishism shows these two phenomena to be mutually illuminating. Implicit in the ascetic denial of materiality and sexuality is a dialectic through which the material world becomes objectified, as it is reduced to the formal features by which it rigidly rules the world of human affairs. As Weber points out, the ascetic intention to divest oneself of material goods ultimately results in the domination by material goods over human life in the form of commodity production.

Viewing commodity fetishism as a form of asceticism, furthermore, points to the erotic component of commodity relations. Not only do commodities become invested with the erotic properties that are detached from our immediate activity, but human relations themselves bear the stamp of this distorted erotic interest. Erotic relations between persons become mediated by commodities. Moreover, one's own sexual being becomes subject to the reifying dynamic of the marketplace. Not only do we seek to possess others as sexual objects, as Kant's discussion of marriage makes clear, but our own bodies also become objects for us to be standardized and exchanged in the sexual marketplace.

Therefore, Kant's philosophical theory, which stands at the juncture of the practices of asceticism and fetishism, must be construed in a context broader than its claims about knowledge. It refers to a social system in which a lack of sensual gratification in our immediate relations with persons and things propels us toward an obsessive interest in an objectified form of material and erotic existence.

The attempt to formulate any remarks that may stand in for a conclusion may well be more intimidating than the project of writing this study in the first place. In the effort to establish a connection of significance in the preceding chapters, the whole imperative of the philosophical tradition comes down as a counterweight. In the particular portions of this study—for example, in the reading of a Platonic dialogue, in the interpretation of Kant's moral theory—the specific tools of philosophical analysis come into play: textual exegesis, clarification of ambiguities, elaboration of contradictions internal to the philosophical theory. But in stepping back and attempting to formulate the general concerns of this study, it is difficult to escape the sense that this project itself is a violation of traditional philosophical concerns, that it trespasses the boundaries of what has been established as legitimate philosophical discourse. This sense of violation and illegitimacy addresses precisely the philosophical issues that lie at the heart of this project.

Philosophy's own self-understanding, as it has been articulated in major strains of the philosophical tradition, assumes that the task of acquiring knowledge is indifferent to history. Truth, according to the dominant view, itself has no history. This idea enables philosophers like Kant to write, "Before the critical philosophy arose there was no philosophy at all" (intro., *MM* 5). Kant's approach to philosophical knowledge presumes that the work of philosophy takes place in an arena that is independent of both the history of philosophical notions and the material conditions of life. Only by self-consciously distancing itself from both the history of its ideas and the concerns of phenomenal life can philosophy claim to achieve knowledge that is pure and everlasting.

The goal of this project has been to examine critically this claim that philosophical reflection can be purified both of its own history—the history of human beings' self-interpretation—and of the conditions of existence in which this interpretation takes place. The question arises whether this commitment to pure truth genuinely provides us with the essential conditions of knowledge. Rather than accepting these philosophical claims about knowledge, the task here has been to consider why this impulse toward purity has maintained such a powerful hold on the philosophical imagination, and to consider whether factors other than a purely rational commitment to truth have motivated this conception of knowledge. By pursuing a genealogical approach—thereby violating the very boundaries of "legitimate" philosophical discourse—it is possible to examine the origin of the impulse to purity and the transmutations that it has undergone. This attempt to recover philosophy's own origins and history makes visible the interests that have defined the parameters of philosophical inquiry. By appearing as "natural" assumptions, these concerns themselves have largely escaped philosophical scrutiny.

Specifically, the attempt of philosophical knowledge to purify itself of the temporality and sensuousness of phenomenal existence originates in Greek religious and philosophical thought. In this context, the value of purity is a response to the threat of mortality implicit in the life of the body, to the interconnection between sexuality and death, and to women's role in the life cycle. This commitment to purity has been transmitted to the modern world through the organization and practices of ascetic religion. Christian thinkers have articulated the church's commitment to asceticism in their adherence to the view that the body, symbolically associated with women's nature, must be subordinated to the rational intellect, with which men were identified. Thus, the quest for purity has a history that is embedded in conceptions about the relation between soul and body, reason and passion, male and female.

The historical connection between the church and the university has led to a philosophical analogue of these ascetic commitments. The philosophical paradigm of knowledge articulated by Kant formulates epistemological conditions by which purity can be attained. Purity characterizes the forms of knowledge, which are universal and unchanging and thus remain indifferent to the empirical context in which knowledge occurs. Moreover, the subject of knowledge is also purified of empirical determinants, insofar as the subject (the transcendental unity of apperception) is constitutive of the objective world. This reduction of the knower to abstract conditions insures that all individuals will have the identical form of knowledge. Even the apprehension of an object through the senses becomes decontaminated of the pleasurable component of sense experience. Hence, the subject qua knower must be detached from the empirical features of subjective identity, from the sensuality of the body, and from the emotional context in which relations with others occur. The object, likewise, is treated solely in terms of its formal features, removed from the context in which it appears to individuals as an object of knowledge.

Thus, the philosophical quest for purity has expressed the attempt to escape from the sensual components of human existence. In light of these commitments, the project of exploring the origin of the significance of purity appears as a double violation. Not only must one proceed historically, in opposition to the prevailing claims that philosophy is ahistorical, but one makes visible the erotic component of human existence, which the philosophical tradition has taken great pains to negate.

But precisely through this transgression, it becomes apparent that philosophy's claim to have escaped erotic life is suspect. Rather than providing a liberation from the body, the philosophical paradigm has made normative a deformation of erotic interest, an objectification of our sentient being. The philosophical imperative to eliminate sensuality from one's apprehension of oneself, of other persons, and of objects creates a split between an embodied and a reflective self. Rational consciousness becomes detached from feelings or desires, indicating a fundamental alienation within the subject, which is manifested in the relation to the body inscribed in philosophy. The body becomes reduced to its status as a mere physical object. Because of the ascetic commitment in both religious and philosophical traditions, when pleasures and desires are recognized by consciousness they appear as a dehumanizing force, a natural contamination that is opposed to the qualities of personhood. Although the ascetic demand to distance reflection from embodied existence seeks to maintain rational control over physical desires and passions, it has not resulted in the control of pure rationality over the polluted body. Instead, these ascetic commitments have resulted in an inherent objectifying dynamic within philosophical thought. Not only does the material world become depersonalized, but thinking itself is viewed only under the aspect of objectivity. Moreover, in the modern world this philosophical orientation has been buttressed by powerful objectifying forces in the social world. Since philosophy has refused to acknowledge its relation to historical reality, it has precluded the possibility of a critical orientation toward this world. Instead, reflection has become subordinated to reifying purposes which it has refused to acknowledge.

The detachment from the body made normative in the philosophical enterprise corresponds to an aperspectival view of knowledge, in which one is forced to exclude much of one's sensible apparatus from contributing to knowledge. Through escaping the confines of the particularity of bodily existence, the ascetic mode of philosophy has attempted to speak with the voice of universal reason. According to this view, to speak from any concrete vantage point is to be guilty of subjectivism; one is charged with importing into the logic of abstract inquiry concerns that belong to the realm of strictly personal existence. This adoption of an apparently universal standpoint has disguised the actual standpoint from which philosophers have initiated their inquiries. But for a woman entering the philosophical tradition, the question concerning the standpoint of the philosopher is inevitable. A woman cannot ignore the fact that her voice is not the voice with which the philosophical tradition has spoken. This inability to identify wholly with the historical standpoint of philosophers forces to mind the issue of perspective. *Who* philosophizes? What set of interests motivate these inquiries? What are the consequences of this systematic work? Philosophy can no longer appear to function in a free-floating realm of abstraction that has no correlation to the material world of experience. Underlying the philosophical claim for universality is the articulation and validation of particular kinds of experience that characterize specific groups of individuals. Marxists, and others sharing a "critical" perspective, have pointed to the economic basis of interests, which motivate philosophical thought, and to the ideological consequences of theory, which legitimate the distribution of economic and political power. Critical theorists have provided guides for understanding the relation of theory and practice and for considering the ideological function of philosophy. But they themselves have overlooked the sexual relations between men and women, which these theories have justified.[20] Thus, even the philosophical heritage that guides us to interrogate the standpoint of the knower and that situates philosophy in sensuous existence obliterates the sexual identity of the knower. In order to answer the question of *who* philosophizes, one must legitimate not only the turn to sensuous existence in general as part of the philosophical enterprise, but one must also include in this scope the concrete relations between men and women.

This work has begun to explore the philosophical significance of relations between men and women. I have argued that the philosophical commitment to purity cannot be understood apart from attitudes and practices that associate women with the "pollution" of the body. Thus ascetic philosophy is not only a response to general features of bodily existence, but it is also a response to specific kinds of bodies—that is, to women's bodies, and their perceived role in the life cycle.[21] Although there is some philosophical precedent for thematizing "concrete" relations between individuals, analyses such as Sartre's sweep over major features of material existence, including class and sexual differences. Yet to be concrete and not just raise the call for concreteness, to situate philosophy in its historical context and not speak abstractly of the historical nature of concepts leads one to examine the particular experience of men and women. Contemporary feminist philosophy takes up this challenge to situate philosophical reflection in the context of sexual relations and thus opens avenues for formulating philosophical concepts that do not reflect an exclusively masculine perspective.[22]

By examining the context of sexual relations in which philosophy has operated, two central themes have emerged at the core of this study: the philosophical significance of women's absence from philosophy, and the social implications of a philosophy constructed on this basis. A historical connection is manifested between women's absence from philosophy and the suppression of the erotic theme of human existence from philosophical contemplation. The original meaning of this philosophical linkage can be discovered by turning to the myths and social practices of the period in which these concepts emerged. Women have been thought to signify not only sexuality, but through the life-giving capacity of their sexuality, they are viewed as embodying the threat of death. The philosophical response to mortality has sought to transcend death through the purity and immortality of eternal knowledge. Therefore, philosophers have sought to defend against the "dangerous" elements of human existence by distancing themselves from women as far as possible, by excluding women from the domain of reflection. Within the compass of philosophical dialogue, these defenses against the threat posed by the erotic and mortal nature of human bodies, represented by women's bodies in particular, have led to the conception of thought as detached from bodily existence.

Moreover, this exclusion of women from the philosophical en-
deavor has implications that extend beyond the nature of the concepts that are formulated. On the one hand, the philosophical commitment to purity has served to rationalize and justify women's
absence in general from other spheres of knowledge and public activity.[23] Philosophy has historically reflected a male perspective,
which has become anchored in universal claims about knowledge,
morality, and beauty. Consequently, women have been viewed as
deficient, according to these standards, and as justly subordinated
to men not only in the realms of thought, but in other practical
spheres as well. Since women have been interpreted as cognitively
and morally inferior, their current increased presence in philosophy, science, theology, and law is still sometimes viewed with suspicion, as an incursion into these all-male arenas. Therefore, the
philosophical commitment to purity does articulate a truth about
the world, but not in the sense that philosophy claims for itself. It
does not provide us with the essential constitutive conditions for
knowledge; it does, however, reflect the distribution of sexual roles
and power that exists in the social world and that urges itself on us
as a natural and necessary phenomenon.

By making normative this ascetic stance, the philosophical suppression of erotic existence has implications not only for women's
social status, but also for human beings generally. The suppression
of erotic facets of existence forces the ascetic to seek gratification
in distorted ways. Instead of allowing an explicit avowal of sensual
interest in other persons, this conscious prohibition against sensuality redirects interest toward the object world. The projection of
desire toward things, in this ascetic mode, is manifested by an interest in the detached, formalized object. With the priority given
this posture toward objects, not only other persons, but the ascetic himself, his own body, becomes subsumed under the logic of
things. Thus, the ascetic paradigm results in the perception of
one's body as an object and not itself as a mode of consciousness,
that is, as a means of apprehending the world or expressing an attitude toward it. In particular, this philosophical idealization of
alienated embodiment has justified the social phenomenon of reification in the contemporary world. The reified world creates constraints by which the body is reduced to its function as an instru-

ment of production, comparable to other such instruments, but it is not treated as an expression of one's humanity or one's sociality.

Although this philosophical commitment to asceticism has implications for human beings generally, feminist philosophy may be in a unique position both to display its significance and to suggest avenues for change. From women's standpoint it becomes evident that theories about knowledge have embedded within themselves conceptions of what it means to be a human male or a human female. What is manly has been defined by its inclusion in the domain of rationality—the capacity for detached, dispassionate, reflection, which is considered necessary for the pursuit of science. Womanly attributes, on the other hand, have been defined at the boundaries of this domain. Women appear to embody the emotional, passionate, sexual features of existence, which pose a threat to the paradigm of objectivity, and which must at all costs be excluded from the pursuit of knowledge. Thus, the conception of rationality has split apart these human attributes and projected them onto different poles of sexual existence. Only those attributes taken to belong exclusively to men have been included in the compass of objectivity.

Therefore, with the inclusion of women in philosophical dialogue that has begun in the contemporary world, a question arises concerning the consequences both for women and for philosophy. Can women accept this paradigm of objective knowledge that has been correlated with their exclusion both from philosophy and from spheres of public power in general? Or does this transformation of the sexual organization of the philosophical world entail at the same time a challenge to the ascetic ideal of rationality?

When women enter the academy, it is impossible for them, despite the "best" of intentions, to fully divest themselves of those qualities by which women generally have been defined as women by others and by themselves in their own self-interpretation. Although they may attempt to fully assume the philosophical ideal of detached and dispassionate inquiry, women's existence outside the academy is still bound up with their identification as passionate, emotional, and nurturing beings.[24] Thus, women experience a discontinuity and incoherence in the attempt to integrate their situations within and without the academy. Their experience is analogous to the dilemma of a colonized people, which Frantz Fanon discusses in *Black Skin, White Masks*. Fanon describes the tensions experienced by black Africans who attempt to adopt the ways of the imperialist culture—in this case, the French. They can neither avoid the discomfort in encounters with childhood friends, who doubt the genuineness of their new manners, nor find acceptance within the imperalist culture. The black man who seeks to become French will find himself excluded both from French and African culture. Insofar as he succeeds in identifying himself as French, he will internalize the contempt of the imperialist for the colonized within himself. Similarly, women who engage in philosophical work are subject to particular conflicts, precisely because philosophy has historically demanded their subordination. Women can never be entirely at home within this academic world as long as it remains a predominantly male institution.[25] Moreover, women can never make themselves entirely at home outside of this world by divesting themselves of their philosophical roles. Since the identity of women in this situation encompasses their intellectual pursuits, to separate these from one's sexual and emotional being is to create a damaging split within oneself. Not only does the dominant philosophical tradition hold women in contempt, but insofar as women imbibe these views, they also suffer from self-abnegation.[26]

Although these conflicts may be a handicap for women in easing themselves into the philosophical world, this very incoherence in women's experience may contain the germ necessary for establishing a new philosophical coherence. These conflicts can be used to challenge the ascetic ideal in philosophy. They can be used to bring into view the sexual differentiation of attributes on which the ascetic ideal is based, to illumine the negative consequences—for both men and women—of splitting off the emotional and the sexual from the intellectual features of existence, and to begin the project of reformulating our conception of the relation between cognition and eros.

However, this project, to which the present study has attempted to contribute, is not without its difficulties. One is faced by the need to call forth into philosophical purview issues that have not been validated as philosophically relevant; for example, those concerning the origins of particular modes of thought, the formation and significance of sexual desire, the relation between sensuality and sensuousness, and the concrete nature of relations between men and women. To raise the issue of legitimacy is itself a useful tactic for thematizing issues that have been excluded from philosophical discourse. But by acknowledging the problem of legitimacy, one does not thereby eliminate the conflicts that gave rise to it. Just as philosophical influence extends beyond the realm of ideas by justifying particular social relations, so the reevaluation of philosophical categories must also extend beyond the world of ideas. Philosophical change must ultimately root itself in the transformation of the inherited social roles of men and women through the elimination of the sexual polarization of rationality and emotion, which the philosophical notion of objectivity has made normative.

This call to legitimate the significance of sexuality and sexual relations within the scope of philosophical inquiry does not merely add to the categories of things about which we can now philosophize; it poses a challenge to traditional modes of thought, such as the paradigm of objective knowledge discussed in this study. But the objection may be raised, what is left for philosophy? Does this redefining of the philosophical project entail a reduction of philosophy, not now to history or sociology, for which Marxist critics are blamed, but to sexuality? And if the history of Western philosophy and science has been dependent on an ascetic response to embodiment, is this response a requisite defensive measure for the development of scientific knowledge?

The question concerning the reduction of philosophy to sexuality is motivated by the same conception of sexuality that underlies the ascetic mode of thought. The body appears as a brute physiological fact, a natural substratum, which, if given its due, will reduce all intellectual activity to what is given and predetermined in physical existence. In arguing for an orientation that accepts philosophical activity as springing from the same source as erotic feelings, one must recognize erotic existence not as a strictly natural, biological fact or as a domain that is itself impenetrable to consciousness. Instead, sexuality must be viewed as a theme of existence, which pervades the multiple relations of our lives, and which itself reflects other, "nonerotic" interests. In elaborating a theory of erotic life, one might follow the lines suggested by Merleau-Ponty in the

*Phenomenology of Perception.* He speaks, for example, of sexuality as an "atmosphere" that is at all times present in the totality of one's existence.[27] Not only do actions and relationships express our sexual being, which we can never outstrip, but also sexuality itself embodies the drama of our whole personal life.[28] Our sexual being cannot be compartmentalized into one corner of our existence, but it itself reflects postures taken up in other dimensions of our lives. From this point of view, thematizing the erotic significance of philosophy no more reduces philosophy to sexuality than it reduces it to existence. Rather, philosophy is understood as the articulation and self-interpretaton of human experience, which is inalienably the experience of sexual beings.

At this point it is appropriate to consider the implication of this critique of objectivity for the possibility of gaining knowledge. By criticizing the existing paradigm as objectifying, have we eliminated all claims for philosophical or scientific knowledge? Is our only remaining option to follow Nietzsche's and Foucault's path in claiming that all truth is interpretation, and there is no objective basis for preferring one interpretation to another? The recent controversies between modernists who defend "truth" and "norms" and post-modernists who reject these categories crystallize the issues present in the on-going philosophical debates between objectivists and relativists. Objectivists view knowledge in terms of universal, ahistorical standards; they therefore create the antithesis between objectivity based on such standards and mere interpretation. Relativists agree with their opponents that they cannot provide objectivity in this sense. They cannot even, as their critics point out, prove that relativism is true transhistorically.[29] However, they also argue that there are no such permanent, ahistorical standards, except as figments of our metaphysical imagination. The polarization between these positions effectively cedes the concept of knowledge to the objectivists and precludes on both sides the question of alternative conceptions of cognition.

The objectivists' insistence that knowledge can be construed only on the basis of ahistorical standards leads one to raise the question of motivation. Richard Bernstein describes the objectivist as moved by a Cartesian anxiety, which seeks a secure anchor to defend against the chaos and irrationality of existence. Impulses such as these, as I have noted, can be traced back to early ascetic attempts to escape the threat of change implicit in temporal and mortal existence. In the twentieth century this impulse has no doubt been strengthened by the palpable irrationality and danger represented by the Second World War, and by the proliferation of weapons that can destroy life together. For those who think wholly intellectual means can defend against such destructive forces, the demand for binding objective norms has especial appeal.

But in suggesting that basic features of knowledge or morality exist independently of concrete temporal conditions, this approach treats knowledge as an insulated sphere that requires the participation of ideal knowers. Rather than treating the mind as if it were animated independently of life, however, one can begin to consider alternative approaches to knowledge by situating cognition in the context of life as it is lived. With such a move, entirely different philosophical questions are foregrounded, which examine the role of emotion, sensuality, and concrete social conditions in knowing. Such a reorientation not only leads to a changed theory of knowledge but requires a changed praxis as well. Since epistemological objectivism is rooted in reifying social conditions, a critique of this paradigm of knowledge is ultimately effective only if it is linked to efforts to change these material conditions as well. Yet short of achieving these radical social changes it may be possible to develop an alternative praxis of knowing that begins to subvert this distorting epistemological procedure and the objectified posture that it demands in daily existence. Although we cannot in our immediate existence either reconstitute the world or our own identity in it, we can cease to bracket out those elements of our experience that have been insistently excluded by the prevailing approach to cognition.

A changed praxis of knowing has implications for research and teaching in the contemporary university as well. Within the university, the corollary to the social relations in the marketplace has been an academic practice that measures intellectual worth in terms of quantitative achievements. These academic norms have been reinforced by an epistemological paradigm that views knowledge as an objective, fully rationalized system. Challenging this epistemological paradigm calls into question the assumption that these academic practices are necessary for the furthering of knowledge. Moreover, it also challenges entrenched pedagogical methods that treat education as a process of depositing an objective body of knowledge in learners' heads. As feminists, among others, have pointed out, an alternative to this banking concept of knowledge can be found in a "midwife" model of teaching, which seeks to draw knowledge out of learners.[30] Such an approach emphasizes knowing as a process of both intellectual and emotional maturation, which develops students' abilities to value their own insights as well as to understand the perspectives of others.

Although I do not seek to offer here an alternative to this objectivist paradigm, I will sketch some general parameters that we might fruitfully explore for furthering our understanding of cognition. Resituating a theory of cognition within lived experience entails examining the experience of concrete, qualitative subjects rather than seeking formal, transcendental conditions of subjectivity. This epistemological shift focuses interpretive authority in the actual subject rather than in an objective system of knowledge. However, validating the subject's perceptions, feelings, and responses as cognitively relevant does not ignore the social context in which one exists. Since individuals are constituted in part through intersubjective experience, the distribution of power among individuals shapes not only one's perceptions and feelings, but also one's ability to assert them as cognitive. Thus, cognitive issues for those who are disempowered may be different than for those who are empowered. For women and blacks who have been devalued in our culture, one's ability to name knowledge is constantly undermined not only by limited resources, but also by the unremitting critical voices that represent entrenched social interests. External struggles invariably bring in their wake internal questions of doubt. But those whose power derives from their identification with objective authority may be even further removed from honoring the subjective component of cognition. The individual who has become what Nietzsche calls an "objective thinker" has few tools to understand how emotions, desires, and defenses direct and inhibit his or her inquiry. Thus, developing an analysis of the subjective component of knowledge must be linked to an analysis of the differential constitution of subjectivity by existing relations of power.

In concretizing the subject of knowledge, one also brings into the cognitive realm dimensions of sensuous experience that generally have been excluded from models of knowledge. For example, vision has been the privileged metaphor of knowledge in the philosophical tradition since Plato. As already discussed, the approach to knowing as seeing promises a desensualization of apprehension that assures the possession of an atemporal perspective.[31] Thematizing the role of sensuous existence in knowledge enables one to explore not only the erotic dimension of seeing, but also the contribution of other senses, such as hearing or touch, to apprehension. An inquiry into the cognitive role of hearing may find a philosophical antecedent in Heraclitus.[32] Merleau-Ponty also points to the importance of touch,[33] as in perceiving the texture of the object, and he emphasizes the role of familiarity and practical knowledge in his account of perception. Although these aspects of perception have been excluded from the scientific analysis of the spatiotemporal features of an object, they are primary features of our existence, and the scientific model itself must be viewed as distanced from sensuous experience.[34]

Situating cognition in the context of lived experience also entails examining the concrete intersubjective relations in our past and present that shape the contours of our erotic and affective lives. Moreover, it foregrounds the philosophical problem of knowing persons and does not treat cognition primarily in terms of knowledge of objects. Knowing another person is not merely a theoretical question but is a practical relation that depends on reciprocal relations between individuals. We can know others, in some sense, only to the extent that they allow themselves to be known. Where the practical relation of reciprocity is lacking, one's knowledge of another person may be confined to what can be learned through observation.[35] This observational posture is based on a relation of detachment or even antagonism between individuals. Insofar as we have taken observation as primary for knowing persons, we have endorsed as normative this detachment between persons. However, in friendships, for example, mutuality generates both an ease with oneself and a receptivity toward the other, through which qualities not evident to a detached observer become revealed. Moreover, feelings of care between individuals may not only bring one greater self-understanding but may also bring changes within oneself. Emotional life contributes a depth to knowledge that is wholly lacking when persons are treated either as objects of observation or as purely rational beings. Cognition encompasses the multiplicity of our responses to another person. There are invariably tensions and contradictions in these responses (e.g., one might at moments be physically attracted to someone one dislikes). But by viewing cognition as drawing on our total apprehension of a person, we resist the Kantian compartmentalization that segregates the moral "person" from the physical "body."

However, recognizing the subjective and intersubjective contributions to cognition does not entail a flight into interiority and a rejection of the objective parameters of existence. Subjective, intersubjective, and objective dimensions coexist dynamically in the process of gaining knowledge. Knowledge of the material world is a precondition for our continued existence as both sensuous and cognitive beings. Moreover, objective conditions inform the human realm and are shaped by it as well. But instead of prioritizing the objective horizon of knowledge, as occurs in traditional accounts, the objective realm should be situated as one aspect of cognitive processes. Sometimes it is even necessary to bracket this objective dimension. At moments we physically remove ourselves from external stimulation and demands in order to develop our reflection or our intimacy with another. But we return to the world informed by these insights and experiences.

Just as it is necessary to concretize the subject of knowledge, so one must also concretize the object that is known.[36] A theory of knowledge could be elaborated that contributes to our understanding of the emotional and sensual significance of objects we experience. Such a theory would also consider the historical conditions that make something an object of knowledge for us.[37] Moreover, one must examine how individuals are situated differently in relation to objective conditions. The subject's relation to the world is more complex than that of an observer vis à vis a world of scientific objects, but it is mediated by possibly conflicting cultural patterns. For example, one's daily life can be occupied with activities that are marginalized by prevailing cultural norms or that are evaluated differently in the competing cultural spheres in which one might live. Both subjectivity and intersubjective relations are informed by this complex situation.

Two kinds of objections might be raised to this approach to knowledge. Thinkers who have identified themselves as defenders of modernism would reiterate the need for legitimating universal, rational norms in order to safeguard against the threat of irrationality. They would argue that abandoning the prevailing paradigm of objectivity undermines the possibility of establishing objectively binding norms. One might respond to this objection by questioning why the issue of the legitimation of norms is foregrounded by these thinkers. In focusing attention on metaethical questions of justification, this philosophical strategy diverts attention away from the content of the political situations that gives rise to questions of choice and action. Furthermore, this search for binding norms appears to be motivated by the view that morality is possible only through enforced restraint. Such an approach construes rationality either as a means of controlling the irrational, unruly aspects of human nature, or as an independent cognitive and moral faculty that leaves untouched nonrational aspects of existence. However, both versions posit a fundamental compartmentalization of rational forms and affective or erotic existence, which this work has questioned. This split between cognition and eros not only generates distortions in human existence, but it also precludes questions concerning the historical construction of rationality and of the social relations that this paradigm validates. The emphasis given to legitimating the power of rational rules displays the inheritance of ascetic philosophy, which seeks certainty and control through a disengagement from concrete existence.

Post-modernist thinkers, on the other hand, would object that investing the concrete subject with cognitive authority reiterates Christian and romantic notions of the individual.[38] In their view, a return to the language of subjectivity implies a return to the notions that authenticity is repressed and seeks liberation, and that meaning should be located in subjective intentionality. Critics like Foucault argue that primary consideration should be given instead to how subjects and norms about subjectivity are constituted, how subjective meanings are used and interpreted, and how the concept of the authorial subject itself serves a historical function in indicating what is accepted as meaningful discourse.[39]

Although one must examine the social function of the configuration of subjectivity and authorship, as Foucault suggests, one must examine the function of the rejection of these concepts as well. There is a peculiar irony in the fact that theoreticians now consider the "author" to be dead when female and black authors have finally attained strong voices. One must consider whether the reception of the post-modernist displacement of subjectivity contributes, contrary to these thinkers' intentions, to the validation of the existing distribution of power among subjects. Moreover, although subjectivity is not necessarily unitary or originative of meaning, we nonetheless live our subjectivity. To discuss cognition on the level of concreteness means to refer to this lived experience, and not to privilege one's cognitive perspective as transcending this horizon.

One consequence of treating cognition in the context of lived experience is the recognition of an openness in the field of epistemic problems. Problems of knowledge themselves are generated by particular historical constellations and events. Moreover, in acknowledging the cognitive role of emotion and sensuousness, one also challenges the view that argumentation is the primary form of knowledge.[40] Since argumentation involves advancing reasons for a position one already holds, it is not the only or even the primary avenue by which cognitive judgments are made. Insofar as rational argumentation has served as the model for the acquisition of knowledge, it has reinforced the presumption that knowledge is purely rational and that it is to be treated primarily in terms of the formal features of justification.

Instead of pursuing a strictly rationalistic approach to knowledge, we can begin to consider what is entailed in "passionate" knowing.[41] Knowledge need not be viewed as rigid and dispassionate, but rather as a process of encountering the world and communicating with others on a multifaceted level. As the hermeneutics of suspicion has taught us, the rational claims of individuals and social groups often belie the meanings they claim to represent. Emotional apprehension is a valuable source for understanding purposes that may be operative, whether or not they are explicitly acknowledged. Even physical objects can be encountered empathetically. Barbara McClintock movingly describes her scientific inquiry as involving patience to "hear what (the corn) has to say to you" and the openness to "let it come to you." She wrote, "I know them intimately, and I find it a great pleasure to know them."[42] The practice of knowledge can cultivate the sense of possibility and openness that may lead to a redefinition of epistemological concerns as new problems demand our attention. Cognitive practice need not be built primarily on the impulse to control, but on the qualities of receptivity and responsiveness. Ultimately, such a reorientation of knowledge entails recognizing our responsibility in defining and selecting epistemological issues and in acknowledging the existential and political parameters that inform these choices.

In this final moment of stock-taking, it is necessary to consider the critical import of this project for the prevailing form of "objective knowledge." One might argue, for example, that displaying the erotic undercurrents of objectivity does not invalidate either the achievements of objective knowledge or the necessity of these erotic deflections for acquiring knowledge. It is well to remember, at this point, that the purpose of this project was merely to investigate the origins of the commitment to objectivity and to indicate the manner in which objectivity, despite its own claims, is not based on purely intellectual motivations. In the course of this study, the negative consequences of the operation of objectivity became evident both for women in particular, and for erotic existence in general. This inquiry, therefore, has not attempted to invalidate the achievements of "objective knowledge." Nor has it offered an alternative formulation of cognition. But it does suggest that this practice of objectivity does not encapsulate the only and essential features of knowledge, and that scientific objectivity is itself ideological. Such a realization opens the door to considering how alternative values and goals might contribute to different directions for scientific and philosophical inquiry. These factors must be kept in view in evaluating the achievements of "objective knowledge" in the modern world.

# NOTES

## CHAPTER ONE

1. Susan Moller Okin, *Women in Western Political Thought*, pp. 46 ff. The status of the female guardians in the *Republic* will be discussed below.

2. Ibid., pp. 37–38.

3. For example, the passage at 457a in the *Republic* has been translated as referring to the "women of the guardians" (Shorey translation in *The Collected Dialogues of Plato*) or the "wives of the guardians" (Jowett translation in *Plato's The Republic*).

4. Arlene Saxonhouse introduces the term "desexualization" in her discussion of the women guardians. See "The Philosopher and the Female in the Political Thought of Plato," p. 196.

5. Okin argues that Plato's treatment of motherhood is not constricting but rather is liberating for women. She writes, "The real significance of the treatment of the subject of women in Book V of the *Republic* is that it is one of the very few instances in the history of thought when the bio-

logical implications of femaleness have been clearly separated out from all the conventional, institutional and emotional baggage that has usually been identified with them" (*Women in Western Political Thought*, p. 41). Although Okin is clearly right in challenging the biological justification for women's traditional role, this challenge need not be based on that detachment from the body that has characterized the male philosophical tradition.

6. Jean Bethke Elshtain is similarly critical of Plato's abstraction from bodily identity. She writes, "The presumption that whether I am a woman or a man is an uninteresting contingent statement about me rather than the essential or interesting bedrock of my identity is false" (*Public Man, Private Woman: Women in Social and Political Thought*, pp. 37–38).

7. Julia Annas notes that it is hardly a feminist argument to claim that women do not have a special sphere (455b) because men can outdo them at absolutely everything ("Plato's Republic and Feminism," in Martha Lee Osborne, ed., *Woman in Western Thought*, p. 26).

8. This discussion may appear to criticize Plato from both sides of the fence. On the one hand, I have suggested that Plato's attempt to separate out personal from bodily identity is misguided. On the other hand, I have suggested that his failure to make this separation for women is the basis for his view that women are inferior. (Plato's discussion of the gifted and the ungifted at 455b suggests that women's weakness lies in their intellectual dullness combined with bodily interference with the mind's activity.) Although I object to the terms of equality set forth by Plato, which demand a separation between personal and sexual identity, it is telling that he cannot even consistently grant these terms to women.

9. The stark opposition between soul and body drawn in the *Phaedo* is more subtly represented in other dialogues by the tension between different parts of the soul. In the *Republic* Plato sets forth a tripartate division between the appetitive, the spirited, and the rational elements of the soul (441a). In the *Phaedrus*, the need for separating the wisdom-seeking from the pleasure-seeking drives is represented by the image of the soul as winged steeds and their charioteer. The lowest of the souls, when they become incarnate, surrender to pleasure, beget offspring of the flesh, and consort with wantonness (*Phaedrus* 250e). Plato describes the souls for whom the "higher elements of the mind" are victorious in the following way: "Their day will be blessed with happiness and concord, for the power of evil in the soul has been subjected, and the power of goodness liberated; they have won self-mastery and inward peace" (*Phaedrus* 256b).

10. For example, G. M. A. Grube argues that Plato understands the motivating power of all intellectual activity as rooted in sexual attraction. See his discussion in *Plato's Thought*, p. 116.

11. J. M. E. Moravcsik, "Reason and Eros in the 'Ascent'-Passage of the *Symposium*," in John P. Anton and George L. Kustas, eds., *Essays in Ancient Greek Philosophy*, refers to this question in terms of "exclusion"

and "inclusion" (p. 293). Moravcsik leans toward the exclusive inter-pretation of eros. He stresses negative aspects of the erotic movement (e.g., the feeling of disdain or indifference towards the beauty of bodies [*Symposium* 210c]). However, he qualifies his claim by suggesting that the lower types of desire may exist, so long as they do not remain the dominant aspiration of one's life.

12. Ibid., p. 291.

13. Moravcsik prefers the translation of eros as the general term "aspi-ration," thereby emphasizing its nonsexual implications (Ibid., p. 290).

14. Ibid.

15. Gregory Vlastos, "The Individual as an Object of Love in Plato's Dialogues," in *Platonic Studies*, pp. 31–32.

16. See L. A. Kosman, "Platonic Love," in W. H. Werkmeister, ed., *Facets of Plato's Philosophy*, p. 67.

17. Moravcsik, in Anton and Kustas, eds., p. 291.

18. In this respect I differ from Moravcsik's conclusion that though "lower" types of desire are no longer dominant aspirations in an individ-ual's life, they remain as subordinate aspirations. See his discussion, ibid., p. 293.

19. Comparisons have been drawn between Plato's theory of eros and modern theories of sublimation. F. M. Cornford, however, observes that the motivating energy of the soul in Platonic theory resides initially in its spiritual part, which becomes ensnared in flesh. This primordial spiritual origin contrasts with Freud's interpretation of the sexual roots of intellec-tual activity. See Cornford, "The Doctrine of Eros in Plato's *Symposium*," in Gregory Vlastos, ed., *Ethics, Politics and Philosophy of Art and Reli-gion*, p. 129, vol. 2 of *Plato: A Collection of Critical Essays*.

20. Since the sun is a central metaphor for truth in the *Republic*, book 6 (509a), this characterization of male descent indicates men's greater af-finity with truth-seeking.

21. See Chapter 2.

22. Elizabeth Spelman, Metaphysics and Misogyny: Souls, Bodies and Women in Plato's Dialogues, p. 41.

23. The prevalence of male homosexuality among the Greeks might throw doubt on this claim that men's renunciation of sexuality is in any way linked to their relationships with women. One could argue, for ex-ample, that if men found sexual gratification primarily with other men, the demand to distance themselves from desire has no implications for their contact with women. But Greek homosexuality itself can be viewed, in part, as a response to the perceived threat posed by women. The elements involved in this "threat" are discussed in Chapter 2.

24. Martha Nussbaum objects to this identification of Diotima's view with the whole meaning of the dialogue. She reminds the reader that after the close of Socrates' speech, Alcibiades appears as an alternative to Socrates' path of being "excellent and deaf" ("The Speech of Alcibiades:

A Reading of Plato's *Symposium*," p. 152). Alcibiades' story concerns his contingent passion for Socrates, a particular individual. She argues that his presence signifies Plato's recognition of these conflicting paths, and of the ultimately tragic choice we must make between philosophy and our humanity (p. 167). Yet Plato does not seem to be impartial between these two choices. Alcibiades' own speech is in praise of Socrates for his "manliness and self-control" (*Symposium* 219d). Although his love is for Socrates the individual, who is "absolutely unique" (*Symposium* 221c), Socrates' uniqueness lies in his strength to pursue the philosophical ideal.

## CHAPTER TWO

1. Hans-Georg Gadamer, *Philosophical Hermeneutics*, p. 28.

2. Paul Brandt, *Das Liebesleben der Griechen*, vol. 2 of *Sittengeschichte Griechenlands*, p. 10. This observation is especially interesting given the prominence of the visual metaphor for truth in Platonic philosophy, as well as in the subsequent philosophical tradition. The eyes must be transformed from a medium of desire to a medium of truth.

3. This discussion is based on Kenneth J. Dover, *Greek Popular Morality in the Time of Plato and Aristotle*, pp. 208–12. The culpability of this act lay in its offense against the property of the male citizen, whose wife, daughter, or mother was implicated in the act. Okin, *Women in Western Political Thought*, p. 31, discusses the status of Greek women as property.

4. Dover, *Greek Popular Morality*, p. 77.

5. The Greeks distinguished eros, as an exceptionally strong response to sensory stimuli, from love, for which the Greek word was *philia*. Love broadly encompassed the affection, weak or strong, for a sexual partner, a child, a friend, or a colleague. Although love needs other factors to generate it, one of its most effective generators is the fulfillment of mutual desire.

6. Hesiod, *Works and Days*, 373–75, trans. R. M. Frazer.

7. The following discussion is based on Dover, *Greek Popular Morality*, pp. 101–2.

8. Ibid., p. 14.

9. Ibid., p. 209.

10. Ibid., p. 98.

11. Ibid.

12. Rather than attributing the cause of women's oppression to female sexuality, as radical feminists do, I am concerned with illustrating how existing hierarchies between men and women organize sexual beliefs and practices.

13. Brandt, *Das Liebesleben der Griechen;* see his concluding remarks.

14. Jane Harrison, *Prolegomena to the Study of Greek Religion*, p. 284.

15. Marcel Detienne, in *La Cuisine du Sacrifice*, argues that this deceptive play of inside/outside indicates the interdependence of good and evil. He writes of Pandora, "La femme est un mal, mais sans ce mal, on manque le bien qui lui correspond. Impossible d'avoir l'un sans passer par l'autre" (p. 119).

16. Aeschylus, *Eumenides*, 736, trans. Herbert Weir Smyth.

17. Harrison, *Prolegomena*, p. 302.

18. Judith Ochshorn, *The Female Experience and the Nature of the Divine*, p. 74.

19. Harrison, *Prolegomena*, p. 394.

20. Mary Daly, *Gyn-Ecology: The Metaethics of Radical Feminism*, p. 62.

21. Ibid.

22. Lewis Richard Farnell, *The Cults of the Greek States* 4:188–93. The women who filled this function were merely required to be respectable, and to lead a life of abstinence. Originally the oracle was required to be a virgin; in later years, she was usually a woman past child-bearing years. Above all, she was required to possess the capacity to become easily frenzied.

23. Philip E. Slater, in *The Glory of Hera: Greek Mythology and the Greek Family*, attempts to give a psychoanalytic explanation of the Greek fear of women. He speculates that women, sequestered in the household, became the dominant and frustrated force in the lives of their children. Slater suggests that it is this aggressive, hostile mother-figure that provides a prototype of the threatening female, who figures so prominently in Greek literature.

24. Victor W. Turner, "Symbols in African Ritual," p. 1101.

25. Martin Nilsson, *A History of Greek Religion*, p. 83.

26. Ibid., p. 88.

27. Similar beliefs about womens' sexual pollution appear in other cultures. For example, in the New Guinea Highlands, men view women's sexuality as a physical threat to their health and strength. The men of the Highland tribes consider intercourse with women as depleting. Too much of it makes a man sick and old, whereas the woman suffers no ill consequences (Raymond C. Kelly, "Witchcraft and Sexual Relations," in Paula Brown and Georgeda Buchbinder, eds., *Man and Woman in the New Guinea Highlands*, p. 40). Because of its debilitating effects, a woman who encourages a man to engage in intercourse is considered to be a witch (ibid., p. 49). Rather than wasting themselves with women, the Highland men believe that a man's semen is expended more fruitfully with other men. The semen can orally provide a young boy with the maturational fluids he needs. A women's pollution is passed on to the man through any act of physical proximity. A woman may not step over food that is to be eaten by a man, or walk by a seated man, for this "passing over" of the vagina carries with it the pollution of intercourse (Georgeda Buchbinder

and Roy A. Rappaport, "Fertility and Death among the Maring," in Brown and Buchbinder, eds., p. 27).

28. Dover, *Greek Popular Morality*, p. 210. Moreover, most Greek citizens were slaveholders. The ratio of slaves to citizens in Periclean Athens was 3:2; in other cities, the relative number of slaves was even larger. See Perry Anderson, *Passages from Antiquity to Feudalism*, p. 22. The pressure of the growing slave population created a need to expand the citizenry by insuring the *legitimacy* of children. Thus the continued mastery of the citizen over his slaves was in part dependent on his power to sequester women in the household.

29. Dover, *Greek Popular Morality*, p. 210.

30. The anthropologist Mary Douglas offers an interpretation of female pollution based on the structural needs of society. She argues, in *Purity and Danger: An Analysis of Concepts of Pollution and Taboo*, that every social structure defines certain groups or individuals as marginal. Persons whose status and roles are ambiguous, or whose function is defined as outside the legitimate structures of power, are thought to be dangerous. According to this view it is socially necessary that some groups be defined as polluting, as a means of exerting control over threatening elements, such as the changes posed by the death of a member of the community. The specific position groups fill in the social structure determines which individuals are assigned polluting qualities. Women, who are usually outside of positions of power in society, are consequently viewed as polluting. Hence it is appropriate that they be assigned polluting tasks, such as care for the dead, since the dead are also outside the bounds of life. Although this may be a fruitful line of inquiry, it cannot account for the particular beliefs about the relation between birth and death that prevailed in Greek society.

31. Nilsson, *A History of Greek Religion*, p. 83.

32. Ibid., p. 103.

33. The discussion of the Anthesteria is based on Jane Harrison, *Themis: A Study of the Social Origins of Greek Religion*, pp. 288–96.

34. Aeschylus, *The Libation Bearers*, 127.

35. Harrison, *Prolegomena*, p. 80.

36. Harrison, *Themis*, pp. 290–91.

37. Harrison, *Prolegomena*, p. 80. Harrison notes that the Keres embody in primitive form our contemporary understanding of bacilli.

38. Nilsson, *A History of Greek Religion*, p. 170.

39. Harrison, *Prolegomena*, p. 39.

40. In the Highland tribes, women are thought to be highly dangerous and polluting both because of their sexuality and their association with the dead, for it is on women that the funerary responsibilities fall (Buchbinder and Rappaport, "Fertility and Death among the Maring," in Brown and Buchbinder, eds., p. 22). The effects of female pollution, caused by a woman stepping over food eaten by a man or by excessive sexual inter-

course with a woman, are generally similar to the rotting of corpses: they are described as wasting, sores, and the spitting up of phlegm (ibid., p. 27). The common features of pollution resulting from intercourse and death suggest a cyclical relation between fertility and mortality similar to that among the Greeks. Buchbinder and Rappaport observe: "Coldness and wetness are taken by the Maring to induce decay; that is, the dissolution of organic matter and its reabsorption into the earth from which it sprang, and that decay is seen by them to favor fertility. New life grows from the rot of things once living; that which is living will in its turn dissolve, supporting life yet to come. But whether or not it is beneficial to growth, that which is decaying is after all itself dead or dying. Fertility is, thus, closely related to death in Maring cosmology. . . . It may be suggested then that Maring men's fear of pollution by women's sexuality on the one hand, and by the association of women with corpses on the other, are one and the same" (ibid.). Maring cosmology is built on the set of oppositions (hot/cold, growth/decay) that parallel, in Buchbinder and Rappaport's view, the fundamental opposition between male and female. Coldness, attributed to women, is the source of both decay and growth. Consequently, the qualities relating to death and fertility are united in women, in opposition to the qualities that characterize men.

41. Ibid., p. 29.

42. Dover, *Greek Popular Morality*, p. 98.

43. Harrison, *Prolegomena*, p. 95.

44. Lewis Richard Farnell, *Greek Hero Cults and Ideas of Immortality*, p. 297.

45. Harrison, *Prolegomena*, pp. 95 ff.

46. The suggestion that the scapegoat ritual provides the pattern according to which women became associated with the pollution of sexuality does not explain why men, rather than women, have the power to assign pollution to the other. No attempt is being made here to explain the origin of the subordination of women to men. Rather, given this historical fact, one can explain how men have used deeply entrenched rituals to assure themselves of purity.

47. Nilsson, *A History of Greek Religion*, pp. 81–82.

48. In *La Cuisine du Sacrifice*, Detienne interprets the Pandora myth in this way. Pandora brings the evil, without which life could not exist.

49. Nilsson, *A History of Greek Religion*, p. 83.

50. Ochshorn, Douglas, and Harrison all describe rituals in this way.

51. Harrison, *Themis*, p. 20.

52. Ibid., p. 43.

53. W. K. C. Guthrie, *Orpheus and Greek Religion: A Study of the Orphic Movement*, p. 194.

54. Harrison, *Prolegomena*, p. 473.

55. Guthrie, *Orpheus and Greek Religion*, p. 207.

56. Harrison, *Themis*, p. 268.

57. Guthrie, *Orpheus and Greek Religion*, pp. 31–33.

58. Ibid., p. 50.

59. Ibid., p. 83.

60. Ibid., p. 156.

61. Ibid., p. 235.

62. Ibid., p. 201.

63. Harrison, *Prolegomena*, pp. 507–8.

64. Ibid.

65. Guthrie, *Orpheus and Greek Religion*, p. 194.

66. Hence one finds scattered Platonic references to Orphism as primitive. For example, Harrison interprets the passage at the *Republic*, 364b, as a criticism of the Orphic idea that purity in life can be gained through sacrifices and rites (*Prolegomena*, p. 508).

67. Friedrich Nietzsche, *The Genealogy of Morals*, p. 299. Not all commentators of asceticism agree with Nietzsche's assessment that it constitutes a denial of life. In particular, Margaret R. Miles, in *Fullness of Life: Historical Foundations for a New Asceticism*, argues that asceticism enhances life. See the discussion of this interpretation in Chapter 3.

68. Nietzsche, *The Genealogy of Morals*, p. 276.

69. Guthrie, *Orpheus and Greek Religion*, p. 165.

70. Ibid., p. 157.

71. F. M. Cornford, *From Religion to Philosophy: A Study in the Origins of Western Speculation*, p. 252.

72. For example, in the *Meno*, Plato argues that the possibility of discovering truth through recollection is based on the immortality of the soul (*Meno* 86b).

73. Diogenes Laërtius, *Lives of Eminent Philosophers*, bk 3, chap. 46.

74. Nietzsche, *The Genealogy of Morals*, p. 288.

75. Friedrich Nietzsche, *Beyond Good and Evil*, preface, p. xi.

76. Eric Blondel, in "Nietzsche: Life as Metaphor," speaks of Nietzsche's "feminine" ontology, in which woman becomes the privileged metaphor of life (in David B. Allison, ed., *The New Nietzsche: Contemporary Styles of Interpretation*, p. 156). Despite Nietzsche's use of woman as the metaphor for truth in the passage cited above, elsewhere he sets them in opposition. He writes, "Among women—'Truth? Oh, you don't know the truth, do you! Is it not an outrage on all our modesties?'" (cited in Blondel, p. 160). Nietzsche's use of the image of woman in his discussion of truth deserves a much lengthier treatment than is possible here.

## CHAPTER THREE

1. Considerations of time and space have led me to omit discussion of the treatment of women and sexuality in Judaism.

2. Quoted in foreword to "The Happy Life," translated by Ludwig Schopp, in *The Writings of Saint Augustine*, vol. 1, p. 6.

3. Augustine, *The City of God*, bk 14, chap. 15, p. 464. Further references to this work will be by the initials *CG*, followed by book, chapter, and page.

4. Augustine, *Confessions*, bk 10, chaps. 31–36, pp. 234–44. Future references to this work will be by book, chapter, and page.

5. Peter Brown, in his distinguished biography, *Augustine of Hippo*, opposes the view that sexual desire is central for Augustine. Brown notes that although sexual dreams worry Augustine, he is much more disturbed by the problem of greed (p. 179). Brown suggests that sexual sins pale for Augustine in comparison with gratuitous acts of crime, such as the pointless robbing of a pear tree in his youth (p. 172). For reasons given below, I will argue for the importance of sexuality in Augustine's treatment of lust. Brown also suggests that our curiosity about Augustine's concubine stems from a particularly modern preoccupation with sexual relationships (p. 61). Augustine and his friends would have found this interest strange, since woman was created to bear man children. Augustine comments, "If it was company and good conversation that Adam needed, it would have been much better arranged to have two men together, as friends, not a man and a woman" (quoted in Brown, p. 62). Although the task of the modern reader is to understand Augustine in his own context, it is also the reader's task to question assumptions that may be problematic.

6. One of the intriguing aspects of Augustine's anthropology is his recognition of the potentiality for sensuality (or, in his view, the danger of sensuality) that resides in all the senses. Augustine recognized the tendency of the senses (even of the "seeing" involved in "knowing") toward pleasure, which must be subdued by the wise soul. Kant's analysis of the senses, as discussed in later chapters, carries further the ascetic imperative evident in Augustine by denying that the senses naturally tend toward pleasure. When pleasure does occur, it is viewed as a subjective interference with the senses' contribution to knowledge. By contrast, Freud, like Augustine, acknowledged the pleasurable component latent in all sense experience, which led him later to consider sexuality as the general condition of sensuality from which all other forms of pleasures are ultimately derived.

7. Although Augustine was committed to ascetic goals, Brown notes that he could never quite be content with a world of disembodied souls (*Augustine of Hippo*, p. 161). For example, he yearned for the physical presence of his friends. Augustine does not so much argue for the detachment from all feelings of delight, but for their scrutiny and transformation for higher ends.

8. Augustine's account of the Fall echoes earlier Greek themes linking sexuality and death. For Augustine, both are signs of the corruption of the body. It is because man sinned that he faces death (*CG* 13.4.415). Like the Greek ascetics, Augustine thought that overcoming sexual desire brought one closer to the blessed state of immortality. Although abstinence alone did not insure the elimination of lust, as Augustine's own

*Confessions* make clear, sexual activity inevitably bound mortal men closer to concupiscence.

9. Rosemary Radford Ruether, "Misogynism and Virginal Feminism in the Fathers of the Church," in Rosemary Radford Ruether, ed., *Religion and Sexism*, p. 162.

10. Most notably, this viewpoint has been argued by Margaret R. Miles in her book, *Fullness of Life: Historical Foundations of a New Asceticism.*

11. Augustine, *Epistula* 18.13. Quoted in Miles, p. 68.

12. See the discussion of the *Symposium* in Chapter 1.

13. In her study of Christian asceticism, Miles offers a more sympathetic interpretation of Augustine's view of embodiment. She suggests that in order to properly interpret the apparently negative comments of Christian authors on the body, one must distinguish between the "flesh" and the "body." She argues that "flesh" is the theological term that refers to the body deprived of the soul's presence, as when it is dissected or buried (*Fullness of Life*, p. 14). Only in this context is the body referred to pejoratively, as a "stinking corpse." Miles suggests that the qualities we attribute to the body, such as movement and feeling, are best matched by Augustine's notion of the "ensouled" body, the body animated by the life principle of the soul. After clarifying these two distinct meanings of body as lifeless or ensouled, we will be led, Miles argues, to understand that thinkers such as Augustine affirmed, rather than denigrated the body. Although Miles's hermeneutical strategy of distinguishing the meaning of the body in Augustine's context and in our own is valuable, ultimately her analysis does not suggest that Augustine had a positive view even of the animated or ensouled body. As argued above, it is not our conception of the body as an organism that feels, desires, and affirms itself as a sensual being that Augustine embraces. He only endorses the body as it is made over in a state of blessedness. Thus, when Augustine comments negatively about the body, his statements should not be discounted as immature or as referring solely to the "flesh." When Augustine writes of our living body, he comments, "It is stupid to deny that the soul is better than the body" (*Epistula* 18.13, quoted in Miles, p. 68). He also writes that one must withdraw from the flesh in order to seek the image of God: "Leave thou abroad both my clothing and my flesh. . . . For not in the body but in the mind was human being made in the image of God" (*In Joannis Evangelium* 23.10, quoted in Miles, p. 69). These comments indicate Augustine's heirarchical conception of the relation between body and soul. The body is a weight, a corruption of the soul; this view is similar to the view of the body's pollution prominent in Greek thought. Even the animated body must be held aloof, since it incarnates man's disobedience to God. Only when the body is transformed by redemption is it considered fully good. Augustine writes of it as follows: "For it shall no longer be animal, but spiritual, having indeed the substance of flesh, but without fleshly corruption" (*CG* 22.24.855).

14. This point has likewise been made more recently by Genevieve Lloyd in her study, *The Man of Reason: "Male" and "Female" in Western Philosophy*. Lloyd comments, "The use of male-female symbolism to express subordination relations between elements of a divided human nature continued in the Christian tradition of biblical exegesis" (p. 28).

15. Ruether, "Misogynism and Virginal Feminism in the Fathers of the Church," in Ruether, ed., p. 161.

16. Augustine, *Soliloquia* I.10.17, quoted in Kari Elisabeth Børresen, *Subordination and Equivalence: The Nature and Role of Woman in Augustine and Thomas Aquinas*, p. 7.

17. See Lloyd, *The Man of Reason*, pp. 30–33. Lloyd notes Augustine's attempt to upgrade women's position from the earlier misogynist views of the church. Rather than exclusively identifying women with the body, as some of his predecessors had, he strives to include women as spiritual equals with men by demonstrating their rational capacity. Although Augustine includes women into the higher contemplative reaches of reason, they remain uniquely identified in his mind with the lower aspect of reason concerned with practical affairs. Despite women's purported spiritual equality with men, the structural relations of superiority and inferiority between men and women remain.

18. Børresen, *Subordination and Equivalence*, p. 27.

19. Quoted in Ruether, p. 161.

20. Ibid.

21. Augustine, *Soliloquia* 1.10.17, quoted in Børresen, p. 8.

22. Quoted in Ruether, p. 157.

23. Derrick Sherwin Bailey, *Sexual Relation in Christian Thought*, p. 56.

24. Ruether, p. 169.

25. The theme of reason as a mode of domination appears in modern philosophy and science in the context of reason's mastery over nature as well. For example, in Bacon's conception of science, the image of female is assimilated to the treatment of nature. Bacon views the promise of science as "leading to you nature with all her children to bind her to your service and make her your slave" (B. Farrington, "*Temporis Partus Masculus:* An Untranslated Writing of Francis Bacon," quoted in Evelyn Fox Keller, "Feminism and Science," p. 598). Science provides the means that do not "merely exert a gentle guidance over nature's course; they have the power to conquer and subdue her, to shake her to her foundations" (Francis Bacon, "Description of the Intellectual Globe," ibid.) In Bacon's comments, the imagery of servile femininity provides a vehicle for securing the claim to power of a rationality identified with masculinity. For further discussion of the sexualized imagery of nature, see Keller's book, *Reflections on Gender and Science*.

26. Bailey, *Sexual Relation in Christian Thought*, pp. 58–59. Ruether criticizes this claim, pp. 162–63.

27. Eileen Power, *Medieval People*, p. 97.

28. Lucien Goldmann, *The Hidden God: A Study of Tragic Vision in the "Pensées" of Pascal and the Tragedies of Racine*, p. 17.

29. After his conversion, Augustine never saw a woman except in the presence of a witness (Børresen, p. 10).

30. Ruether, p. 162.

## CHAPTER FOUR

1. Eleanor Commo McLaughlin, "Equality of Souls, Inequality of Sexes: Women in Medieval Theology," in Ruether, ed., p. 256.

2. Miles, *Fullness of Life*, p. 87.

3. Richard William Southern, *Western Society and the Church in the Middle Ages*, p. 214.

4. Ernst Troeltsch, *The Social Teachings of the Christian Churches* 1:109.

5. The earlier discussion of Greek religion indicated that worship of female divinities does not necessarily correspond to an elevated social status for women. Athena, for example, appears as a powerful female figure for the Greeks; but her strength draws from her defeminization and her allegiance to the father. In evaluating Mary's position in Catholicism, one must also consider whether this female figure serves ultimately to support male-dominated religious and social patterns. Mary Daly, in *Beyond God the Father: Toward a Philosophy of Women's Liberation*, stresses that the image of virgin birth is an impossible ideal for real women. Consequently, it leaves women to identify with the only other image of woman in Christianity, which is that of Eve. Ultimately, therefore, this elevation of the pure mother serves to reinforce women's subordination to men both within the church and in the world outside of this institution. Moreover, Daly argues that the worship of Mary buttresses the view that woman exists for man. Mary was "immaculately conceived" (p. 82) in order to be worthy of becoming the mother of Jesus. Thus, only by fulfilling their function for men can women become virtuous. Mary's goodness is ultimately derived from the godliness of Jesus. As indicated in the doctrine of Assumption proclaimed in 1950, she remains a passive figure who was "taken up," in contrast to Jesus, who ascended, and "went up" under his own power (p. 87). However, Daly also observes that the image of Mary is not a wholly negative one for women. It may have served a compensatory function; it may, moreover, have served as a safety valve for the church by deflecting women's anger. Daly also suggests that the image of Mary may contain the germ of a liberating view of woman. It carries forth earlier notions of a mother goddess (e.g., of the Greek figure Kore). Furthermore, it suggests the possibility of female autonomy (Daly, p. 87), and the ability to show love that is above the law (pp. 130–31). Henry Adams described Mary's function in the twelfth and thirteenth centuries in the following terms: "The mother alone was human, imperfect, and could love. . . .

the mother alone could represent whatever was not unity; whatever was irregular, exceptional, outlawed; and this was the whole human role . . ." (quoted in Daly, p. 131). More recently, Carol Gilligan, in her work *In a Different Voice: Psychological Theory and Women's Development,* has cited this concern with flexibility and with circumstances in enacting laws as characteristic of women's moral voice.

6. McLaughlin, in Ruether, ed., p. 246.

7. Ruether, p. 164.

8. Southern, *Western Society and the Church in the Middle Ages,* p. 310.

9. Quoted in Southern, ibid., pp. 314–15.

10. McLaughlin, in Ruether, ed., p. 244.

11. Thomas Aquinas, *Summa Theologica,* vol. 1, part 1, question 92, article 1. Future references to this work will be by the initials *ST* and by part, question, and article.

12. Lloyd comments that women's creation "symbolizes" generation, and man's creation "symbolizes" the human vital function of reason (*The Man of Reason,* p. 35).

13. While discussing the nature of God's perfections, Aquinas comments, "Whatever perfection exists in an effect must be found in the producing cause . . . as when man produces man . . ." (*ST* 1.4.2). Therefore the first man, from whom all others are derived, must contain as much perfection as those whom he produces.

14. *ST* 3, *Supplement* question 62, article 4. Future references to this work will be by the abbrevation *Suppl,* and by question and article. Although Aquinas died after writing the first few questions of the *Supplement,* the remainder of it was compiled from his *Commentary on the 4th Book of the Sentences of Peter Lombard,* which Aquinas wrote as a young man. Commentators note that where the *Supplement* contradicts positions in the *ST* (e.g., concerning the church's doctrine on divorce), the latter should be taken as authoritative. Elsewhere, I am using the *Supplement* as an additional source for Aquinas's views of sexual relations.

15. Børresen, *Subordination and Equivalence,* p. 170.

16. Lloyd comments that for Aquinas, unlike other thinkers, woman does not symbolize an inferior form of rationality. But since her meaning is bound up with reproduction, in distinction from intellectual functioning, woman is "symbolically located outside the actual manifestations of reason within human life" (*The Man of Reason,* p. 36).

17. Mary Daly, *The Church and the Second Sex,* p. 52.

18. Aquinas argues that since the intellectual soul has to gather knowledge from individual things by way of the senses, it must be united to a body (*ST* 1.76.5). And since those who are refined in body are well endowed in mind, as Aristotle observes, perhaps in Aquinas's view women's deficiency in exercising reason stems from the less refined nature of her senses.

19. Miles, in *Fullness of Life,* argues that Aquinas provides an "affir-

mation of sexuality as a natural human activity" (p. 130). Moreover, Aquinas stresses that the soul and the body form a psychophysical unity that is the human person, and he rejects the Manichean principle that the body derives from an evil principle (Thomas Gilby, ed., *St. Thomas Aquinas: Philosophical Texts*, pp. 198, 201). He also argues that the union with the body is for the soul's enrichment by providing the possibility of sense knowledge. Yet he treats this union as a strictly hierarchical relation, drawing on Aristotle's discussion of the relation between body and soul (see also Chapter 1). The soul governs the body despotically, like a master governs slaves (*ST* 1.81.3). Thus, the body represents that aspect of the human organism that must be subject to the higher rule of reason.

20. Quoted in *ST* 1.98.2.

21. It may appear difficult to reconcile Aquinas's claim that the goal of human reason is the intelligible truths that angels apprehend, with his insistence elsewhere that the human mind depends on sense perception for natural knowledge. Aquinas argues that human reason must proceed discursively to apprehend the truths that angels know absolutely (*ST* 1.79.8). Thus, human and angelic knowledge do not differ in genus but only in their degrees of perfection. As an *embodied* mind, the human mind is dependent on sense perception as the starting point for knowledge. But natural knowledge is the basis for the higher processes of intellectual reasoning, which can lead to some knowledge of the intelligible world (*ST* 1.12.12). Thus, although the soul depends in this life on sense experience for natural knowledge, its highest activities transcend the material world (F. C. Copleston, *Aquinas*, p. 167).

22. For example, Aquinas writes, "Considered in themselves, passions are neither right nor wrong, for morality depends on the reason" (quoted in Gilby, ed., p. 296). He also notes that "it is better not merely to will good, but also to feel good about it" (quoted in Gilby, ed., p. 297).

23. Aquinas acknowledges that sensible apprehension occurs in animals and is one component in human understanding (in addition to intellectual cognition) (Copleston, *Aquinas*, p. 180). But he does not consider the possibility that emotion itself may be a means of apprehension.

24. *ST* 2.151.4, quoted in McLaughlin, in Ruether, ed., pp. 233–34.


# CHAPTER FIVE

1. Max Weber, *The Protestant Ethic and the Spirit of Capitalism*, p. 121.

2. See Jane Demsey Douglass, "Women in the Continental Reformation," in Ruether, ed.

3. Martin Luther, *Letters of Spiritual Counsel*, p. 209. Future references to this work will be by the initials *LSC* and page number.

4. "Treatise on Good Works" (1520), in *Works of Martin Luther* (Phila-

delphia: Muhlenberg Press), 1.275, 276, quoted in introduction to *LSC*, p. 18.

5. Bailey, *Sexual Relation in Christian Thought*, p. 168.

6. Calvin, *Institutes of the Christian Religion*, bk 2, chap. 8, p. 42. Future references to this work will be by the abbreviation *Insts* and by book, chapter, and page.

7. Quoted in Bailey, *Sexual Relation in Christian Thought*, p. 171.

8. Ernst Troeltsch, *Protestantism and Progress*, pp. 80 ff.; Weber, *The Protestant Ethic*, pp. 118–19.

9. Letter from Calvin to an unknown woman, June 4, 1559, in Philip E. Hughes, ed. and trans. *The Register of the Company of Pastors of Geneva in the Time of Calvin*.

10. Quoted in Douglass, in Ruether, ed., p. 297.

11. Ibid., p. 295.

12. Bailey, *Sexual Relation in Christian Thought*, p. 173.

13. Quoted in Douglass, in Ruether, ed., p. 302.

14. Francois Wendel, *Calvin: The Origins and Development of His Religious Thought*, p. 35.

15. This discussion of Protestant asceticism is based on Weber, *The Protestant Ethic*, pp. 115–19.

16. Ibid., pp. 172, 174. The relation between asceticism and the growth of an economy built on commodity exchange will be discussed in the following chapters on Kant. At this point, however, it is significant to note that asceticism has implications not only for relations between men and women, but also for general economic relations in society.

17. Ibid., p. 181.

18. Foucault suggests that the development of modern science resulted not only in a change in prevailing concepts of the body, but in the body itself, which is constituted by transformed social practices. See, for example, Foucault's comments on *The History of Sexuality*, vol. 1., in *Power/Knowledge*, p. 186.

19. See Chapter 9 on Kant's theory of objectivity.

## CHAPTER SIX

1. The asceticism in Kant's philosophy will be addressed in subsequent chapters.

2. Friedrich Paulsen, *The German Universities and University Study*, p. 4.

3. Hastings Rashdall, *The Universities of Europe in the Middle Ages* 1:26.

4. Ibid., p. 275.

5. This discussion cannot address in detail the development of the universities or the divergencies in the university movements in different parts of Europe. For example, although Rashdall stresses the eccle-

siastical character of northern European education, he distinguishes from this the "free lay system of education" in Italy (*The Universities of Europe in the Middle Ages* 1:222). He argues that northern Europe could draw on only the institutions of the military and of the clergy, of which the latter alone displayed a commitment to education. Italy, however, had an interest in education inherited from the political sphere. Nonetheless, other scholars have noted that Rashdall exaggerated the secular character of Italian education. Manocorda comments that episcopal authority must have been necessary in Italy for the licensing of teachers in the eleventh and twelfth centuries, as everywhere else (see ed. n., 1:231).

6. Ibid., p. 347.

7. Rashdall noted that France did not require specific legislation establishing the necessity of the church's sanction to teachers because education had been so completely confined in practice to the cathedrals and monasteries that official sanctions were unnecessary (ibid., pp. 278–79).

8. The following discussion is based on Rashdall (ibid., 3:368–96).

9. Ibid., p. 419.

10. Ibid., p. 442. Rashdall notes that the association between the church and universities is evident in the impact of the ideal of disinterested knowledge on moral and religious life. Knowledge became valued as an end in itself, not merely as a means for immediate edification or priestly training. The further question to consider is whether these very ideals of disinterested inquiry themselves display the ascetic effect of the church.

11. Charles Homer Haskins, *The Rise of the Universities*, p. 14.

12. Ibid., p. 64.

13. Friedrich Paulsen, *German Education Past and Present*, p. 19.

14. Lina Eckenstein, in *Women under Monasticism*, p. 48, and Eileen Power, in *Medieval English Nunneries, c1275 to 1535*, p. 240, both mention this point.

15. Paulsen, *The German Universities and University Study*, pp. 26–27.

16. Rashdall, *The Universities of Europe in the Middle Ages* 2:233.

17. Paulsen, *The German Universities and University Study*, p. 33.

18. Ibid., p. 38.

19. Ibid., p. 49.

20. Ibid., p. 33.

21. Ibid., p. 27.

22. Ibid., p. 54.

23. One might object that the universities did not preserve and transform their monastic roots, but liberated themselves from these roots altogether. Although there may be progressive tendencies in the development of universities, it is important to note that the argument for progress is typically buttressed by the claim that rationality and science are liberated from religious prejudices and economic interests. My argument is that precisely this interpretation of scientific rationality displays the roots it seeks to deny.

24. Paulsen, *The German Universities and University Study*, pp. 4–5.

25. Immanuel Kant, *The Conflict of the Faculties*, part 1.

26. Charles McClelland, *State, Society and University in Germany, 1700–1914*, p. 116.

27. Ibid., p. 120.

28. Paulsen, *Geschichte des gelehrten Unterrichts*, vol. 2. In the index of Paulsen's two-volume "definitive" work on the German university, there is not a single entry for women.

29. Louis Althusser, "Ideology and Ideological State Apparatuses," in *Lenin and Philosophy*.

30. McClelland, *State, Society and University in Germany*, p. 250.

31. Douglass, in Ruether, ed., p. 304.

32. In "Ideology and Ideological State Apparatuses," Louis Althusser argues that educational institutions in general, including universities, must be understood as ideological systems (see *Lenin and Philosophy*).

33. Althusser, *Lenin and Philosophy*, p. 158.

34. Ibid., p. 132.

35. Althusser stresses that ideology must be understood as a "material component of existence," and in this respect shifts away from Marx's early treatment of the concept. In *The German Ideology*, Marx conceived of ideology as mere illusion. It represents the ideas of the ruling class, articulated by jurists, politicians, and theorists. (Marx, *The German Ideology*, p. 68). These ideas present a distorted picture of the social order, insofar as they present the interests of the ruling class as the general interests of society. In Marx's view, the "real world" is constituted by the "material" conditions of existence, such as production. In *The German Ideology*, ideology appears as a distortion or an inversion of this real world (Althusser, *Lenin and Philosophy*, p. 164). Althusser gives greater weight to the social function of ideology. He views it as constituting the values and rules that structure our relation to production. Therefore, ideology cannot be viewed as merely a false picture of reality, but is itself a clue or guide to how subjects interpret their relation to the real world. In Althusser's terms, ideology is not an "illusion" about the real world, but an "allusion" to reality which must be interpreted (p. 162). Althusser compares Marx's early notion about ideology to the view of dreams that prevailed before Freud. Pre-Freudian dream theorists conceived of dreams as arbitrary and chaotic arrangements of the day's residue. Althusser writes, "For them, the dream was the imaginary, it was empty, null and arbitrarily 'stuck together' (bricolé) once the eyes had closed, from the residues of the only full and positive reality, the reality of the day. This is exactly the status of philosophy and ideology (since in this book philosophy is ideology *par excellence*) in *The German Ideology*" (p. 160). Althusser poses the question of interpretation to ideology that Freud poses to dreams. His explanation follows a path parallel to Freud's own. Through the interpretation of dreams, one learns how the dreamer perceived his or her relation to the world. Similarly, ideology represents the "imaginary" relation of individu-

als to their conditions of existence (Althusser, p. 162). Althusser's view that ideology represents the imaginary relation to the conditions of existence is closely linked to his thesis that it is "material." Like the interpretation of dreams, the analysis of ideology reveals a mode of perception or recognition that constitutes the individual's real, experienced world. The dreamer's thoughts are not just a chaotic jumble of the day's events, but they express unconscious wishes and desires that underlie his or her waking perceptions of the world. Similarly, Althusser suggestively links the function of ideology to the mechanism of the unconscious. Rather than presenting an arbitrarily distorted or unreal picture of the world, ideology expresses individuals' perception of their relation to daily life.

36. For further discussion of Kant's treatment of sexuality and of women, see Chapter 8 on sensibility.

37. Terry Eagleton, *Criticism and Ideology: A Study in Marxist Literary Theory*, p. 48.

38. Althusser, *Lenin and Philosophy*, p. 156.


## CHAPTER SEVEN

1. Quoted in Friedrich Paulsen, *Immanuel Kant: His Life and Doctrine*, p. 42.

2. Ernst Cassirer, *Kant's Life and Thought*, p. 361.

3. Paulsen, *Immanuel Kant*, p. 45.

4. Cassirer, *Kant's Life and Thought*, p. 413–14.

5. Ibid., p. 15.

6. Weber, *The Protestant Ethic*, p. 132.

7. Ibid. Limitations of time and space preclude a fuller discussion of the role of Lutheranism and Calvinism in the development of Pietism. It will suffice to note that although originally Pietism was viewed as a movement within Lutheranism, recent scholars have recognized it as a broader movement within Protestantism in the seventeenth and eighteenth centuries. The experiential tradition in Christianity that Pietism emphasizes can be traced to both Luther's and Calvin's discussion of faith (F. Ernest Stoeffler, *The Rise of Evangelical Pietism*, p. 6).

8. Paulsen, *Immanuel Kant*, p. 29.

9. Quoted in Cassirer, *Kant's Life and Thought*, p. 18.

10. Paulsen, *The German Universities and University Study*, p. 33.

11. Paulsen, *Immanuel Kant*, p. 15.

12. Ibid., p. 38.

13. Cassirer, *Kant's Life and Thought*, p. 16.

14. Paulsen, *Immanuel Kant*, p. 7.

15. Immanuel Kant, *Critique of Pure Reason*, Bxxx.

16. Paulsen, *Immanuel Kant*, p. 7.

17. Ibid., p. 339.

18. Ibid.

19. Ibid., p. 364.

## CHAPTER EIGHT

1. Kant, *Critique of Pure Reason*, A15/B29. All references to the first *Critique* will be to the Kemp Smith translation unless otherwise indicated. Future references to this translation will be by the initials *CPR* and by the pagination in both A and B editions where available.

2. Immanuel Kant, introduction to the *Metaphysics of Morals*, in *The Metaphysical Principles of Virtue*, pp. 9–10. Future references to this work will be by the initials *MM* and by page number.

3. In this context Kant refers both to empirical intuition, which is given through sensation, as well as to space and time as the pure form of sensible intuition.

4. Immanuel Kant, *Anthropology from a Pragmatic Point of View*, Dowdell translation, par. 19. p. 43. All quotations will be from the Dowdell translation unless otherwise indicated. Future references to this work will be by the abbreviation *Anthro* and by paragraph and page number. As Evelyn Fox Keller and Christine Grontkowski note, this depiction of vision itself involves a desensualization of seeing and ignores the way in which a meeting of eyes may be erotic ("The Mind's Eye," in Sandra Harding and Merrill B. Hintikka, eds., *Discovering Reality*, p. 220).

5. Kant gives no examples to support this claim.

6. If parental gratification is wholly self-related, we tend to view it as narcissistic pleasure rather than joy.

7. Immanuel Kant, *Anthropologie in pragmatischen Hinsicht*, in Ernst Cassirer, ed., *Immanuel Kants Werke*, vol. 8, par. 73, p. 141 (my translation).

8. Immanuel Kant, *Lectures on Ethics*, p. 163. Future references to this work will be by the initials *LE* and by page number. If the reader feels there may be something right in Kant's treatment of purely sexual desire, it may be because we have inherited this objectifying interpretation of sexuality from the masculine ascetic tradition. When feminists criticize sexual objectification (such as pornography, for instance), they do not view the problem as lying in our "purely sexual impulses" but in the particular construction of sexuality that prevails in our society.

9. Immanuel Kant, *Foundations of the Metaphysics of Morals*, p. 16. Future references to this work will be by the shortened title *Foundations* and by page number.

10. Cassirer, *Kant's Life and Thought*, p. 413.

11. Kant, *Observations on the Feeling of the Beautiful and Sublime*, sec. 3, p. 78.

12. Ibid., pp. 132–33.

## CHAPTER NINE

1. Karl Marx, *Capital* 1 : 72. In introducing the discussion of Kant, I noted I would follow his use of the masculine form of the subject in order to stress its roots in a male ascetic tradition. In introducing this discussion of Marx, the question arises whether to accept Marx's use of the masculine form in referring to workers, or to substitute instead sex-neutral language. In Marx's analysis of the social division of labor, he depicts men's contribution to the reproduction of society primarily through their productive activity; women's contribution is located primarily in their reproductive function. If wage labor has historically been predominantly male, then the features of production and the experience of alienation that Marx analyzes may also be rooted in a specifically masculine heritage. (Further discussion of this point will be found in Chapter 12 on reification and asceticism.) From this perspective, it appears that Kant and Marx share as the object of their analysis a dimension of existence that has been historically male. In light of this similarity, it may appear more consistent with my discussion of Kant to retain the masculine form of the subject found in Marx's writing. However, I have chosen instead to use sex-neutral language in this context. Although the development of commodity relations itself may be linked to a male ascetic heritage, women in the contemporary world have increasingly become wage laborers, and hence directly subject to the phenomenon of fetishism. Further discussion of the role of sexual identity in Marx's theory must be postponed for a later study.

2. Ibid.

3. György Lukács, "Reification and the Consciousness of the Proletariat," in *History and Class Consciousness: Studies in Marxist Dialectics*, p. 87.

4. Marx, *Capital*, p. 74.

5. Ibid., p. 75.

6. It is important to explain the relation of the terms "objectification" (*Vergegenständlichung*) and "reification" (*Verdinglichung*). These terms are often used synonymously to refer to the process of concretizing or hypostatizing. Since "objectification" has an established place in philosophical vocabulary, it has been suggested that in discussions of alienation this term could supplant the use of "reification" altogether, which has been criticized as jargonistic. However, the concept of reification highlights important features that are not evident in the more general philosophical term "objectification." In English usage, reification refers to the mental conversion of a person or abstract concept into a theory (see the *Oxford English Dictionary*). It occurred in nineteenth-century contexts to refer to the process by which what had hitherto been regarded as a living being becomes converted into an impersonal substance (*Fraser's Magazine*, vol. 49 [1854]). What is central in this term is the mental distortion

that takes place in viewing a person or concept as a thing. This element of mental distortion is central to Marx's analysis, as the passage on fetishism quoted above indicates. Objectification, on the other hand, is defined as making into an object, especially of the senses, or as expressing in external or concrete form (*OED*). Objectification does not necessarily represent a phenomenon of mental distortion. For example, human intention is objectified in our acting upon nature in certain ways. This distinction between the two concepts in English usage points to an important distinction in Marx's thought. In his early writings, Marx attacked Hegel's equation of the existence of objects (*Vergegenständlichung*) with alienation (*Entfremdung*). Objectification, in Marx's view, is the premise of material existence. It is only the alienated form of objectification that occurs in capitalist society, which Marx criticizes. In the *Economic and Philosophical Manuscripts*, he writes: "Labor's realization is its objectification. In the conditions dealt with by political economy this realization of labor appears as loss of reality for the workers . . ." (Robert Tucker, ed., *The Marx-Engels Reader*, p. 71). In other words, the manner in which workers objectify themselves under capitalism results not in a realization of themselves but in an impoverishment of their existence. Thus, in his early writings, Marx implicitly introduced the concept of reification. He elaborates the notion in his later works, especially in *Capital* and *Grundrisse*. Although Marx does not yet give a definition of reification, he introduces the basic elements of this concept in vol. 1 of *Capital*, p. 72, in the passage on commodity fetishism. He explicitly introduces the term reification in vol. 3 of *Capital*. Marx writes, "Im Kapital ist die Mystifikation der Kapitalistischen Produktionsweise, die *Verdinglichung* der gesellschaftlichen Verhältnisse . . . vollendet . . ." (my emphasis; *Das Kapital*, vol. 3, chap. 48). Despite Marx's discussion of reification in *Capital*, his analysis of the concept was long neglected until Lukács' treatment of it in his essay, "Reification and the Consciousness of the Proletariat" (Tom Bottomore et al, eds. *A Dictionary of Marxist Thought*, p. 412). Lukács drew not only on Marx's analysis but also on Max Weber's analysis of bureaucracy and rationalization and on Simmel's discussion in the *Philosophy of Money*. The notion of reification has not been confined to Marxist discussions in this century, although its use may indicate the influence of Marx and Lukács. For example, in the closing passages of *Being and Time*, Heidegger refers to reification as follows: "It has long been known that ancient ontology works with 'Thing-concepts' and that there is a danger of 'reifying consciousness.' But what does this 'reifying' signify? Where does it arise? . . . Why does this reifying always keep coming back to exercise its dominion? What *positive* structure does the being of 'consciousness' have, if reification remains inappropriate to it?" (p. 437). In the context of Marxist discussions, reification generally refers to the most extreme form of alienation, which typifies the commodity relations in a capitalistic society. I have chosen to retain the term reification as a critical concept that depicts the alienated manner in which workers objectify themselves under capitalism. Objectification will also be used in this context in its narrower sense of alienated objectification, as Marx uses it in his early writings.

7. Lukács, *History and Class Consciousness*, p. 92.

8. Ibid., p. 93.

9. Ibid., p. 110.

10. Kant, preface to *The Metaphysical Elements of Justice*, p. 5. Future references to this work will be by the initials *MJ* and by page number.

11. Marx, *Capital*, p. 79.

12. Immanuel Kant, *Kritik der reinen Vernunft*, A50/B74 (my translation). Future references to the German text of the first *Critique* will be by the initials *KRV* and by passage number.

13. Kant writes, "So ist dagegen das Vermögen, Vorstellungen selbst hervorzubringen, oder die Spontaneität des Erkenntnisses, der Verstand" (*KRV* A51/B75).

14. Goldmann, *The Hidden God*, p. 17.

15. In the Deduction, Kant defines an object as "that in the concept of which the manifold of a given intuition is united" (*CPR* B137).

16. Lukács, *History and Class Consciousness*, p. 98.

17. Ibid., p. 87.

18. Lucien Goldmann, *Immanuel Kant*, p. 170.

19. Ibid., p. 188.

20. The relation of the categories to experience is a complicated and thorny problem. In one sense, one would be mistaken to regard the categories as independent of experience. Kant stresses that the categories have no objective meaning apart from appearance. In the "Schematism" he explains that the categories only acquire their objective meaning from sensibility (*CPR* A147/B187). He writes, "Now there certainly does remain in the pure concepts of understanding, even after elimination of every sensible condition, a meaning; but it is purely logical, signifying only the bare unity of the representations" (*CPR* A147/B186). The fact that the categories can only have objective meaning in conjunction with sensibility is essential to Kant's argument that the categories are not applicable to things in themselves (*CPR* A139/B178). Furthermore, the categories in their pure form refer to objects in general; they provide the necessary conditions of experience. Thus, the transcendental logic of the categories is differentiated from general logic, which abstracts from all empirical content. Transcendental logic does not abstract thought from its relation to objects or matter (Norman Kemp Smith, *A Commentary to Kant's "Critique of Pure Reason,"* p. 171).

Yet the pure concepts of the understanding must be schematized: they must be mediated in order for intuitions to be brought under the categories (*CPR* A138/B177). This need for mediation indicates the fundamental independence of the categories from appearance. Kant stresses this independence in his definition of pure, a priori concepts. Knowledge that is a priori is "not knowledge independent of this or that experience, but knowledge absolutely independent of all experience" (*CPR* B3). As in pure knowledge, "there is no admixture of anything empirical" (*CPR* B3).

In other words, although the categories, which provide the form of possible experience, only attain objective meaning in relation to the content of experience, this form is in no way derived from experience. It is the contribution of the human understanding, which is permanent and unchanged by the content of any particular experience.

21. Herbert Marcuse, "The Concept of Essence," in *Negations: Essays in Critical Theory*, p. 52.

22. Lukács' phrase, *History and Class Consciousness*, p. 83, in his discussion of reification.

23. Goldmann, *Immanuel Kant*, p. 152.

24. Weber's terms are *Vergesellschaftung* and *Vergemeinshaftung*, adapting the well-known terms of Tönnies, *Gesellschaft* and *Gemeinschaft*. Weber gives the following definition of his terms: "A social relationship will be called 'communal' if and so far as the orientation of social action . . . is based on a subjective feeling of the parties, whether affectual or traditional, that they belong together. A social relationship will, on the other hand, be called "associative" if and in so far as the orientation of social action within it rests on a rationally motivated adjustment of interests. . . . The purest cases of associative relationships are: (a) rational free market exchange . . ." (Max Weber, *The Theory of Social and Economic Organization*, p. 136).

25. Goldmann, *Immanuel Kant*, p. 128.

26. There is an interesting parallel between this analysis of alienation as a social phenomenon and psychological treatments of the individual's relation to the object of experience. For example, psychologists agree that an individual's idea or image of an object mirrors one's own self-image. This is evident in the relation between the abstraction of the laborer and the abstraction of the commodity. In Kant's thought, this symmetry is reflected in the formal character of both the knower and the object known. Edith Jacobson, in *The Self and the Object World*, explains that the object must serve the ego's purposes. In Kant's thought, the object appears *not* to serve the ego's purposes. Kant claims that the object is constituted by pure concepts and pure intuitions. However, Jacobson argues that there is no strictly conceptual representation of an object. When an object is represented as strictly conceptual, this idealization itself serves the purposes of defense. In other words, the affective component of this idealized presentation of the object in Kant's discussion of knowledge can be viewed as a defensive construct. The conceptual structure reflects the suppression of the erotic feelings demanded by the ascetic ideal. Anna Freud also suggests, in *The Ego and the Mechanisms of Defense*, that instinctual con-

flicts find expression in ideational content. She refers to the asceticism of the adolescent, in whom the instinctual changes at puberty lead to a renunciation by the ego of all pleasure and desire in the name of lofty moral ideals. Thus, it appears that the socially created alienation builds on these potential psychological conflicts within the individual.

27. Lukács, *History and Class Consciousness*, pp. 116–17.

28. Goldmann, *Immanuel Kant*, p. 157.

29. The formalism of Kant's theory of knowledge, in which the forms of intuition and the categories of knowledge are taken to be constitutive of experience, is in some ways reminiscent of the formalism of Plato's theory. Therefore, one might well ask whether Plato assumes a social theory like that evident in Kant's discussion of knowledge. Both Kant and Plato emphasize the purity of the forms of knowledge, which are freed of sensuous content. In fact, this parallel led originally to the inquiry concerning the role of purity in Platonic philosophy. Plato's formalism was discussed as a flight from the perceived pollution of the sensuous world. It articulated an ascetic impulse to escape the corruption of existence and attain purification in the created system of Ideas. Although both Plato and Kant give expression to this ascetic view, there are important differences between the thinkers. The central paradox of fetishism, and the central paradox in Kant's philosophy, is that the world is created by man, yet at the same time experienced as an objective existence, independent of human activity. For Kant, the phenomenal world is constituted by the Ideas, which are produced by man. But the manner in which this occurs results in an alienation within both human activity and its products. For Plato, on the other hand, the Ideas, corresponding to the true Being of the world, are not created by man, and can only at best be approximated by human thought. As Kant remarks in the *Critique*, Plato's Ideas "issued from highest reason . . ." (*CPR*, A313/ B370). Consequently, for Plato the objective world that is accessible to knowledge is not itself produced by the activity of human reason. Although the forms underlie the world of phenomena in Platonic thought, they do not strictly constitute the world. Instead what constitutes the world of appearance is its fallenness from the world of pure Ideas. Kant observes, "For Plato ideas are archetypes of things in themselves, and not, in the manner of the categories, merely keys to possible experience" (*CPR* A313/ B370). Ultimately, Platonic Ideas refer to the Being outside of phenomenal existence, which Kant excludes from human experience.

30. Smith, *Commentary*, pp. lv–lvi.

31. A. C. Ewing, *A Short Commentary on Kant's Critique of Pure Reason*, p. 11.

32. For example, in the preface to the second edition of the *Critique*, Kant refers to science thirty-five times.

33. Max Horkheimer, "Notes on Science and the Crisis," in *Critical Theory: Selected Essays*, p. 8. This discussion draws on Horkheimer's analysis of science in this piece.

34. Lukács, *History and Class Consciousness*, p. 110.

35. Ibid., p. 120.

36. Ibid., p. 105.

37. Horkheimer, "Notes on Science and the Crisis," in *Critical Theory*, p. 4.

38. Lukács, *History and Class Consciousness*, p. 121.

39. Max Horkheimer and Theodor Adorno, "The Concept of Enlightenment," in *The Dialectic of Enlightenment*, p. 22.

## CHAPTER TEN

1. Karl Marx, *The Poverty of Philosophy*, quoted in Lukács, *History and Class Consciousness*, p. 160.

2. Kant gives the following explanation for considering behavior motivated by a selfless joy in other's contentment as lacking "true moral worth." Such behavior is motivated by inclination and hence must be judged on the level of all actions from empirical motives. Although some inclinations, like the inclination to honor, may fortunately accord with duty, they do not arise from it. Thus, in Kant's view these actions deserve "praise and encouragement but no esteem" (*Foundations* 14). Some interpreters hold that an action can give satisfaction and still have moral worth, as long as it is done from duty. Unfortunately, where satisfaction is present, neither the agent nor the philosophical observer can verify that an action is done solely from duty and hence has moral worth.

3. The only feeling that Kant considers moral is the respect for the law. But since this feeling is caused by a rational concept (*Foundations* 17 n.), it is different from all other feelings and inclinations. The moral feeling is the "subjective *effect* which the law has upon the will" (*Foundations* 80); hence it does not itself act as a motivation to obey the law.

Perhaps the claim that inclinations are totally put aside in the Kantian moral system is too strong, but Kant allows them to provide no direct motive or object for moral behavior. For example, Kant recognizes happiness as a necessary natural end for all rational creatures with a dependent will (*Foundations* 33). Kant comments that "all men have the strongest and deepest inclination to happiness, because in this idea all inclinations are summed up" (*Foundations* 15). In order to achieve the natural end of happiness, one must have a good will. Kant writes, "This will must indeed not be the sole and complete good but the highest good and the condition of all others, even of the desire for happiness" (*Foundations* 12). Thus, morality is the condition of happiness and in that sense can be said to promote this natural end. But the relation between happiness and morality remains an indirect one. It is an indirect duty to promote one's happiness, because misery could be an inducement to transgress other moral duties (*Foundations* 15). But it is entirely possible that serving the end of reason may be counter to the empirical principle of happiness (*Founda-*

*tions* 12); such a conflict in no way diminishes the beauty and obligation of the moral law.

4. There is, moreover, a problematic relation between the cognitive and the moral subject in Kant's thought. For example, in the third Paralogism, Kant retains the concept of personality in the transcendental sense, as referring to the unity of the subject in apperception (*CPR* A365). Does this transcendental unity, which founds the cognitive subject, serve as the basis for the freedom of a rational being? In other words, are the cognitive and moral subjects identical? If so, is it possible for the cognitive subject to put aside all moral concerns in his pursuit of objective knowledge?

5. It is debatable whether the categorical imperative also establishes a universality in the content of a moral act. For example, would every individual, in a given situation, make the same moral decision on the basis of the universal law? Whether or not this is the case, Kant maintains that the form of the act, which is determined by a universal law, is the essential feature of a moral action; and this *form* is identical for all consciousnesses.

6. Lukács, *History and Class Consciousness*, p. 125.

7. Lukács suggests that the principle of noncontradiction is an attempt, on Kant's part, to find a formal principle which will "both determine and preserve content—at least negatively . . ." (ibid., p. 125).

8. Herbert Marcuse, *Studies in Critical Philosophy*, p. 94.

9. From *The Holy Family*, quoted in Lukács, *History and Class Consciousness*, p. 149.

10. Wilhelm Reich, in *The Mass Psychology of Fascism*, discusses this middle-class identification with authority as central to the development of fascism in Germany.

11. Marcuse, *Studies in Critical Philosophy*, p. 92. This criticism echoes Hegel's critique of Stoicism in the *Phenomenology of Mind*.

12. Lukács, *History and Class Consciousness*, p. 124.

13. Goldmann, *Immanuel Kant*, p. 170.

14. Horkheimer and Adorno, in their essay, "Juliette or Enlightenment and Morality," refer to the Stoicism that Kant embraces in his moral theory as "the bourgeois philosophy." They write: "Stoicism (which is the bourgeois philosophy) makes it easier for the privileged, confronted with the suffering of others, to steel themselves to their own threats. It confirms the general by elevating private existence, as a protection from the generality, to the condition of a principle" (in *The Dialectic of Enlightenment*, p. 96).

15. In her book *In a Different Voice*, Gilligan criticizes the formal Kantian ethics, adopted by the psychologist Kohlberg, as displaying a masculine bias. She argues for an approach to ethics that considers the concrete context in which moral issues occur and examines the particular consequences of actions. She broadens moral thinking to encompass feelings of care, which are prominent in women's approach to moral ques-

tions. From the Kantian point of view, such an approach, in which morality is not entirely determined by abstract rational principles, is morally deficient. Gilligan argues, however, that the Kant-Kohlberg approach itself is morally deficient and must be revised to include elements of morality associated traditionally with women's perspective.

16. Both Goldmann and Lukács agree that Kant's analysis fails in its attempt to escape the reified relations of bourgeois existence.

17. The first *Critique* is generally understood to be an attempt to build knowledge on the foundation of Newtonian science. The paradigm of scientific knowledge, with its objectifying consequences, is particularly appropriate as a model of knowledge in a world of reified social relations. In his moral philosophy, Kant likewise examines the pure, "rational part of the science of ethics, which is comparable to the pure rational part of the science of nature" (*Foundations* 4). His laws of morality thus carry the same consequence that is evident in the cognitive sphere: the subordination of the personal subject to the objective, universal law. Kant's attempt to treat morality in scientific terms has a historical antecedent in Hume's philosophy. For example, Charles William Hendel argues that Hume not only constructs his science of the mind on the objective laws of Newtonian science, but that these laws underlie his moral system (in *Studies in the Philosophy of David Hume*, pp. 192, 258). One might well consider whether Hume's philosophy is characterized by the same reification and depersonalization that is evident in Kant's thought.

## CHAPTER ELEVEN

1. Immanuel Kant, *Critique of Judgement*, intro, par. 7, p. 30. Future references to this work will be by the initials *CJ* and by paragraph and page number.

2. Immanuel Kant, *Kritik der Urteilskraft*, in Cassirer, ed., *Immanuel Kants Werke*, vol. 5, par. 7, p. 260 (my translation). All future references to the German text will be by the initials *KU* and by paragraph and page. The German text is cited where the English translation appeared too unwieldy. In such cases, the English translation is my own.

3. Robert L. Zimmerman, "Kant: The Aesthetic Judgement," in Robert Paul Wolff, ed., *Kant: A Collection of Critical Essays*, p. 400.

4. Although Kant considers the beautiful and the moral to be analogous, he does not mean that particular moral judgments are relevant to judgments of beauty. His suggestion that beauty is a symbol of morality implies that the beautiful teaches the transcendence of sensibility necessary for morality (*CJ* 59.251).

5. Marcuse, in his essay, "The Affirmative Character of Culture," points out the contradiction between the bourgeois claims for universal happiness and the social conditions that make for unequal material gratification in reality (in *Negations*, p. 98).

6. Ibid., p. 94.

7. Horkheimer and Adorno, "The Culture Industry: Enlightenment as Mass Deception," in *The Dialectic of Enlightenment*, p. 137.

8. Ibid., p. 121.

9. Ibid., p. 139.

10. Adorno and Horkheimer note, moreover, that the principle of "purposefulness without purpose" hides the social function of bourgeois art, which is "purposelessness for the purposes declared by the market" (ibid., p. 158).

11. This understanding is not taken to be actual; but the idea of such an understanding serves as a principle for reflection (*CJ* 4.19).

12. Similarly, Horkheimer and Adorno comment that the culture industry in contemporary capitalist society manipulates images of green trees, blue skies, and moving clouds. They write, "Nature is viewed by the mechanism of social domination as a healthy contrast to society, and is therefore denatured" (in "The Culture Industry," *The Dialectic of Enlightenment*, p. 149).

13. Marx, *The German Ideology*, p. 62.

14. The question being discussed here applies primarily to the phenomenon of compulsive consumption. Why do individuals often seek to acquire commodities, not just for the basic needs of life, nor even just for the luxury of indulging oneself by acquiring pleasant things, but for the sake of consumption? Marxists in general approach the problem of consumption through a discussion of the social creation of needs by new forms of production. But one might further ask how such external pressures as availability of goods and advertising create the subjective desire for commodities. My suggestion here is that the appeal of consumption is the promise that everyone will find the commodity, and hence the individual who possesses it, an object of pleasure.

15. Sigmund Freud, "Sexual Morality and Modern Nervousness," in *Sexuality and the Psychology of Love*, p. 34.

16. Marcuse, for example, introduces the notion of "repressive desublimation" to argue that the forms of erotic gratification in our society are repressive ones. Desires and the means for gratifying them, far from threatening the status quo, have become socially controlled. Thus, "gratification" only strengthens individuals' allegiance to, or harmony with, the established order (see *One-Dimensional Man*).

## CHAPTER TWELVE

1. Marcuse, "The Concept of Essence," in *Negations*, p. 43.

2. Marx, *Capital*, p. 79.

3. This repression of sexuality in bourgeois society is evident, as indicated above, in the desensualization of the process of production. More-

over, theorists have suggested that sexual relations between individuals in bourgeois society themselves occur in repressed form. Freud's work has been seminal for these views in pointing to the repression and sublimation of sexuality entailed in the process of maturing into an achievement-oriented adult. Reich points to the repression of children's sexuality and the continued restrictions placed on women's sexuality in the family in bourgeois society. Feminists such as Adrienne Rich stress that the prevalence of heterosexuality itself is based on institutions such as marriage, which demand the repression of women's homosexual feelings. The discussions of both Reich and Rich indicate once again the connection between the demand that sexuality be controlled and the justification of women's subordination to men as a means of such control.

4. Karl Marx, *Grundrisse: Foundations of the Critique of Political Economy*, p. 105.

5. Ibid., p. 106.

6. Although I have not sought to develop a philosophy of the erotic, throughout this work I have examined historical practices and assumptions that cast doubt on this view that eros and rationality are independent domains.

7. Eric Blondel, "Nietzsche: Life as Metaphor," in Allison, ed., *The New Nietzsche*, p. 157.

8. Sigmund Freud, "The Sexual Aberrations," in *Three Contributions to the Theory of Sex*, p. 17.

9. Ibid, p. 19.

10. Maurice Merleau-Ponty, *Phenomenology of Perception*, p. 16.

11. Ibid., pp. 157–58.

12. Kant, *Metaphysische Anfangsgrunde der Rechtslehre*, in *Immanuel Kants Werke*, Cassirer, ed., vol. 7, par. 24, p. 81 (my translation).

13. Kant, *The Conflict of the Faculties*, pp. 201–5.

14. Michel Foucault, *The History of Sexuality* 1 : 123.

15. Kant, *The Conflict of the Faculties*, p. 213.

16. Foucault discusses the "scientia," or knowledge of sexuality that developed especially in the nineteenth century. He argues that the scientific discourses and strategies concerning sexuality belie the theory that modern society has been sexually repressive. However, the "scientization" of the body and of sexuality, for which Foucault argues, is not in opposition to sexually repressive rules of behavior. On the contrary, this scientific interest postulates an objectified form of the body which itself results from the ascetic suppression of sensuality. This scientific posture also underlies the objectification of the body in certain forms of pornography. For example, Adorno and Horkheimer discuss the Marquis de Sade as a typical Enlightenment figure. His heroine Juliette would make any scientist proud of her precision and rationality in dissecting the possible permutations of bodily pleasure and torture. If indeed modern pornography rests on the same objectification that characterizes Enlightenment ra-

tionality, then this ascetic posture is damaging in a cultural context that extends beyond the boundaries of philosophy and science.

17. Herbert Marcuse, *Eros and Civilization: A Philosophical Inquiry into Freud*, p. 46.

18. Quoted in Marcuse, ibid., p. 213.

19. Sigmund Freud, "Repression," in the *Standard Edition of the Complete Psychological Works* 14:149.

20. Michèle Barrett refers to the "sex-blind" character of Marx's analysis of production in *Women's Oppression Today: Problems in Marxist Feminist Analysis*, p. 8.

21. This attempt to situate philosophy in the context of human sexuality does not lead in the direction of formulating an ontology of sexuality, such as Sartre envisions. For example, Sartre explicitly claims that sexuality should lead us back to ontology. He views sexuality as a "necessary structure of being-for-itself-for-others" (*Being and Nothingness*, p. 499). Sartre considers human beings to be fundamentally sexual, in contrast to the traditional conceptions that treat sexual desire as a "contingent accident" (ibid., p. 499), separated from fundamental attitudes of human existence. But his turn toward ontology leads him to incorporate into his analysis of being in general claims that in fact describe a particular male perspective. Sartre's treatment of the body begins from that position of alienated embodiment which this essay has tried to delineate. An ontology of sexuality, like an analysis of the universal features of rationality, makes illicit claims for universality that cover over the real divergences of experience that arise from the different social positions of men and women.

22. Feminists have treated sexual relations not only under the aspect of power, drawing on the concepts of subordination and exclusion that have been emphasized in this work. Many theorists approach the question of sexual relations through the concept of gender and the analysis of the development of masculinity and femininity. Drawing on the work of, e.g., Nancy Chodorow, writers such as Sandra Harding and Evelyn Fox Keller consider philosophical concepts of objectivity and autonomy as reflecting a particularly masculine ego development, which stresses psychological separateness at the expense of relatedness to others.

23. For example, historically women have been either totally absent or starkly underrepresented in the natural sciences, mathematics, etc. (women have made greater advances in those disciplines, such as literature, which are not considered forms of "scientific" knowledge). However, to speak of women's absence from these socially legitimated spheres of knowledge does not imply that women had no access to knowledge. For example, Barbara Ehrenreich and Deirdre English's study, *Witches, Midwives and Nurses: A History of Women Healers*, shows the importance of women's medical knowledge in the nineteenth century prior to the professionalization of medicine, which excluded women. In this context, it is

interesting to note Mary Daly's analysis of the European witchcraze as an attempt by professional men to retain control of knowledge in the face of the challenge to this control represented by women healers (*Gyn/Ecology*, p. 194).

24. It is important to stress that I do not embrace the traditional stereotype of women as emotional, passionate, and irrational. In my view, this definition of women's identity is premised on the traditional splits, e.g., between cognition and eros, which themselves need to be questioned. As indicated elsewhere, I view both men and women as emotional, sexual beings. However, given certain cultural patterns, those emotions have become oriented in different ways. (For example, Chodorow and Gilligan consider the family constellation, which leads women to be more relationally oriented and men to be oriented more toward separateness.) Although the posture of objectivity itself expresses a stance of distancing and detachment, the emotional significance of this posture is generally not acknowledged.

It may also be true that internalizing prevailing cultural interpretations about sexual identity leads women generally to greater attentiveness to human emotion than men. (Women often give this quality a positive valence, whereas men give it a negative, or indifferent valuation.) This awareness may be used fruitfully by women to reevaluate certain philosophical constructs.

25. The male character of the academy is evident today despite the entry of women into the university in this century. On a practical level, women are still underrepresented in disciplines such as philosophy, and there are disproportionately few women at senior professorial and administrative levels. Furthermore, women students are often not treated as "seriously" as their male peers; sometimes they are made "invisible" by professors' attitudes, sometimes they are treated paternalistically. Moreover, as indicated above, these institutional constraints are manifested in the content of university study. For example, insofar as the philosophical canon has excluded women, women can find no validation for themselves in the content of their study. Women can accept the "universal" formulations of philosophers only at the cost of excluding from philosophical reflection their concrete identity as women.

26. This existential conflict is the source of the difficulties and even paralysis experienced by many women in writing. One's ideas become threatened with obscurity because they derive from experiences and sensibilities that have not been legitimated within philosophy, and whose legitimation is so badly needed.

27. Merleau-Ponty, *Phenomenology of Perception*, p. 168.

28. Ibid., p. 171.

29. Richard Bernstein, in *Beyond Objectivism and Relativism*, gives a useful account of these competing positions.

30. Mary Field Belenky, Blythe McVicker Clinchy, Nancy Rule Gold-

berger, and Jill Mattuck Tarule, *Women's Ways of Knowing: The Development of Self, Voice and Mind*, p. 217. Plato also understands the role of the philosopher-teacher to be that of a midwife. However, his view that knowledge consists in understanding the pure forms means that this midwife approach to knowledge is bound up with a theory of recollection and reincarnation by which the soul, through its affinity with the forms, could gain knowledge of reality.

31. Evelyn Fox Keller and Christine R. Grontkowski, in their essay "The Mind's Eye," note that the eyes can also be a keen source of erotic pleasure, as in meeting the eyes of another in a moment of communication (in Harding and Hintikka, eds., p. 220). The early Greeks acknowledged this quality when they considered the eyes as the entryway of eros. Thus, the desensualization associated with vision is not entailed by the nature of this sense itself, but rather is a feature of the particular philosophical treatment of vision.

32. Ibid., p. 221. For example, Heraclitus states, "Not understanding, although they have heard, they are like the deaf" (#34). And "When you have listened, not to me but to the Law (Logos), it is wise to agree that all things are one" (#50). Yet he also adds, "The eyes are more exact witnesses than the ears" (#101a). See Kathleen Freeman, trans., *Ancilla to the Pre-Socratic Philosophers*, pp. 27–31. Perhaps this path leads to the distinction between knowledge as observation and knowledge as understanding.

33. The role of touch also has been explored by recent French feminists, such as Luce Irigaray, who examine the sexual substructure of certain cognitive postures, and consider the philosophical implications of articulating women's sexuality. Irigaray's discussion of women's sex as "neither one nor two" leads to an exploration of the multidimensionality of subjectivity, and of the role of desire in overcoming the rigidity of the prevailing subject-object split. (See *This Sex Which is Not One*.) The weakness in Irigaray's approach, in my view, is the residue of naturalistic commitments in her discussion of sexuality and of consciousness.

34. However, Merleau-Ponty's distinction between phenomenological description, which is his concern, and reflective analysis does not challenge the existing model of knowledge, but rather supplements it with an examination of prereflective experience.

35. Blacks have typically known whites better because it was necessary to observe them in order to survive.

36. This view need not commit oneself to the Kantian claim that the subject constitutes the object of knowledge. Some French feminists have suggested that such an assumption itself displays a masculine orientation, which puts the male ego at the center of the world.

37. The objects that surround us, like our watches and our radios, were created by industry, which entailed particular forms of social relations. Moreover, industry itself shapes our sensibility in certain ways.

When the only timepiece in a town was on the tower of the city hall, individuals had a different relation to time than they have now, where most people carry watches.

38. Charles Taylor, "Foucault on Freedom and Truth," in David Couzens Hoy, ed., *Foucault: A Critical Reader*, pp. 77–78.

39. Michel Foucault, "What is an Author?" in Josué V. Harari, ed., *Textual Strategies: Perspectives in Post-Structuralist Criticism*, pp. 159–60.

40. It is interesting to note in this context that argumentation is central for both Habermas's and Arendt's concept of rational discourse, although they develop it through their concepts of cognition and judgment, respectively (Bernstein, *Beyond Objectivism and Relativism*, p. 222).

41. Belenky et al., *Women's Ways of Knowing*, p. 141.

42. Ibid., p. 144.

# REFERENCES

Aeschylus. *Aeschylus.* Vol. 2. Translated by Herbert Weir Smyth. Loeb Classical Library. London: William Heinemann; New York: G. P. Putnam's Sons, 1926.

Allison, David B., ed. *The New Nietzsche: Contemporary Styles of Interpretation.* New York: Dell Publishing Co., Delta Book, 1977.

Althusser, Louis. *Lenin and Philosophy.* Translated by Ben Brewster. New York and London: Monthly Review Press, 1971.

Anderson, Perry. *Passages from Antiquity to Feudalism.* London: New Left Books, 1974. Reprint. London: Verso Editions, 1978.

Anton, John P., and George L. Kustas, eds. *Essays in Ancient Greek Philosophy.* Albany: State University of New York Press, 1971.

Aquinas, Thomas. *Summa Theologica.* Translated by the Fathers of the English Dominican Province. Vols. 1, 3. New York: Benziger Bros. Inc., 1947.

Aristotle. *The Basic Works of Aristotle.* Edited by Richard McKeon. New York: Random House, 1941.

———. *The Generation of Animals.* Translated by A. L. Peck. Loeb Classical Library. Cambridge, Mass.: Harvard University Press, 1942.

Augustine. *The City of God*. Translated by Marcus Dods. Modern Library. New York: Random House, 1950.

———. *Confessions*. Translated by R. S. Pine-Coffin. Baltimore: Penguin Books, 1961.

———. *The Writings of Saint Augustine*. Vol. 1. New York: Cima Publishing Co., 1948.

Bailey, Derrick Sherwin. *Sexual Relation in Christian Thought*. New York: Harper and Bros., 1959.

Barrett, Michèle. *Women's Oppression Today: Problems in Marxist Feminist Analysis*. London: New Left Books and Verso Editions, 1980.

de Beauvoir, Simone. *The Second Sex*. Translated by H. M. Parshley. New York: Random House, Vintage Books, 1974.

Beck, Lewis White. *A Commentary on Kant's Critique of Practical Reason*. Chicago: University of Chicago Press, 1960.

Belenky, Mary Field, Blythe McVicker Clinchy, Nancy Rule Goldberger, and Jill Mattuck Tarule. *Women's Ways of Knowing: The Development of Self, Voice and Mind*. New York: Basic Books, 1986.

Bernstein, Richard J. *Beyond Objectivism and Relativism*. Philadelphia: University of Pennsylvania Press, 1985.

Børresen, Kari Elisabeth. *Subordination and Equivalence: The Nature and Role of Woman in Augustine and Thomas Aquinas*. Translated by Charles H. Talbot. Washington, D.C.: University Press of America, 1981.

Bottomore, Tom, Laurence Harris, V. G. Kiernan, and Ralph Miliband, eds. *A Dictionary of Marxist Thought*. Cambridge, Mass.: Harvard University Press, 1983.

Brandt, Paul. *Das Liebesleben der Griechen*. Vol. 2 of *Sittengeschichte Griechenlands*. Dresden u. Zurich: P. Aretz, 1925–26.

Brown, Paula, and Georgeda Buchbinder, eds. *Man and Woman in the New Guinea Highlands*. Washington, D.C.: American Anthropological Association Special Publication 8, 1976.

Brown, Peter. *Augustine of Hippo*. Berkeley and Los Angeles: University of California Press, 1967.

Calvin, John. *Institutes of the Christian Religion*. Translated by Ford Lewis Battles. Library of Christian Classics, vols. 20, 21. Philadelphia: Westminster Press, 1960.

Cassirer, Ernst. *Kant's Life and Thought*. Translated by James Haden. New Haven and London: Yale University Press, 1981.

Copleston, F. C. *Aquinas*. Middlesex: Penguin Books, 1955.

Cornford, F. M. *From Religion to Philosophy: A Study in the Origins of Western Speculation*. Cloister Library. New York: Harper and Row, Harper Torchbooks, 1957.

Daly, Mary. *Beyond God the Father: Toward a Philosophy of Women's Liberation*. Boston: Beacon Press, 1973.

———. *The Church and the Second Sex*. New York: Harper and Row, Harper Colophon Books, 1968.

————. *Gyn/Ecology: The Metaethics of Radical Feminism.* Boston: Beacon Press, 1978.

Detienne, Marcel and Jean-Pierre Vernant. *La Cuisine du Sacrifice en pays grec.* N.p.: Éditions Gallimard, 1979.

Diogenes Laërtius. *Lives of Eminent Philosophers.* Translated by R. D. Hick. Loeb Classical Library. Cambridge, Mass.: Harvard University Press, 1925.

Douglas, Mary. *Purity and Danger: An Analysis of Concepts of Pollution and Taboo.* London: Routledge and Kegan Paul, 1966.

Dover, Kenneth J. *Greek Popular Morality in the Time of Plato and Aristotle.* Oxford: Basil Blackwell, 1974.

Eagleton, Terry. *Criticism and Ideology: A Study in Marxist Literary Theory.* London: NLB; Atlantic Highlands, N.J.: Humanities Press, 1976.

Eckenstein, Lina. *Woman under Monasticism.* New York: Russell and Russell Inc., 1963.

Ehrenreich, Barbara, and Deirdre English. *Witches, Midwives and Nurses: A History of Women Healers.* London: Writers and Readers Publishing Cooperative, 1973.

Elshtain, Jean Bethke. *Public Man, Private Woman: Women in Social and Political Thought.* Princeton, N.J.: Princeton University Press, 1981.

Ewing, A. C. *A Short Commentary on Kant's Critique of Pure Reason.* Chicago: University of Chicago, 1938.

Fanon, Frantz. *Black Skin, White Masks.* Translated by Charles Lam Markmann. New York: Grove Press, 1967.

Farnell, Lewis Richard. *The Cults of the Greek States.* Vol. 4, Oxford: Clarendon Press, 1907; vol. 5, New York: Caratzas Bros., 1977.

————. *Greek Hero Cults and Ideas of Immortality.* Oxford: Clarendon Press, 1921.

Foucault, Michel. *The History of Sexuality.* Vol. 1, *An Introduction.* Translated by Robert Hurley. New York: Random House, Pantheon Books, 1978.

————. *Power/Knowledge: Selected Interviews and Other Writings 1972–1977.* Edited by Colin Gordon. Translated by Colin Gordon, Leo Marshall, John Mepham, and Kate Soper. New York: Random House, Pantheon Books, 1972.

Freeman, Kathleen. *Ancilla to the Pre-Socratic Philosophers: A Complete Translation of the Fragments in Diels, "Fragmente der Vorsokratiker."* Cambridge: Harvard University Press, 1971.

Freud, Anna. *The Ego and the Mechanisms of Defence.* Translated by Cecil Baines. London: Hogarth Press for the Institute of Psycho-Analysis, 1968.

Freud, Sigmund. *Group Psychology and the Analysis of the Ego.* Translated by James Strachey. New York: W. W. Norton and Co., 1959.

————. *Sexuality and the Psychology of Love.* New York: Macmillan Co., Collier Books, 1963.

————. *Standard Edition of the Complete Psychological Works of Sig-*

*mund Freud*, Vol. 14. Translated and edited by James Strachey. In collaboration with Anna Freud. Assisted by Alix Strachey and Alan Tyson. London: Hogarth Press, 1957.

————. *Three Contributions to the Theory of Sex.* Translated by A. A. Brill. New York: E. P. Dutton and Co., 1962.

Gadamer, Hans-Georg. *Philosophical Hermeneutics.* Translated and edited by David E. Linge. Berkeley and Los Angeles: University of California Press, 1976.

Gilby, Thomas, ed. *St. Thomas Aquinas: Philosophical Texts.* London: Oxford University Press, 1951.

Gilligan, Carol. *In a Different Voice: Psychological Theory and Women's Development.* Cambridge, Mass.: Harvard University Press, 1982.

Goldmann, Lucien. *The Hidden God: A Study of Tragic Vision in the "Pensées" of Pascal and the Tragedies of Racine.* Translated by Philip Thody. London: Routledge and Kegan Paul, 1964.

————. *Immanuel Kant.* Translated by Robert Black. London: New Left Books, 1971.

Grube, G. M. A. *Plato's Thought.* Boston: Beacon Press, 1958.

Guthrie, W. K. C. *Orpheus and Greek Religion: A Study of the Orphic Movement.* New York: W. W. Norton and Co., 1966.

Harari, Josué V., ed. *Textual Strategies: Perspectives in Post-Structuralist Criticism.* Ithaca, N.Y.: Cornell University Press, 1979.

Harding, Sandra, and Merrill B. Hintikka, eds. *Discovering Reality: Feminist Perspectives on Epistemology, Metaphysics, Methodology and Philosophy of Science.* Dordrecht: D. Reidel Publishing Co., 1983.

Harrison, Jane. *Prolegomena to the Study of Greek Religion.* New York: Meridian Books, 1955.

————. *Themis: A Study of the Social Origins of Greek Religion.* Cambridge: Cambridge University Press, 1912.

Haskins, Charles Homer. *The Rise of the Universities.* New York: Henry Holt and Co., 1923.

Hegel, G. W. F. *Hegel's Lectures on the History of Philosophy.* Translated by E. S. Haldane and Frances H. Simson. Vol. 3. New York: Humanities Press, 1955.

————. *The Phenomenology of Mind.* Translated by J. B. Baillie. New York and Evanston: Harper and Row Publishers, Harper Torchbooks, 1967.

Heidegger, Martin. *Being and Time.* Translated by John Macquarrie and Edward Robinson. New York and Evanston: Harper and Row Publishers, 1962.

Hendel, Charles William. *Studies in the Philosophy of David Hume.* Princeton, N.J.: Princeton University Press, 1925.

Hesiod. *The Poems of Hesiod.* Translated by R. M. Frazer. Norman: University of Oklahoma Press, 1983.

Horkheimer, Max. *Critical Theory: Selected Essays.* Translated by Matthew J. O'Connell and others. New York: Seabury Press, Continuum Book, 1972.

Horkheimer, Max, and Theodor W. Adorno. *The Dialectic of Enlightenment*. Translated by John Cumming. New York: Seabury Press, Continuum Book, 1972.

Hoy, David Couzens, ed. *Foucault: A Critical Reader*. New York and Oxford: Basil Blackwell, 1986.

Hughes, Philip Edgcumbe, ed. and trans. *The Register of the Company of Pastors of Geneva in the Time of Calvin*. Grand Rapids, Mich.: William B. Eerdmans, 1966.

Irigaray, Luce. *This Sex Which Is Not One*. Translated by Catherine Porter with Carolyn Burke. Ithaca, N.Y.: Cornell University Press, 1985.

Jacobson, Edith. *The Self and the Object World*. New York: International Universities Press, 1964.

Kant, Immanuel. *Anthropology from a Pragmatic Point of View*. Translated by Victor Lyle Dowdell. Carbondale and Edwardsville: Southern Illinois Press, 1978.

———. *The Conflict of the Faculties*. Translated by Mary J. Gregor. New York: Abaris Books, 1979.

———. *Critique of Judgement*. Translated by J. H. Bernard. London: Macmillan and Co., 1931.

———. *Critique of Practical Reason*. Translated by Lewis White Beck. Indianapolis and New York: Bobbs-Merrill Co., 1956.

———. *Critique of Pure Reason*. Translated by Norman Kemp Smith. London: Macmillan and Co., 1958.

———. *Foundations of the Metaphysics of Morals*. Translated by Lewis White Beck. Indianapolis and New York: Bobbs-Merrill Co., 1959.

———. *Immanuel Kants Werke*. Vols. 3, 5, 7, 8. Edited by Ernst Cassirer. Berlin: Bruno Cassirer, 1922.

———. *Kritik der reinen Vernunft*. Edited by Erich Adickes. Berlin: Mayer and Muller, 1889.

———. *Lectures on Ethics*. Translated by Louis Infield. New York: Harper and Row, 1963.

———. *The Metaphysical Elements of Justice*. Translated by John Ladd. Indianapolis and New York: Bobbs-Merrill and Co., 1965.

———. *The Metaphysical Principles of Virtue*. Translated by James Ellington. Indianapolis and New York: Bobbs-Merrill and Co., 1964.

———. *Observations on the Feeling of the Beautiful and the Sublime*. Translated by John T. Goldthwait. Berkeley: University of California Press, 1960.

———. *On History*. Edited by Lewis White Beck. Translated by Lewis White Beck, Robert E. Archor, and Emil L. Fackenheim. New York: Bobbs-Merrill Co., 1963.

Keller, Evelyn Fox. "Feminism and Science." *Signs: Journal of Women in Culture and Society* 7 (Spring 1982): 589–602.

————. *Reflections on Gender and Science*. New Haven: Yale University Press, 1985.

Kierkegaard, Søren. *Concluding Unscientific Postscript*. Translated by David F. Swenson and Walter Lowrie. Princeton, N.J.: Princeton University Press, 1968.

Lloyd, Genevieve. *The Man of Reason: "Male" and "Female" in Western Philosophy*. Minneapolis: University of Minnesota Press, 1984.

Lukács, György. *History and Class Consciousness: Studies in Marxist Dialectics*. Translated by Rodney Livingstone. Cambridge, Mass.: MIT Press, 1972.

Luther, Martin. *Letters of Spiritual Counsel*. Translated and edited by Theodore G. Tappert. Philadelphia: Westminster Press, 1955.

McClelland, Charles E. *State, Society and University in Germany 1700–1914*. Cambridge: Cambridge University Press, 1980.

Marcuse, Herbert. *Eros and Civilization: A Philosophical Inquiry into Freud*. Boston: Beacon Press, 1966.

————. *Negations: Essays in Critical Theory*. Translated by Jeremy J. Shapiro. Boston: Beacon Press, 1968.

————. *One-Dimensional Man*. Boston: Beacon Press, 1964.

————. *Studies in Critical Philosophy*. Translated by Joris De Bres. Boston: Beacon Press, 1973.

Marx, Karl. *Capital: A Critique of Political Economy*. Vol. 1. Translated by Samuel Moore and Edward Aveling. New York: International Publishers, 1967.

————. *Grundrisse: Foundations of the Critique of Political Economy*. Translated by Martin Nicolaus. New York: Random House, Vintage Books, 1973.

————. *Das Kapital*. Vol. 3. Berlin: Dietz Verlag, 1957.

————. *Writings of the Young Marx on Philosophy and Society*. Edited and translated by Lloyd D. Easton and Kurt H. Guddart. New York: Doubleday and Co., 1967.

Marx, Karl, and Friedrich Engels. *The German Ideology: Part One with Selections from Parts Two and Three and Supplementary Texts*. Edited by C. J. Arthur. New York: International Publishers, 1970.

Merleau-Ponty, Maurice. Phenomenology of Perception. Translated by Colin Smith. London: Routledge and Kegan Paul, 1962.

Miles, Margaret R. *Fullness of Life: Historical Foundations for a New Asceticism*. Philadelphia: Westminster Press, 1981.

Nietzsche, Friedrich. *Beyond Good and Evil*. Translated by Marianne Cowan. South Bend, Ind.: Henry Regnery Co., Gateways Editions, 1955.

————. *The Birth of Tragedy and The Genealogy of Morals*. Translated by Frances Golffing. Garden City, N.Y.: Doubleday and Co., 1956.

Nilsson, Martin P. *A History of Greek Religion*. Translated by F. J. Fielden. Oxford: Clarendon Press, 1925.

Nussbaum, Martha. "The Speech of Alcibiades: A Reading of Plato's *Symposium*." *Philosophy and Literature* 3 (Fall 1979): 131–72.

Ochshorn, Judith. *The Female Experience and the Nature of the Divine*. Bloomington: Indiana University Press, 1981.

Okin, Susan Moller. *Women in Western Political Thought*. Princeton, N.J.: Princeton University Press, 1979.

Osborne, Martha Lee, ed. *Woman in Western Thought*. New York: Random House, 1979.

Paulsen, Friedrich. *German Education Past and Present*. Translated by T. Lorenz. New York: Charles Scribner's Sons, 1908.

———. *The German Universities and University Study*. Translated by Frank Thilly and William W. Elwang. New York: Charles Scribner's Sons, 1906.

———. *Geschichte des gelehrten Unterrichts auf den deutschen Schulen und Universitäten vom Ausgang des Mittelalters bis zur Gegenwart*. Vols. 1 and 2, Leipzig: Veit and Comp., 1897.

———. *Immanuel Kant: His Life and Doctrine*. Translated by J. E. Creighton and Albert Lefeure. New York: Charles Scribner's Sons, 1902.

Plato, *The Collected Dialogues of Plato*. Edited by Edith Hamilton and Huntington Cairns. Princeton, N.J.: Princeton University Press, 1961.

———. *The Republic*. Translated by B. Jowett. New York: Modern Library, 1941.

Pomeroy, Sarah B. *Goddesses, Whores, Wives and Slaves: Women in Classical Antiquity*. New York: Schocken Books, 1975.

Power, Eileen. *Medieval English Nunneries c1275 to 1535*. Cambridge: Cambridge University Press, 1922.

———. *Medieval People*. London: Methuen and Co., 1924. Reprint. New York: Harper and Row, 1963.

Rashdall, Hastings. *The Universities of Europe in the Middle Ages*. 3 vols. Oxford: Clarendon Press, 1936.

Reich, Wilhelm. *The Mass Psychology of Fascism*. Translated by Vincent R. Carfagno. New York: Simon and Schuster, 1970.

Ruether, Rosemary Radford, ed. *Religion and Sexism*. New York: Simon and Schuster, 1974.

Sartre, Jean-Paul. *Being and Nothingness*. Translated by Hazel Barnes. New York: Washington Square Press, 1973.

Saxonhouse, Arlene. "The Philosopher and the Female in the Political Thought of Plato." *Political Theory* 4 (1976): 195–212.

Slater, Philip E. *The Glory of Hera: Greek Mythology and the Greek Family*. Boston: Beacon Press, 1968.

Smith, Norman Kemp. *A Commentary to Kant's "Critique of Pure Reason."* London: Macmillan and Co., 1918.

Southern, Richard William. *Western Society and the Church in the Middle Ages*. New York: Penguin Books, 1970.

Spelman, Elizabeth V. Metaphysics and Misogyny: Souls, Bodies, and Women in Plato's Dialogues. Amherst College, 1979. Typescript.

Stoeffler, F. Ernest. *The Rise of Evangelical Pietism.* Leiden: E. J. Brill, 1965.

Troeltsch, Ernst. *Protestantism and Progress: A Historical Study of the Relation of Protestantism to the Modern World.* Translated by W. Montgomery. Boston: Beacon Press, 1912.

———. *The Social Teachings of the Christian Churches.* 2 vols. Translated by Olive Wyon. London: George Allen and Unwin, 1931; New York: Macmillan Co., 1931.

Tucker, Robert C., ed. *The Marx-Engels Reader.* 2d ed. New York, London: W. W. Norton and Co., 1978.

Turner, Victor W. "Symbols in African Ritual." *Science* 179 (March 16, 1973): 1100–5.

Vlastos, Gregory. *Platonic Studies.* Princeton, N.J.: Princeton University Press, 1983.

Vlastos, Gregory, ed. *Plato: A Collection of Critical Essays.* Vol. 2, *Ethics, Politics, Philosophy of Art and Religion.* Garden City, N.Y.: Doubleday and Co., Anchor Books, 1971.

Weber, Max. *The Protestant Ethic and the Spirit of Capitalism.* Translated by Talcott Parsons. New York: Charles Scribner's Sons, 1958.

———. *The Theory of Social and Economic Organization.* Translated by A. M. Henderson and Talcott Parsons. New York: Macmillan Co., Free Press, 1947.

Wendel, Francois. *Calvin: The Origins and Development of His Religious Thought.* Translated by Philip Mairet. New York and Evanston: Harper and Row, 1963.

Werkmeister, W. H., ed. *Facets of Plato's Philosophy.* Amsterdam: Van Gorcum, 1976.

Wolff, Robert Paul, ed. *Kant: A Collection of Critical Essays.* Garden City, N.Y.: Doubleday and Company, Anchor Books, 1967.

# INDEX